BIRMINGHAM

by

BIRMINGHAM UNIVERSITY LIBRARY
THIS BOOK MUST BE RETURNED
IMMEDIATELY IF RECALLED FOR
THE USE OF ANOTHER BORROWER,
OTHERWISE ON OR BEFORE THE
LATEST DATE BELOW

BOOK

AVAILABLE

D1355963

£6.00

PERGAMON INTERNATIONAL LIBRARY
of Science, Technology, Engineering and Social Studies
The 1000-volume original paperback library in aid of education,
industrial training and the enjoyment of leisure
Publisher: Robert Maxwell, M.C.

BETWEEN THE LINES
OF THE BALANCE SHEET

The plain man's guide to published accounts

THE PERGAMON TEXTBOOK
INSPECTION COPY SERVICE

An inspection copy of any book published in the Pergamon International Library will gladly be sent to academic staff without obligation for their consideration for course adoption or recommendation. Copies may be retained for a period of 60 days from receipt and returned if not suitable. When a particular title is adopted or recommended for adoption for class use and the recommendation results in a sale of 12 or more copies, the inspection copy may be retained with our compliments. If after examination the lecturer decides that the book is not suitable for adoption but would like to retain it for his personal library, then a discount of 10% is allowed on the invoiced price. The Publishers will be pleased to receive suggestions for revised editions and new titles to be published in this important international Library.

Other Titles of Interest

BETWEEN THE LINES
OF THE BALANCE SHEET

The plain man's guide to published accounts

by

MICHAEL GREENER

Second Edition

PERGAMON PRESS

OXFORD · NEW YORK · TORONTO · SYDNEY · PARIS · FRANKFURT

U.K.	Pergamon Press Ltd., Headington Hill Hall, Oxford OX3 0BW, England
U.S.A.	Pergamon Press Inc., Maxwell House, Fairview Park, Elmsford, New York 10523, U.S.A.
CANADA	Pergamon of Canada, Suite 104, 150 Consumers Road, Willowdale, Ontario M2J 1P9, Canada
AUSTRALIA	Pergamon Press (Aust.) Pty. Ltd., P.O. Box 544, Potts Point, N.S.W. 2011, Australia
FRANCE	Pergamon Press SARL, 24 rue des Ecoles, 75240 Paris, Cedex 05, France
FEDERAL REPUBLIC OF GERMANY	Pergamon Press GmbH, 6242 Kronberg-Taunus, Pferdstrasse 1, Federal Republic of Germany

Copyright © 1980 M. Greener.

All Rights Reserved. No part of this publication may be reproduced, stored in a retrieval system or transmitted in any form or by any means: electronic, electrostatic, magnetic tape, mechanical, photocopying, recording or otherwise, without permission in writing from the publishers.

First edition 1968

Second edition 1980

British Library Cataloging in Publication Data
Greener, Michael
Between the lines of the balance sheet.
2nd ed. — (Pergamon international library):
1. Balance sheets
I. Title
657′. 3 HF5681.B2 79-40910

ISBN 0-08-024071-2 (Hard cover)
ISBN 0-08-024072-0 (Flexicover)

1190845

HF 5681.B2
G

Printed and bound in Great Britain by
William Clowes (Beccles) Limited, Beccles and London

to my father

Contents

Preface to the Second Edition

WHEN asked in 1978 to revise, if only marginally, a book written in 1966 I was filled with misgivings. Twelve years is a long time in economics. However, although facts and figures have a habit of changing rapidly from one year to the next, ideas and attitudes tend to endure. Most of modern philosophy is little more than a confirmation of the adage that there is nothing new under the sun. The greater part of it is fairly easy to find, albeit differently presented, in the writings of the ancient Greeks.

This book is by no means a philosophical treatise, it is merely a discussion of the ideas underlying accountancy and its application to investment decisions. None the less it is concerned with basic concepts and these, it seems, are not prone to sudden shifts.

Had space allowed it would have been instructive to explore the extraordinary contrast, at least in the medium term, between the manufacturing and distributive sectors of industry in this country. The disparity in rates of return seems to underline the claim that Britain is, and possibly should continue to be, a nation of shopkeepers. Even in the area of inventions we seem to profit more from their sale than their development — though the reason is doubtlessly attributable to our lack of the space, the money and the natural resources to develop them.

As explained in the introductory chapter the time and trouble that would have been incurred in replacing the figures taken from accounts dated in the early 1960s with similar figures from the late 1970s would have had no noticeable effect on the arguments which those figures were used to support. They have therefore been left unchanged, though current figures have been introduced in the new chapter where a point seemed to need underlining.

Finally, may I express my gratitude to the companies included in the text for the help they have afforded — particularly those which now own or represent the few corporate bodies that have ceased to exist as separate entities since 1963. I must also afford space to thank Corrie Coughlan and Pauline Thomas for the time they gave to all the necessary retyping and to my son, Matthew and his friend Jay for help with the proofs.

Michael Greener
Barry, 1979

Preface to the First Edition

THE reason for this preface is the obligation on my part to acknowledge in some permanent manner the help received from so many persons in the writing of this book. Much was of that indirect kind that is not always apparent to those who provide it. There were many such people: friends, acquaintances and comparative strangers. If I do not mention each by name it is for reasons of space, not absence of gratitude.

As for specific assistance, the donkey work was the responsibility of three people: Jean Thomas, who made a superb job of the typing from handwriting that was almost unreadable, and Barbara Harvey and Angela Tarling who ploughed through the calling over, a tedious business. The latter, in addition, acted as an unpaid secretary and organising genius.

The book was read by three people: Mr. John C. W. Day of the College of Commerce, Wednesbury, Mr. Michael Quinn and Mr. Gwyn Ingli James of Cardiff University. Mr. Gwyn James took on the formidable task of correcting the worst of my punctuation. He also tried unsuccessfully to dissuade me from some obscure grammatical constructions; for these he takes no responsibility. His greatest contribution, however, was probably founded in a long friendship and showed itself in continual encouragement and a willingness to listen to tales of woe and weariness.

My wife took the brunt of my temper throughout the period, in addition to having the living room littered with a multitude of accounts and working papers.

Perhaps it is only fitting that the final remarks should be reserved for the place wherein the book was originally conceived. The years spent at Wednesbury were probably the most intellectually rewarding of my life, apart from being the happiest. It is impossible to single out individuals without seeming to show a preference not necessarily felt. However, it is essential that I mention the names of Mr. E. George Smith and Mr. Eric Cockson-Jones, two men as different as those in the preface to *Hills and the Sea,* yet whose acquaintanceship, or rather friendship, has been a singular source of strength, both in the times we lectured together and since. Those days were truly memorable. They were followed by a long period of ill health — also memorable in a rather different way. It was during convalescence from this that the book was written.

Michael Greener
Barry, 1968

An Introduction (with hindsight) to the Second Edition

SINCE this book was first published just over a decade ago there have been many changes on the industrial scene. There have been two new Companies Acts and a considerable revamping of fiscal legislation concerning the taxation demanded of corporate bodies. The United Kingdom has also become, not without much heart-searching, a full member of the European Economic Community. None the less, despite all these legal and commercial commotions and volte-faces; the basic arguments and themes discussed in this book and the conclusions drawn need very little revision. The figures used for illustration may seem a little out of date but the arguments that they illustrate are as relevant and topical today as they were when first put forward.

The fact that three of the eight companies initially selected for scrutiny have ceased to exist as separate businesses is symptomatic of the industrial centralisation by way of mergers, acquisitions and amalgamations that has been much in evidence over the intervening period. The gobbling up by larger groups or by the State of the three companies referred to, namely William Hancock Ltd., The Lancashire Cotton Corporation and Harland & Woolf Ltd., is indeed consistent with many of the observations made in the text. The Lancashire Cotton Corporation was shown to be in possession of a high proportion of liquid assets — resources which were no doubt welcomed by Courtaulds Ltd., a highly successful company in the textile world, which bought the complete capital of the Corporation shortly after the book was written and, in fact, prior to its publication. Today, The Lancashire Cotton Corporation is still registered as a company but no longer trades as one.

Harland & Woolf, the Belfast Shipbuilders, stand out prominently in each chapter as a company in straightened circumstances. Conditions did not improve in the years following and had it not been for the substantial amounts of money provided by Parliament at Westminster, which regarded the continuation of business in such a high employment industrial sector as an over-riding consideration, the company would never have survived. Between 1966 and 1974 it received state aid in the region of £68 million (six times the 1977 share capital and almost five times the average capital employed for 1963, shown in Table A). In 1974 pressure for even more finance led to the Government deciding to acquire a majority interest and thereby assuming ultimate control. In 1975 it went on to acquire the balance of the ordinary share capital still in private hands, and eventually by September 1978, according to the Directors Report attached to the 1977 accounts, the total issued share capital of the company became vested in the State through the Department of Commerce for Northern Ireland or its nominees.

Although the company was not subject to the state takeover of British shipbuilding through the Aircraft & Shipbuilding Act 1977 that Act ensured that British Shipbuilders (the new state body) would consult with and co-ordinate its activities with companies, such as Harland & Woolf, registered in Northern Ireland. *De Facto* nationalisation of Harland & Woolf was thereby rendered *de jure*.

None the less in the years ended 31 December 1976 and 31 December 1977 the company continued to trade at a fairly substantial loss and little respite from such an unhappy state of affairs was projected by the chairman in his report of 21 September 1978. In such circumstances there seems little need to qualify comments and conclusions contained in the text as it stands.

The crude fact is that the halcyon days of British supremacy in the shipbuilding world are long gone and, in so far as such industries can now rarely be viable under private enterprise, the national interest demands that rather than be abandoned they should be supported by the public purse.

So, of the three smaller companies, two, namely Lancashire Cotton and Harland & Woolf, are accounted for. The first was swallowed, or in view of its super liquidity perhaps one should say drunk, by Courtaulds. The second, after a catalogue of misfortune, has become state supported and controlled. This leaves us with William Hancock & Co. Ltd., the popular brewers who, in 1968, yielded to the advances of one of the fast-emerging mammoth brewery groups, namely Bass Charrington Ltd. As a result of an offer closing on 18 March 1968 they were taken over lock, stock and barrel with no protest from the Monopolies Commission.

The price paid by Bass Charrington reflected the considerable extent to which the Fixed Assets of Hancocks were undervalued. As pointed out in Appendix B, note 3, of the original text the estimated surplus on licensed properties arising from a revaluation in 1963 was in the region of 125% of the value shown in the accounts at that date.

By 1968 this surplus was possibly much greater and, in so far as it had never been incorporated in the books, it represented a substantial "secret reserve" appertaining to the owners of the company's equity.* To this must be added the 81% increase in the value of the actual brewery premises disclosed in a revaluation made in 1967.

It might be interesting to recalculate the true rate of return being earned from 1960 to 1963 by Hancocks in the light of these figures which are noticeably higher than the conservative estimates made in Chapter 7, but such an exercise would, at this date, serve little purpose except perhaps to indicate the overwhelming need at the time for the injection of new working capital in order to bring the return on real capital employed up to a respectable level.

It is the inability of the smaller companies to make these cash injections which leads them to seek the shelter and protection of a large group, though on the basis of the real capital worth, as measured by the 1967 equity interest plus "secret reserves" contained in the undervaluation of fixed assets, the purchasing group was not being over-generous in its offer price. But then altruism has no role to play in the risk business and the tendency has long been for the large national companies to call the tune to which the lesser provincial businesses dance.

The distinction so far made between the small companies and the others is based not so much on the 1963 figures but on their size and the manner in which they are seen by the public in 1978. On the basis of the 1963 figures there were only three noticeably large public companies

---

*The estimated surplus of £3·58 million would, on the basis of the general index of prices over the period, have risen to £4·8 million approximately; i.e. a further £1·22 million being an additional 35% of the 1963 equity capital, making the total apparent hidden equity profit some 170% of the 1963 average equity capital.

among the eight selected; namely I.C.I., Courtaulds and Imperial Tobacco. Of the remaining five, Lancashire Cotton was the biggest in terms of total capital, well ahead of Harland & Woolf, Newton Chambers and George Wimpey who vied for second place, whilst William Hancock was way down in a minor league. Such ratings were hardly supported by profitability. Had those companies been ranged in order of average profits earned then Wimpey would have shot to the top — far ahead of Lancashire Cotton in second place with Newton Chambers third, Hancocks fourth and Harland & Woolf far off in the distance.

By 1978 the picture had changed dramatically. Though still lagging behind the big three capitalwise, George Wimpey had earned a place alongside them. Of the remaining four companies, three had virtually disappeared in ways we have already discussed, leaving only Newton Chambers to be accounted for.

The story of Newton Chambers between 1963 and 1978 has not been one of epic proportions. Certain changes have taken place, Subsidiaries have been bought and sold and in December 1972 the parent company itself became a subsidiary of Central & Sherwood Ltd., an old-established investment company. If the tests applied to the "big four" companies were brought in to bear on Newton Chambers itself then it becomes apparent that far from expanding wildly it has kept a rather low profile and, in terms of price indices, its total capital employed has actually fallen over the period — though in view of the fact that the last-available accounts are, at the time of writing, to December 1976, it is just possible that some sudden explosion has occurred during the past eighteen months (possible but unlikely as the message of the past decade has been that the main emphasis has been on keeping a steady course in an industry which has long been beset by economic troubles). The British engineering sector of industry has been severely challenged by both foreign competition and domestic misfortune over the past fifteen years and it can only be to the credit of a company such as Newton Chambers that it has not only survived the storms but has managed to maintain a comparatively healthy profit record. It is worth noting that although the 1976 total capital was well short of the 1963 figure updated according to the general price index, the profit figure for 1976 was about level with the updated 1960–3 average. Unfortunately the latest accounts do not include a ten-year review so it is difficult to state whether this commendable result was a freak or a confirmation of a general trend.

The four remaining companies are those which might be thought of as in the big league, being household names by virtue of who they are or, particularly in the case of Courtaulds, what they produce. Those unfamiliar with the name Courtaulds will probably find that they wear a considerable amount of clothing made by that group of companies or with the fibres and textiles they provide. In fact, subsidiaries such as Kayser-Bondor Ltd. and Wolsey Ltd. are possibly better known than the holding company itself.

One very pertinent factor in the development of these four giant companies whose combined total assets exceed £8,000 million is the manner in which they have grown both horizontally and through diversification over the period 1963–78. Diversification is particularly noticeable in the case of the Imperial group which, by the very fact of abandoning its old title of Imperial Tobacco Company Ltd., has given notice to the world that it no longer wishes to be considered as just a tobacco giant with outside interests but as a major producer or supplier of a variety of goods. In fact, at present, over one-half of its income is generated by its interests in food and drink, processing and packaging, etc.; for example, Ross Foods, Golden Wonder, Courage and John Smith's ales, general paper and board packaging and retail and wholesale outlets. It is not without interest that the other tobacco giant, British American Tobacco, is also becoming equally well known for its other activities through such subsidiaries as Wiggins Teape, International Stores and those companies producing Yardley and other popular cosmetics.

It is probably this continual broadening of horizons and the determination not to be bound by the vaccilations in demand for one particular product which has made these two groups, whose shares are known colloquially as Imps and Bats, such a consistently safe investment and the nearest thing to a gilt-edged security on the company scene. Not for the adventurous and spirited punter perhaps but a reasonable choice for the more conservative.

The growth in the other three companies, Courtaulds, Imperial Chemicals and Wimpeys, has been quite as dramatic as in Imperial

Tobacco even if they do not seem to have bounded off in quite so many different directions. Unlike the moguls at Imperial, the Directors of the other three companies have tended to restrict their expansionist policies to areas of the market which border on those with which they have long been familiar and although the need to diversify has been accepted it has been, for the greater part, modified by an apparent determination to stay within those new enterprises which are technically compatible with the old. Quite apart from an understandable preference to continue doing that which they had already proved they could do well, one excellent reason for keeping to traditional paths lay in the fact that, unlike Imperial Tobacco, their primary bread-winner was not being continually condemned by well-meaning, if not always well-informed, pressure groups within the society in which they operated.

Consider certain representative figures for the four companies:

	£000	£000	£000	£000	£000			%	%
	(1)	(2)	(3)	(4)	(5)	(6)	(7)	(8)	(9)
I.C.I. Ltd.	898	4647	76·3	511	639·5	5·2	6·6	10·1	13·76
Courtaulds Ltd.	229	1280	20·5	67·3	101·6	5·6	3·3	9·5	8·1
Imperial Group Ltd.	299	1842	29·8	130·2	181·4	6·2	4·4	11·4	9·8
G. Wimpey & Co. Ltd.	33	463	3·5	47·9	56·1	14·0	15·9	11·1	12·2

Key: (1) average capital Table N; (2) average capital last two available years; (3) average profit; (4) average profit last two available years; (5) adjusted average profit last two available years; (6) increase in capital over period shown as a multiple; (7) equivalent increase in profit shown as a multiple; (8) mean return Table N, col. 9; (9) comparative figure at present.

Every picture tells a story and a statistical table is little more than a picture. First impressions are never the most reliable guide. Reverting to Table N and the mean deviation in rate of return (col. 9) expressed as a percentage, the apparent value of I.C.I. shares as an investment in 1977 is immediately suspect. A return of 13·76 may seem more than usually attractive but the percentage deviation noted was as high as 9·7%. Although even a subtraction of 9·7% in the return disclosed would still put this company well ahead of the game, the fact of such a high percentage deviation must inevitably raise question marks. The profit has indeed multiplied well beyond the average capital, thus accounting for the increase in the return, but nothing in recent history, nor in the performance of that company during the past decade, gives good ground for believing that the deviation observed has noticeably declined and, to that extent, whatever the present may appear to offer, investment in the company must continue to be seen as a calculated risk rather than as a punters' dream. This viewpoint can certainly not be assuaged by the ubiquitous threat of nationalisation which still hovers even though it appears less a prospect for the immediate future than a gleam in the ultra-left eye. The mark of the socialist finger is never easy to erase.

The risk element in I.C.I. Ltd. is further underscored by looking at the trend of the profit before tax figure over the past decade. Taking 1968 as 100 the profit expressed as an index for the succeeding nine years began by rising to 109 in 1969 and then showing 95, 85, 92 over the years to 1972. In four years it had fallen eight points whilst the general index of retail prices rose by more than 30% over the same period. The year 1973 showed a vast improvement, the index jumping from 92 to 203, a promise underlined by another leap, to 297 in 1974. The following year hopes were rather damaged if not dashed by a fall of 88 points. Then in 1976 came a record leap to 353, a rise in one year of 144 points, only to be followed in 1977 not by another increase but by a sharp if not massive fall to 315. Over the period 1974–7 when inflation was running at an excessive rate, averaging around 25% per annum and prices in general rose by some 74 points, I.C.I.'s profits increased by a mere 6%.

Actually, although the profit figure over the decade 1968–77 went up some 215% the retail price index over the same period went up from 65 to 182, some 280%. When this is allied with the erratic behaviour of the profit figure over that same period the conclusions previously made do not seem to merit any revision. Note that the figure of "Total Assets Employed" increased fairly consistently throughout the period, from 1,487 million in 1968 to 3,680 million in 1977. The 1977 figure expressed as an index is 248 which is more than the comparative increase in the profit index.

As the rise in profit over the longer period, 1963 to 1977, was observed to be greater than that of capital, the only obvious conclusion must be that the years 1963–8 showed a more than average increase in efficiency as measured by the profit/capital ratio.

If this is accepted, there is no escaping the corollary that the performance of the company over the past decade has not lived up to the expectations generated by the results of the previous half decade. The fact, already established, that the present two-year average return on capital is noticeably up on the comparative figure for 1963 does not upset this corollary but it does give further weight to the overall verdict expressed earlier, i.e. that I.C.I. shares are not for the cautious investor or at least not in the short term.

The second company on the list is Courtaulds. In terms of capital this company has grown slightly more than has I.C.I. but comparative profit growth is far from encouraging. Over the fifteen-year period capital has been multiplied five and a half times, mostly by adding to reserves and increasing borrowings, both at a fairly steady rate. However, over that same period profit has been far from steady and the average for the last two years was only just over three times that in 1963. Thus it is not surprising that the rate of return as shown in the table has taken a downward turn.

The 1969/70 Annual Report contained a delightfully phrased reference to the interference of the government in the structure of the Textile Industry, interference which the directors received with "a mixture of exasperation and patience". It might not be an inapt description of the manner in which the average investor must view the profit record of the group over the past fifteen years. Exasperation with the unpleasant effect world trading conditions in the textile and fibre market have on sales trends and patience induced by the obvious efforts made to overcome these adverse outside influences. It is worth noting that the group's venture into the paint industry has borne more than a little fruit — as evidenced by the fact that the profit/sales ratio in the paint division is well above that in the textile division and still climbing. When one considers the erratic behaviour of the profit figure over the past fifteen years, particularly the last ten where a graph would take on the appearance of a terrifying "big-dipper", one can only admire the skill of the management in bringing the group through relatively unscathed.

Although the Directors' Report never appears to risk looking ahead, maybe with good reason, the future would seem to rest as much as anything with the establishment of a safe bread-and-butter base through greater diversification, a field in which the Imperial Group are well-equipped to advise.

As noted above, Imperial have diversified considerably over the fifteen-year period. The fact that their sixfold growth owes more to the building up of non-tobacco divisions has affected the profit picture slightly but this is inevitable as they move into areas where demand for goods is rather more elastic. The rate of return may have dropped from 11·4 to 9·8 but it still retains the quality of stability to which other companies aspire.

The remaining company of the big three is George Wimpey & Co. Ltd. Wimpeys have not just expanded over the fifteen years, they have exploded. Capital has been multiplied fourteen times and profits nearly sixteen times. On these facts alone it is hardly surprising that the Table N rate of return has risen from 11·1 to 12·2. What is more the chairman shows in his latest statement to shareholders a healthy enthusiasm for the coming years. Alas, unlike most other companies, Wimpeys prefer not to include a review of past years in their Annual Report and this fact must invite caution on the part of the prospective investor. He must inevitably be wary of forecasts that are not well supported by records of past performance, suspect as any figures, by their nature, must be. Another aspect, made more important by the chairman's apparent need to refer to it, is the spectre of nationalisation, a spectre more ominous than that lurking in the wings of I.C.I. by the very nature of Wimpeys role as a major company in the world of building contracting. Such considerations must diminish the immediate impact of what appeared, at first light, to be the success story of the post-1963 epoch.

Nationalisation, the transfer of a company from the private sector into public ownership, has been mentioned as a possibility in the case of two of the four "big league" companies discussed above. The respective boards of directors seem to regard this possibility as something much to be dreaded not just because it may cost them their jobs but because the public sector has become associated with inefficiency.

It might be argued that such attitudes are untenable in so far as they arise from the premise that efficiency is equated with profitability, a premise that has no application whatsoever in the context of state ownership where the corporation would be run not for private gain but for the public good.

The principal fault with this argument lies in its tendency to be used empirically. It may hold good for certain service industries which by their nature must, barring crass ineptitude, be far more efficient when run on a monopoly basis; for example, the provision of light and power and a national transport network. In such cases, where competition is adjudged wasteful, it is sensible that the only corporation in the field should be a nationally owned one — though the records of public bodies in the U.K. like British Rail, the Post Office Corporation and the N.C.B. are not entirely reassuring. It is in the realms of manufacturing that the advantages of nationalisation are more than dubious.

It could be suggested that the reason why state take-overs in the manufacturing sector seem inevitably to end in disaster — for example, British Steel, British Leyland,* etc. — lies not so much in the fact that Public Bodies that lack the profit motive are born to fail but in the fact that any very large organisation, whether publicly or privately owned, is a prey to the inefficiencies which inevitably flow from the very size of the business. Large corporations, like large animals, are cumbersome things and tend not only to lose sight of where they are heading but equally are unsure of exactly when or why they have arrived. The elephant may have great strength and certainly carries considerable weight but he is not the most graceful of creatures nor is he adept at pulling up short on the edge of a precipice.

Another disease from which the mammoth organisation suffers concerns communications. As the active part becomes further and further removed from the control centre there is an immediate problem with keeping clear the lines of communication. Both orders and messages, which have to be relayed through a myriad of channels and as many distinct link-men, have an irritating tendency to become distorted with consequences that could, in certain cases, be catastrophic. Conversely and looking at the position from the other side, the passing of the buck up an ever-growing line of management can result in its becoming somewhat battered even if it is not, as too often happens, lost on the way.

Bigness is not necessarily bad any more than small is necessarily beautiful, other factors must always be taken into account, but it is not unreasonable to suggest that in all businesses there is an optimum size after which efficiency must suffer. Why state-owned businesses are seen with distrust is because, by and large, they are always bigger than this

*Leyland is not a nationalised concern in the strict sense, but is run mainly on state funds.

optimum size, though it is worth remembering that in a considerable number of instances the State takes over an already oversized corporation in the private sector. British Leyland prior to 1974 was possibly too big whether run publicly or privately. The major error was probably made when the motor industry was centralised in the private sector — well before it became, in 1975, effectively a State-run enterprise.

There is one other aspect of nationalisation that seems to merit attention. It is too frequently supposed that once a large enterprise in the private sector is taken into public ownership society must automatically benefit if only because there will be no more dividends to pay and state ownership means public control of output, prices, etc. Nothing could be further from the truth. The man in the street has this unhappy tendency to overlook the importance of capital in industry, not to mention its efficient use. Nationalisation does not abolish capital when it removes capitalism, all it does is change the nature of the capital and call the price of borrowing it interest rather than dividends and, in many cases, the former is rather more tough on the purse-strings than was the latter.

As for public control of output, prices, wages, etc., the public knows only too well how little control it actually acquires — and that little is vested in some department of state which is as far removed from the public eye as was the old Board of Directors. What is more, the general public also likes to forget that when, through socialist legislation, they take power over industry then they must also accept the responsibility that goes with it. It is sad but instructive to note how eager the man in the street was to blame a company in the private sector for the damages that resulted from the introduction of the thalidomide drug and how the same man would never have dreamed of apportioning to himself, as part-owner of the nationalised coal industry, the horrors of Aberfan.

CHAPTER 1

By Way of an Introduction

A BALANCE sheet is not a document specifically designed for the conveying of information; it is rather a by-product of the system of double entry accounting. It has never held much interest for the person who provides it other than to confirm by content and state of balance that all book-keeping entries have been correctly made. The man-in-office, be he company executive or club secretary, who desires information on the financial position of his organisation has many other and more suitable sources on which to draw. Nevertheless, despite its inadequacy as a guide from the point of view of those within the organisation it is still of particular interest to those without. This because it is the one point at which contact is made between those on either side of the company or club wall. It is in fact the only window on a world in which the gazer may have considerable interest. The purpose of this book is to discuss ways in which that person can maximise his appreciation of the doings of the organisation of which he is a member, or prospective member, through the window of this balance sheet, and how he may see through the many and convincing attempts at both window-dressing and curtaining that may be made by those within. In so doing it has been assumed that the investor is working from the minimum of information. A full-scale analysis, based on facts culled from various sources and not necessarily generally available, would be interesting to compile but would, if the various arguments developed in the book were adopted, involve a work of immense proportions.

The immediate aim is to give a more general guide to the shareholding or interested public as to the content of the average company report or for that matter any set of accounts and the scope and limitations of the information that may be extracted from them. Attention has been focused on the balance sheet as containing the most relevant material, though recourse is made to other documents when necessary.

It has been argued that what is often referred to as the operating account is of far more interest. This may be true were a full operating account provided, but the normal content as dictated by law is insufficient to make any kind of reliable judgement. It has therefore been used only to extract the profit figure and, where necessary, to obtain such information as is necessary to make adjustments to that figure.

The period chosen is one of four years. This is quite arbitrary — it might have been two, six or more. Generally speaking, unless a great deal of statistical work on the figures presented is being attempted — the value of which is in any event doubtful (as shall be made clear later) — then a long period merely multiplies the time taken in computation and adds little to the strength or stability of the argument. The reason is because, barring a few instances, companies tend to follow a fairly consistent line of success or failure or else are subject to sudden and apparently quite arbitrary fluctuations. In either case the short term is likely to give as useful a picture as the long. Again it is sufficient to show immediate prospects, which the investor is usually concerned with, particularly if he tends to invest on a short-term basis. From the long-term investor's viewpoint it may be less valuable; but he is either looking for a safe holding, which will be by definition apparent on a four-year assessment, or he is gambling on some particular stock which he expects to show considerable improvement some time hence. This would be unlikely to be apparent from any analysis, either short or long term. All in all then, it can be assumed that the choice of a short period is not as valueless for the drawing of general conclusions as might at first be assumed. In addition, instead of taking the full accounts for the four years, and as a further example of economy, the accounts for the years ending in 1961 and 1963 only have been taken, using the comparative figures to supply the missing items. As we were taking averages it was necessary to have the opening figures for 1960, which on the data were not of course available. In these cases, by working backward from the 1961 comparative figure and the profit shown, it has been possible to arrive at a rough estimate — at least in those companies, Lancashire

Cotton and Imperial Tobacco — for which the information was not otherwise to hand.

As for the companies chosen these were taken quite at random. To be specific, they represent a random selection from the investments held by a widow of moderate means who understands nothing of the information contained in the reports she receives. It was for persons such as she that the book was originally written. Originally, because, in the course of the work, ideas have been introduced and developed which, in some cases from their novelty and in others from their controversial nature, may make the book rather complex in parts and the lay reader may tend to dismiss it as written for the specialist. However, the complexity of ideas does in no way forbid their understanding and every attempt has been made to avoid jargon and keep the arguments as detailed as possible.

It was for the benefit of the lay reader that Chapter 2 was written at the risk of deterring the specialist. The point was to introduce the lay reader, whose occupation afforded him no knowledge of balance sheets, to the terms and contents of such phenomena.

As far as the companies selected for analysis are concerned, apart from the genuine randomness of the selection, they have been used not as the subject matter of the book but merely as, as it were, guinea pigs on which to show the extent of the effect which the various hypotheses made may have on the assessment made of any company that might be chosen.

There is no doubt that many approaches which are feasible have been ignored — concentration has been focused particularly on return on capital as the finest indication of prosperity; but this is extensively discussed in the text. All that is noted here is that the analysis is not claimed to be exhaustive in extent, or even for that matter in depth, but merely a sign-post to the way that may best be taken if any sound conclusions are to be drawn, whether they be of positive value or only confirmation of the suspicion that the uses of this type of analysis are few and the possible interpretations of the figures and ratios that are collected are rather limited.

It is admitted that certain chapters could be usefully developed, particularly those on solvency and turnover — but as has been pointed out this was never intended as an exhaustive thesis. Again, the chapters on depreciation and revaluation are controversial and the premises adopted may be denied — the reader must judge for himself on the basis of the arguments used. That on depreciation is in conflict with generally accepted principles. That on revaluation may be criticised not so much in theory as in the methods adopted to put it into practice — these, however, can be corrected as soon as companies are prepared to set about providing the necessary information.

The chapters on capital gearing and taxation are again no more than sketches of the influence of these items and could no doubt be developed considerably. To do so in the present context would be to lengthen the book and risk detracting from the principal thesis. The long chapter on reform will again persuade senior members of professions connected with investment and finance to emulate the "fretful porpentine". It is unfortunate as it would mean reaction of the type that debars rethinking. It is hoped it will not be so. The commentary though hard is well intended and the changes recommended though fundamental are seriously suggested as necessary.

If there is a tendency to shout it is not in hope than persuasion can be made easier that way, but more in anticipation that the noise may awaken those to action whose general tendency is to sleep.

Finally it must be stated that the book is written, not as an aid to the accountant in industry, though he is welcome to accept certain of the ideas put forward in preparing accounts; it is meant principally for the investor, the man who knows nothing of the company he partly owns but what is provided in the annual report and what he may hear at the general meeting, assuming he has not accepted the offer by the directors to vote in his stead.

It may again be said that in attempting to write for the layman we are hoping for the impossible. This is quite absurd. Even if it were true, it would be a poor reflection on the companies concerned, inasmuch as they were giving information to their proprietors in a form which they knew those persons could not comprehend.

Apart from certain additional chapters included for clarification, the book follows a certain pattern. It begins, as we have said, with an elementary explanation of the structure of a balance sheet. It then goes on to a discussion of solvency, inasmuch as the liquid position of the company is of vital importance and must affect any further analysis.

From then on the argument centres on return on capital — beginning with accepted forms and proceeding to discuss, discard and add to them — until some degree of complexity is reached. There is some discussion of the underlying ethic of business as it applies to the results shown in the tables that have been prepared. This is fairly thin in content and represents little more than a suggestion on which an investigation might be based.

Then follow chapters on the incidence of taxation and the nature and influence of such items as capital gearing. The turnover figure and its relevance is discussed briefly and the final chapter is that on the possibilities of reform with reference to the 1967 Companies Act, etc.

The book closes with a sort of *envoi* which is an admission not of the weakness of the arguments developed, nor of the methods of analysis used, but of the limitations necessarily imposed on any sensible discussion of the position and prospects of a particular company unless far more information is provided in a form which excludes ambiguity. This will not occur until both the accounting profession and, through it, the law, awake to the real responsibilities of the company toward the shareholder.

In tables where specific companies are listed, the years quoted indicate the end of the financial year, and not the actual calendar year.

CHAPTER 2

The Anatomy of a Balance Sheet

A BALANCE sheet is a statement of affairs. It attempts to portray the financial position of an enterprise at a particular date. It is divided into two parts, assets and liabilities, meaning the things possessed by the organisation and the persons to whom they belong or to whom they are owed.

Take a simple illustration. Suppose Richard Robot commences business as a small manufacturer with a capital of £5,000. His opening balance sheet reads:

Liabilities	£	Assets	£
Capital	5,000	Cash at bank	5,000

His assets are £5,000, all of which is owed to Robot himself by the business. He now buys premises and materials. The new balance sheet reads:

Liabilities	£	Assets	£
Capital	5,000	Premises	2,000
		Stock	2,500
		Cash	500
	£5,000		£5,000

The business now has various assets still totalling £5,000, all of which constitute capital owed to Robot. Suppose he buys and sells, partly for cash and partly for credit. At any time there will be debtors and creditors and the balance sheet will read:

Liabilities	£	Assets	£
Capital	5,000	Premises	2,000
Creditors	1,750	Stock	3,000
		Debtors	1,500
		Cash	250
	£6,750		£6,750

Robot finds another £3,000 to introduce as capital and after the first year, as a result of successful trading, he finds that his assets exceed his liabilities by £1,000. This represents profit. His balance sheet now also includes work in course of completion, referred to as work-in-progress.

Liabilities	£	Assets	£
Capital	8,000	Premises	2,000
Profit	1,000	Stock and work in	
Creditors	1,250	progress	4,800
		Debtors	3,400
		Cash	50
	£10,250		£10,250

The assets are now £10,250, of which £1,250 is owed to creditors. The balance, being capital and profit, belongs to Robot himself.

Business continues and expands. In order to finance this expansion and to purchase two vans Robot borrows £2,000 from the bank, secured on his premises. Profit for the second year is £1,500 after allowing £250 for depreciation of the vans. Robot draws £1,000 out of the business for his own use. The new balance sheet is:

Liabilities	£	£	Assets	£	£
Capital		8,000	Fixed assets		
Profits	2,500		Premises		2,000
less drawings	1,000		Vans at cost	900	
		1,500	depreciation	250	
Bank loan		2,000			650
					2,650
Current liabilities			Current assets		
Creditors		1,400	Stock and w.i.p.	5,800	
			Debtors	2,900	
			Cash	1,550	
					10,250
		£12,900			£12,900

Note the sub-headings. A distinction is made between fixed assets, which are purchased for permanent use within the business, and current assets, which are continually turned over in the course of business and the constitution of which is forever changing.

So far tax has been ignored. Because of the method of payment of taxation there may be two items of tax on the liability side of any commercial balance sheet. There may be a current liability for the amount payable on the following 1st January and based on the profits for the preceding year. There may also be a liability for the sum due at a future date and based on the profits of the current year.

Introducing these items into our balance sheet, and assuming another successful year we have:

Liabilities	£	£	Assets	£	£	£
Capital		8,000	*Fixed assets*			
Profit	4,800		Premises		2,000	
drawings	2,250		Vans at cost	900		
	——	2,550	depreciation	500	400	
				——	——	2,400
		10,550				
			Current assest			
Bank loan		2,000	Stock and w.i.p.		6,800	
Corporation tax payable		250	Debtors and payments			
			in advance		4,800	
Current liabilities			Cash		1,300	
					——	12,900
Provision for tax	200					
Sundry creditors and						
accrued liabilities	2,300					
	——	2,500				
		£15,300				£15,300

Of the assets, now £15,300, £2,500 is due to various creditors, including the Commissioners of Inland Revenue (C.I.R.); £2,000 is owed to the bank; £10,550 belongs to Robot; and £250 at present is at the disposal of Robot but will sometimes be needed for tax.

Complicating the position, suppose that Robot, wishing to raise more money for expansion, turns his business into a limited company. He registers 25,000 £1 ordinary shares of which 10,800 are issued to himself, in exchange for his capital and profits, and 4,200 are sold to his friends. Profits after tax for the next year are quite high at £5,000. The company decides to hold £3,000 in what it calls a "general reserve" and distributes £1,000 in dividends. Assuming the new capital was used in extending the premises and installing machinery, the balance sheet now reads:

Liabilities	£	£	*Assets*	£	£	£
Share capital			*Fixed assets*			
Authorised 25,000			Premises			5,000
shares of £1 each		25,000	Plant and machinery			2,500
			Vans	900		
Issued 15,000 shares			depreciation	750		150
of £1 each		15,000				
General reserve		3,000				7,650
Profit and loss a/c		1,000	*Current assets*			
Bank loan		2,000	Stock and w.i.p.		8,200	
Corporation tax payable		1,500	Debtors and payments			
			in advance		5,900	
Current liabilities			Cash		4,650	
Creditors and accrued						18,750
liabilities	2,550					
Taxation	350					
Dividends	1,000					
		3,900				
		£26,400				£26,400

As a further step, assume the following:
1. An interest in a supplying company is purchased for £3,000.
2. A further amount of £3,000 is raised from the bank and a debenture, secured on the premises, is issued for the whole £5,000.
3. Surplus funds of £1,500 are invested in quoted shares.
4. The vans are replaced and their number increased.
5. Profits allow the transfer of a further £2,500 to reserve.
The balance sheet at the end of another year might then be:

Liabilities	£	£	*Assets*	£	£
Share capital			*Fixed assets*		
Authorised 25,000			Premises		5,000
shares of £1 each		25,000	Plant and machinery	2,500	
Issued 15,000 shares			depreciation	250	
of £1 each		15,000			2,250
			Vans	1,950	
General reserve	5,500		depreciation	450	
Profit and loss a/c	1,000				1,500
		6,500			
			Trade investment		3,000
		21,500			
8% Debentures		5,000			11,750
Corporation tax payable		1,800	*Current assets*		
Current liabilities			Quoted investments		
Sundry creditors and			(market price		
accrued liabilities	2,850		£2,200)	1,950	
Taxation	1,400		Stock and w.i.p.	8,600	
Dividends	1,200		Debtors and payments		
		5,450	in advance	7,250	
			Cash	4,200	
					22,000
		£33,750			£33,750

This balance sheet could be added to almost indefinitely, but it would not necessarily serve the stated purpose, which is to arrive at a representative, but necessarily simplified, example of the average commercial or industrial balance sheet.

As a final step, assume the years roll on and

(a) Further shares are issued, being 5,000 ordinary, at a premium of 50p per share, and 2,500 5% preference shares.

(b) The premises are revalued and, due to inflation of property values, are found to be worth £10,000.

(c) Further purchases of machinery are made.

Our final balance sheet now reads:

Liabilities	£	£	*Assets*	£	£
Share capital			*Fixed assets*		
Authorised: 25,000			Premises at valuation		10,000
shares of £1 each		25,000	Plant and machinery		
Issued: 2,500 preference			at cost	14,800	
shares of £1 each		2,500	depreciation	1,400	
20,000 ordinary					13,400
shares of £1 each		20,000	Motor vans	3,560	
			depreciation	1,190	
Capital reserves					2,370
Share premium a/c	2,500		Trade investment at		
Surplus on re-			cost		3,000
valuation of					
premises	5,000		Total fixed assets		30,770
		7,500			
Revenue reserves			*Current assets*		
General reserve	12,000		Investments		
Profit and loss	2,400		(market value		
		14,400	£11,300)	8,870	
Total capital and			Stock and w.i.p.	18,400	
reserves		44,400	Debtors and payments		
Corporation			in advance	12,780	
tax plus			Bank balances	1,280	
amounts set					41,330
aside for deferred					
taxation		4,700			
8% 1st mortgage					
debentures		5,000			
Current liabilities					
Sundry creditors and					
accrued liabilities	5,150				
Taxation	4,100				
Bank overdraft	3,500				
Dividends	3,250				
		16,000			
		£70,100			£70,100

One or two items in this balance sheet deserve comment. The first point to note is the distinction between two categories of reserve: capital and revenue. Capital reserves are those which by law or custom are not available for immediate distribution to shareholders. Other reserves are revenue reserves.

Secondly, an amount has now been set side for deferred tax. This is made necessary by the fact that fixed assets are written off more quickly for tax than for financial purposes. Less tax is therefore paid in the early years of an asset's life than in later years. In order to spread the incidence of taxation more evenly over the whole of an asset's life, additional amounts in lieu of tax are reserved from profits in the early years and made available for meeting tax demands in later years.

It has been noted that stock refers to raw materials and finished goods, whereas work-in-progress refers to goods in course of production. A point to remember, and which will assume a greater degree of importance as the argument proceeds, is that both these items are difficult to value for balance sheet purposes. This is partly because an accurate physical count is almost impossible and partly due to the fact that it is far from easy to value stock of various ages and work in different stages of production.

Finally a word on group accounts. Where one company holds a controlling interest in another, it is necessary for the first company to publish group accounts. This will mean a consolidated balance sheet, which is a combination of the balance sheets of the holding company and its subsidiary or subsidiaries. The various comments and criticisms we make as we proceed will apply to this type of balance sheet as to all others, except that it is as well to remember that conclusions drawn, for example as to solvency, would apply to the group of companies taken together and not to the holding company alone.

In a fairly short space of time progress has been made from a simple balance sheet containing two items to one fairly complicated in character. Nevertheless, whatever the size, the principle remains the same. The assets side still gives the things possessed by the company and the liability side details the persons or groups to whom they belong. In the case of the balance sheet which was recently compiled, of assets worth £70,100, £16,000 will shortly be paid to various creditors; £5,000 is owed on a longer term to debenture holders; £4,700 is put aside for tax, and the balance of £44,400 belongs to the shareholders.

To say that £X belongs to shareholders is perhaps dangerous inasmuch as it is seldom true. It would depend upon the assets being realisable at the values shown in the balance sheet. It would be pointless to waste time on reasons why they are not. The process of book-keeping does not generally concern itself with the market value of an item. It is more interested in the value of that item in the business. The distinction can be seen in an item such as stock in trade. The stocks are worth to the business, as a going concern, far more than they would fetch on quick realisation — we are speaking now more of raw materials, but the same can be true of finished goods. A retailer closing down is forced to sell at a low price to clear his goods.

Generally speaking the amount at which an asset is shown is its original cost. This is why the prevailing system of accounting is known as the historical cost system. When an asset is purchased it is recorded at cost price and appears in the accounts at this figure until sold or disposed of. Adjustments are made in various ways but not to offend the original principle. Depreciation is written off fixed assets but shown as a separate item and thought of more as a provision for a replacement. There is one other principle of accounting which sometimes conflicts with the historical cost idea and that is the assertion that no asset should be shown at above its value to the business. For this reason it has long been customary for stocks to be shown at cost or selling price whichever be the lower. Again work in progress is often valued at less than cost to allow for any possible loss. In fact it is an unwritten law that whilst no count is taken of profits not yet realised, allowance must be made for all anticipated falls in value or losses expected, usually by way of a provision in the profit and loss account (or a deliberate mis-statement of stocks) which has the effect of bringing the loss forward into the present year.

Such is the historical cost system in outline. There are many nuances which have not been described, but there is little to be gained by introducing details that would confuse more than clarify.

The protagonists of this method claim that it is the only satisfactory and practicable method of keeping accounts. One is continually coming across phrases such as "the balance sheet is not a statement of current worth", as if this somehow solves all problems. In fact it begs the outstanding question.

Is there any point in publishing a balance sheet which purports to be for the benefit and information of the recipient, who as shareholder is theoretically the owner, when the items on the balance sheet are in some important part wrongly valued? In a time of inflation as has been experienced in recent years, the currency of a country effectively changes from one chosen period to the next. To state, say, property purchased in 1920 at cost in the accounts of 1963 is therefore to state that asset in terms of an alien currency. 1963 pounds are not equivalent to 1920 pounds. To pretend they are is to make mockery of economics and to show an asset at 1920 cost in the balance sheet, particularly without stating date of purchase, is, apart from being ridiculous, dangerously misleading.

If the market value, however this term is defined, is greater than the value as given in the balance sheet, and if the figure is material to a proper appreciation of the accounts, then the present value of the asset, if sold to a willing purchaser, should be stated. The shareholder has a right to know the value of the assets he partly owns. The matter will be discussed in more detail in a later chapter. Suffice it for now to say that the historical cost system, unchallenged for so long, is beginning to feel the force of new ideas and its defenders, albeit reluctantly, are beginning to find their arguments falling upon barren ground.

One point which should be noted is that many companies today publish balance sheets in what is known as vertical form. Instead of a two-sided account, the assets are listed, fixed assets first, then current assets from which are deducted current liabilities, the total being shown as net assets employed.

As a separate item the various elements of capital are then also listed (with appropriate sub-totals) to give total capital employed, which is of course equal to net assets. This though considered a modern and more imaginative way of displaying a balance sheet has, as shall appear later, certain disadvantages and at times can be misleading.

Having examined the structure of a balance sheet the question must now be asked, what does it tell us about the state of a business? The answer can only be discovered by dissection and examination. This will be attempted under various headings, beginning with the matter of solvency.

CHAPTER 3

The Question of Solvency

PERHAPS the most important thing about a business is that it should be solvent; that is to say, it should be in a position to pay its debts as and when they become due. An organisation with valuable assets well in excess of external liabilities may still be insolvent if it cannot realise those assets, or borrow on the security they offer in time to pay debts. Insolvency leads normally to bankruptcy or liquidation. In such an event all assets are sold. They may not realise the prices that their book value suggested, and consequently, after external liabilities have been met, the proprietors, whether they be partners or shareholders, may find their capital considerably depleted if not entirely consumed.

What are the symptoms of insolvency or its approach? Can they be recognised on the face of the average balance sheet?

Except in cases where a business is well on to the rocks any really satisfactory assessment of solvency requires rather more information than is usually given. What is more, inquiries are hampered by the inevitable window dressing practised by so many businesses at the time the balance sheet is produced. Be that as it may, there are certain tests that may in most cases be made.

In the first place it is necessary to distinguish between current assets and liquid assets. Liquid assets are cash and those current assets readily convertible into cash, e.g. marketable securities and debtors. These must be sufficient to pay immediate current liabilities and provide a fund for the payment of such operating expenses as wages. Note that if sales are partly for cash, then stock itself may be considered partially liquid; but in most manufacturing businesses stock is only convertible into finished goods and debtors and is not therefore a liquid asset.

In the search for solvency, then, is it sufficient to compare the total of liquid assets with current liabilities? The answer is a qualified yes;

qualified because of certain unknowns:

(a)   Are all debts due for collection in the following month?

(b)   What is the length of credit allowed by creditors?

(c)   How much is needed for operating expenses?

Having a figure of total sales it is possible to obtain a rough estimate of sales per month by straightforward division, assuming sales are not seasonal. Comparing the answer with the debtors figure it is not difficult to estimate the approximate length of the collection period.

Courtaulds sales in 1962/63 were £185,431,899, giving an average monthly figure of £15,452,658. Debtors were stated as £30,836,139 suggesting a two-month collection period. I.C.I.'s 1963 accounts reveal average monthly sales of £52,011,000. Comparing this with the debtors figure of £131,098,000, a collection period of slightly over two months is indicated. Much will, of course, depend on the nature of the business. Where capital equipment is being produced and sold then payments may be made in instalments over a longer credit period. This would favour a longer collection period. Massey-Ferguson accounts, for instance, suggest a period of over four months.

On such a slender base as this it is of course impossible to draw a firm conclusion, but as in most manufacturing businesses accounts receivable are not due for settlement until the end of the month following the month in which the sale occurs; it is then not unreasonable to work on the assumption that the debtors figure in the average balance sheet represents two months' sales. It might seem from this that only 50% of the debtors could be considered liquid at any one time. However, inasmuch as the later debts will theoretically be settled at the beginning of the second month, it follows that all could be due within five weeks and all may for present purposes be considered liquid.

We come now to creditors. The difficulty here is that certain accounts for capital items may be on an extended credit basis. It is, however, impossible to allow for this, and better to suppose that all accounts will in fact be due for payment within four weeks. This will be true even if, for window dressing purposes, the payment of accounts due before balance sheet date has been put forward into the next year (having the effect of bolstering the cash position). The basis for the supposition is that any purchase is normally due for payment at the end of the month following the date of acquisition.

So much for collection periods. What about operating expenses? How much of the liquid assets do they demand? Although some of these expenses are effectively contained in the figure of creditors one important item not so included (except for perhaps a small provision for the part week to the balance sheet date) is wages. During the following month at least four payrolls must be met. In any manufacturing business this is likely to amount to a relatively large sum of money.

Unfortunately wage figures are seldom published and it is impossible in a particular case to estimate the amount of money that will be needed. However, these payrolls are a claim on available liquid assets in addition to the current liabilities listed in the balance sheet.

It would be instructive at this point to examine the ground so far covered with a view to the drawing of one or two conclusions. It has been stated that the liquid assets, mainly debtors, marketable investments and cash, are realised within the following five weeks and must be adequate to meet both the current liabilities which are payable during that period (principally trade creditors and tax) and also the monthly payrolls.

This is the premise. How does it fit with the facts? Consider the group accounts of Imperial Tobacco for 1963. This is a company which might fairly be assumed solvent, yet liquid assets are quite insufficient to pay current liabilities, let alone leave anything over for operating expenses. The figures are as follows:

	£		£
		Debtors	68,512,521
		Loan to L.A.s	400,000
		Bank balance and	
		cash	257,841
			69,170,362
Bank overdraft	26,792,385		
Other borrowings			
in U.S.A.	12,508,376		
Acceptance credits	5,000,000		
Deposits by			
assoc. and other			
companies	2,803,145		
	47,103,906		
Creditors tax, etc.	31,628,270		
Dividends	5,783,139		
			84,515,315
		DEFICIT	£15,344,953

How is this explained? The answer probably lies in the bank overdraft. For four successive years this has been over £20 million. It has become a permanent feature of finance. It might be assumed, then, that it is not due for immediate repayment and consequently could be excluded from quick current liabilities. Should this be done a surplus of £4–5 million appears.

There are two other points to note. Firstly it cannot be known whether the creditors figure is an average for the year or whether purchases are made seasonally, thus perhaps inflating creditors at balance sheet date.

The second point is that there are trade investments of £20½ million. These have a stated market value of almost £122 million. Although they are not bought for resale they do form a useful reserve. The company could hardly approach insolvency with such a backing. True, some might be sold to extinguish the overdraft, but presumably the interest paid on the overdraft is more than outweighed by the revenue and other advantages accruing from the investments.

Another company that denies the initial premise is William Hancock & Company Limited. The group accounts for 1963 show current liabilities of £1,697,163 and quick current assets of only £507,684. The position seems far from satisfactory: a deficit of almost £1,200,000. The profits before depreciation for 1963 were £435,000. This means that if all profits were ploughed back into quick assets it would take three years to balance the cash position. It would seem from the facts that solvency is at a premium. How can the company continue to exist and why has it allowed itself to get into such a position?

The answer to the first part of the question lies in the bank. The company will only pay its creditors by increasing the bank overdraft. Is this feasible? It is, where the company can offer the bank plenty of security, as Hancock's obviously can with properties costing over £3 million and probably worth a great deal more.

When it comes to the question of why this position has arisen the solution is found in the Chairman's Statement. The company have spent a great deal of money, and intend to spend more on modernising their licensed premises. It is a long term policy which will bring benefits that outweigh embarrassment arising from temporary shortage of liquid funds.

From the two cases we have examined the conclusion to be drawn is that the original premise is of itself not entirely sound. It is apparently not reasonable to state that a company will not remain solvent where quick current appear less than current liabilities. It is necessary, then, to look for other signs of financial insecurity.

So far the tendency has been to juggle with absolute figures. More useful tests can be applied by using ratios. Two ratios are relevant: the current ratio and the liquid ratio. The first is the ratio of total current assets to current liabilities. The second relates quick current assets to current liabilities.

These ratios are not usually so instructive themselves as when featured in comparisons. It has already been seen that though the liquid ratio should in theory be greater than one, this is not always essential to solvency. Similarly with the current ratio. There was an opinion at one time that for a healthy business this should exceed two. However, it will be found that a business can be far from the rocks even where it is less than one.

There are two relevant comparisons. Firstly that between the equivalent ratios of firms within an industry. In the U.S.A. there are charts available showing the normal ratio in any of many particular types of business. Unfortunately, such things are not available in this country, except to a more limited extent in certain publications of the Dept. of Trade.

The more important comparison is between successive years. Watch, for example, the trend of a ratio in the business being reviewed. Presuming balance sheets are available for more than one year (note that because of comparative figures all balance sheets cover two years), the current ratio can be calculated over a period, and the way it is moving noted. So also with the liquid ratio. What are the trends to look for? Here again it is difficult to be precise.

The ratio may be doing one of three things. It may be steady, it may be rising or it may be falling.

If the balance sheets disclose a steady ratio, then much depends upon the level which the ratio has found. Generally speaking, lack of movement is a healthy sign. But suppose the business is in fact becalmed in the doldrums. Here there is nothing healthy about consistency; what one would wish to see would be both ratios rising. The best that can be said by way of a generalisation is that if both ratios are steady and both above unity, then one can be reasonably satisfied and there is no real need to look further into the question of solvency.

If either ratio is rising then there is no real occasion for anxiety, but a little inquiry would be relevant. The business may be recovering from a bad patch; if so, good. However, it is well to remember that a high ratio could indicate too much liquidity. It may suggest that too much of the company's resources are being retained in quick assets when they could be more usefully invested.

If both ratios are falling there is indeed a reason for anxiety. Except in rare cases, where the fall is from a peak to a good average, a fall indicates one of two things. Either sales and profits are falling, or, although they are rising, there has been overtrading: i.e. too much being attempted on too slender a capital base. In either case there is the danger of going the road that leads to insolvency.

It is not necessary for both ratios to move in the same way. It may be found that the liquid ratio falls while the current ratio remains fairly steady. This could suggest re-stocking: i.e. debtors and cash are falling but stocks are increasing, due perhaps to over-production and/or lack of sales.

Again the current ratio may be rising while the liquid ratio remains constant. This could indicate a build-up of stocks, which again may indicate overproducing.

It would be unusual to find a falling current, and a steady liquid ratio, unless stocks are deliberately being run down.

So much for the theory. As an illustration, take the accounts of eight limited companies. The ratios diclosed are shown in Tables A and B.

The first three ratios in each case do not (as might have been expected) call for much comment. I.C.I.'s liquid ratio has been rising for four years; but 0·9 was probably on the low side and the rise is thoroughly healthy. The current ratio has remained fairly constant. The case of Imperial Tobacco has already been discussed.

Courtaulds have suffered a fall in the current ratio and a slight drop in the liquid. Neither calls for much comment, particularly as these both seem to have now levelled out. The fall is possibly explained by certain steps taken at that time to forestall a possible take-over bid by I.C.I.

The case of Lancashire Cotton Corpn. is more interesting. Here both

TABLE A
CURRENT RATIOS

	1960	1961	1962	1963
I.C.I.	2·0	2·0	2·2	2·2
Imperial Tobacco	3·2	3·0	3·1	2·8
Courtaulds	2·7	2·8	2·2	2·2
*Lancashire Cotton Corpn.	7·5	6·0	6·7	7·5
George Wimpey	1·8	1·6	1·8	1·6
Harland & Woolf	2·0	1·7	1·4	1·5
Newton Chambers	2·7	2·6	1·9	2·6
William Hancock	0·96	1·0	0·87	0·68

TABLE B
LIQUID RATIOS

	1960	1961	1962	1963
I.C.I.	0·9	1·0	1·2	1·3
Imperial Tobacco	0·93	0·89	0·95	0·82
Courtaulds	1·2	1·3	1·0	1·1
*Lancashire Cotton Corpn.	4·9	3·5	4·4	4·6
George Wimpey	0·62	0·52	0·62	0·68
Harland & Woolf	0·76	0·91	0·57	0·56
Newton Chambers	1·0	0·79	0·64	0·89
William Hancock	0·41	0·49	0·46	0·30

ratios are unusually high. There is no apparent reason for running a present liquid ratio of 4·6. Of course there might be some reason connected with the type of business; but unless this is known it can only be imagined that the company is not using its available assets to the best advantage. It is carrying in near liquid form funds which could be more permanently and profitably invested.*

George Wimpey & Co. are, of course, constructional engineers. The reason for their low liquid ratio (which is quite steady) lies in the enormous figure for stocks and work in progress, much of which is in

*See Appendix B, note 1.

fact liquid, as customers are normally required to pay regular amounts on account of the work so far done.

Harland & Woolf show a falling current ratio to a low point of 1·4 in 1962. The liquid ratio is a little erratic, but that too is at a dangerously low figure in 1962. Looking at the accounts one finds that in fact the company's profits fell from 1960 to a considerable loss in 1962. Thereafter things improved. The current ratio has now begun to rise and the liquid ratio has levelled out. This is another company that seemed, for a time, to exist on a very low liquid ratio. In fact shortly after this period a receiver and manager was appointed.

Newton Chambers show a fall in both ratios to 1962 and a rise thereafter. Profits actually fell during the whole period, though in 1963 the drop was fairly marginal. The reduction in dividends probably helped the liquidity position toward the end of the period.

The case of William Hancock has already been discussed. Here both ratios have fallen below what might have been thought of as safe. However, profits have been rising throughout the period concerned. The answer lies in the fact that liquid funds are continually being taken out of current assets and ploughed into improvements to licensed premises. Day-to-day business is being financed by a continually increasing bank overdraft. This is possibly well secured, but there is always the danger of a credit squeeze and a tendency for the source of funds to dry up. Should this happen the company might well find itself in difficulties. Though with such a horde of properties, probably undervalued, the difficulties should be only temporary.

A general point that may reasonably be made here is that a company can alleviate temporary financial difficulties by mortgaging or selling fixed assets, preferably real property. Remember, however, that less fixed assets will likely lead to less profits. Business may be put on an even footing again, but only on a lower level than previously.

So much for the question of solvency. Though it is difficult to be dogmatic about absolute figures, movements of ratios can be significant. What must be remembered is that the figures produced are not always instructive in themselves; rather, they may prompt inquiries where none were thought initially to be necessary. As with Hancock's so with many other companies — low or falling liquidity does not necessarily foreshadow insolvency. It may be a temporary embarrassment due to the implementation of a policy as a result of which a period of poverty must precede the promise of plenty.

Whatever the reason for the lack of liquidity, it can in most cases be restored at a cost, and it is with this cost that the investor must be chiefly concerned.

In the first place, if the company is still making profits, then those profits can be ploughed back into working capital until some sort of equilibrium is restored. If, due to insufficiency of profits, this does not seem an adequate solution, then other steps can be taken.

Firstly, funds can be borrowed either on short or long term. Short-term borrowing is usually a stop-gap measure. Its immediate effect is to raise the ratio; but as the funds must of their nature soon be repaid, it can only serve to tide over difficulties which are merely temporary. It is also expensive and has an adverse effect on profits. Long-term borrowing again has the effect of mortgaging future profits; and in any event there must be promise of sufficient future profit to pay the interest and eventually repay the loan; else the last state may be worse than the first. There is an exception when inflation is running at a very high rate, as in the U.K. from 1974 to 1977, then the fall in the real value of the capital to be repaid may exceed the interest payable over the period of the loan.

Secondly, funds can be raised by selling fixed assets. There are two possibilities to be considered. In the first place part of the business can be sold, the proceeds enabling the remainder to be carried on more satisfactorily but at a lower total earnings level than before. Alternatively, real property can be sold and rented back. This is a popular device for raising funds, but it is a "once only" measure. The rent will, however, be a further charge against future profits.

Whatever course is adopted, it is apparent that distributable profits are going to be less in the foreseeable future, and the likelihood of attractive dividends is small.

This is even more true if the fall in liquidity was due not to temporary difficulties but to more deep-rooted faults in the anatomy of the business, such as a serious falling off in the demand for its products. Such a position is obviously indicated by (a) falling profits; (b) long-term movements in the ratios; (c) general knowledge of the state of the market; and (d) trends in other ratios, which will now be discussed.

CHAPTER 4

Return on Capital Employed

THE solvency of the company having been ascertained, the next two questions of importance are firstly — How is it possible to arrive at some idea of the efficiency of the company? and secondly, What manner of return is it making on the money invested by the shareholders?

In tackling these questions there is one term, much used in balance sheets, which must be more closely examined, for it occurs on different occasions meaning quite different things. This term is what is known as "capital employed".

It is sometimes used to denote the total of share capital and reserves, sometimes including tax payable*, sometimes not. At other times it is used to describe the net assets. Obviously they will be equal to share capital and reserves if there is no loan capital — but this is to beg the question.

For present purposes we shall use the term to mean the total capital belonging to the shareholders: that is to say, issued share capital plus *all* reserves.

Turning now to the questions originally asked, and dealing with the second first: i.e. how to measure the return the ordinary shareholder is making on his investment. It is basically a matter of comparing profit with capital employed.

It is, of course, nothing to do with dividends. The rate of dividend quoted by a company is of little significance. It merely relates the profit *distributed* to the nominal value of the shares — ignoring reserves altogether. This is, or should be, of little interest to the investor. He may relate the dividend to the amount he is paying or has paid for his shares to note how much he is receiving as interest on his initial investment. But this is unimportant. It ignores the fact that in buying ordinary shares one

* See Appendix B, note 2.

is also buying an entitlement to an equal part of the company's reserves.

It is essential to remember that the real return on capital invested, as far as the ordinary shareholder is concerned, is the total profit of the particular year *available* for distribution, and not the amount actually distributed. Undistributed profits are the shareholder's savings; albeit involuntary due to a State policy of dividend restraint.

It is the ratio of total profit to capital employed that indicates the comparative adequacy of the return the company is making on the capital that appertains to the shareholders. And it is by watching the movements in this ratio that it is possible to judge the future prospects of the business. Dividends are often a matter of policy not a measure of success.

It is, of course, true that the main concern of the investor who buys in the market is the ratio that the annual dividend bears to the amount that he originally invested. But to think solely along these lines is to be most unrealistic. If the company is continually accumulating reserves then this fact means that part of the investor's profit is being reinvested without his express authority, and he should expect a dividend which represents a reasonable return on this also. This applies to ordinary shares though occasionally preference shares do have a right to participate in the reserves.

The point can be further emphasised (for it is a matter of no little moment) by considering the original purchase of a £1 share in a new company. In a number of years' time the investor may be receiving 25p each year. This sounds a more than satisfactory return. However, if the company has accumulated reserves equivalent to £4 for every £1 of nominal capital, the return the investor is really obtaining is 25p on £5; that is to say, 5% against the stated return of 25%. The present market price of the share will of course give some indication of this.

The position could also be stated in another way by saying that, inasmuch as reserves are being amassed, so are additional assets. Therefore the break-up value of the £1 share is now much greater than £1 and the investor would be most foolish to imagine that his stake in the company is still £1 and to proceed to compare his dividend with this. Were the company to be wound up, or were he to sell his share the amount he would receive would be far in excess of the nominal amount of his capital.

In order to be precise, at the expense of pedantry, it is necessary to make two points qualifying to a certain extent the previous paragraph. Firstly the break-up value of a share is not an aliquot part of the total assets as stated, for individual assets will not of course realise the amount at which they are shown — sometimes very much more, sometimes very much less, depending on the circumstances in which the business is sold, the methods of valuation previously employed and whether the sale is piecemeal or as a going concern.

Secondly, when referring to the price the share might fetch if sold, although the main concern of the buyer, and the primary factor that determines the price, is the dividend currently paid, so many other factors must be taken into account that the market price is not always a fair indication of the real value of the share. Such factors are consideration of future prospects; distrust in management; doubts as to government policy; and many more including one which particularly merits discussion, the possibility that assets are very much undervalued in the balance sheet.

Obviously the value at which assets are stated determines the "capital employed" figure which is being sought. If a building or plot of land was revalued and found to be worth five times the amount stated, then the increase in value represents of course a similar increase in the effective capital employed. The fact that the increase in value is no more than a measure of the fall in the value of money is for present purposes irrelevant — for in so far as the assets are inflated so generally will be the profits.

The important point is that, in considering return on capital employed and comparing either its movement within one company over a period or its record *vis-à-vis* other companies in the same or other lines of business, then it is quite absurd to relate profits which are stated in the language of present-day purchasing power to capital which may be stated in terms of the purchasing power of money from anything from one to fifty years ago.

The trouble arises from the accountancy profession's obsession with what is known as historical cost.* Assets are stated at what they cost at the time they were purchased, less any depreciation written off to date.

*Despite many committees and commissions, reports and recommendations, the position in 1979 is much the same as in 1963.

To illustrate the effect this has on the ratio we are seeking, consider the case of I.C.I. They have revalued their assets three times since 1948, the total surplus disclosed being about £150 million. This compares with a stated nominal capital at the time revaluations commenced of £85 million (of which £60 million were ordinary shares). The 1958 revaluation disclosed something like £54 million. This on the nominal stated capital in 1957 of £144 million — equivalent to a dividend of 38% tax free. The effect of the revaluations is illustrated by the statistical record shown in I.C.I.'s 1963 account, where the group income before tax as a percentage of funds invested dropped from 11% in 1957 to 8% in 1958.

Accounting-wise I.C.I. are a company which take their responsibilities seriously. Unfortunately the other companies chosen for analysis, with the exception of Newton Chambers, do not reflect quite so much credit. Hancock's assets are at cost; Harland & Woolf — freehold land, etc., at 1936 valuations with additions at cost; George Wimpey — at cost; Imperial Tobacco — at a mixture of cost and valuation; Courtaulds — at valuation 1939. Newton Chambers are the only company compatible with I.C.I. inasmuch as their assets were revalued at 1st January 1959; incidentally, the works, land and buildings of the holding company showed an increase of nearly 200%.

It is obvious that in considering the return on capital, present conditions make inter-company comparisons misleading. For instance, though Courtaulds may at present show a higher return than I.C.I., were their assets revalued at 1959 prices then the return may drop well below. These are fairly prosperous companies. What of those companies whose present earning power is less? It would be interesting to see the effect if all public companies were to restate their balance sheets in present-day values. It would not be surprising to find that a very great number of such companies were not only making a totally inadequate return on their capital, but in doing so, actually wasting both the shareholder's money and the country's limited resources. It is true of course that certain essential industries have, as a point of economic policy, to be run at an apparently unfavourable return (though the ratio will still indicate relative efficiencies within that industry). In order to do so government assistance or control may be necessary. However, so far as the companies outside this category are concerned (and these are surely in the majority), from the point of view of the shareholder, the rate of return on capital is, basically, the only measure of success — whether he is considering the progress of the company itself or comparing it with other companies within or without the same industry. Alas it seems, and that is the rub of all things, that all statements so far made must needs be qualified. In making the seemingly reasonable point that success is in effect measured by the ratio of profit to capital, two factors have been argued. These are of equal but intangible importance. This is not the time or place to indulge in political or philosophical musings: for if it were, the book would become of a far different nature. Suffice it to say that profit is no virtue if it be made at the expense of efficiency or social obligation. In the present context this means that the rate of return is no measure of efficiency. A company having a monopoly of a particular type of business may be making high profits and a high return on capital; but this is no gauge of its efficiency. With better employment of resources maybe the profits could be very much higher.

Secondly, suppose there are two companies, one of which is for a period showing a higher average rate of return than the other. That other company may be far more successful in the long run. It may be earning a much greater income but giving at the same time far greater benefits to employees in the form of high wages, bonuses, pensions, etc. This, besides being a social duty, could be an insurance policy for the future. It could make for far greater loyalties within that company and the avoidance of disputes and disagreements which could in the long run severely disable the company we first mentioned. It is a pity that benefits to employees over and above things common to all companies, are not shown as appropriations of, rather than charges against, profit.

So much for the various arguments, qualifications and comments. Perhaps now, knowing the reservations that are necessary, it is possible to examine the accounts we studied in the previous chapter and see how their various rates of return vary from year to year and between companies.

The first column (*see* Table C1) gives the method of valuation of fixed assets applied in each case, as this is of vital importance to any assessment that may be attempted. The second column gives the approximate proportion that net fixed assets bear to total assets employed (in 1963). This is so that we are better able to estimate the

TABLE C1

RATE OF RETURN ON CAPITAL EMPLOYED

Company	Basis of valuation of fixed assets	Fixed assets %	1960 %	1961 %	1962 %	1963 %
I.C.I.	Holding company 1958 others at cost	68	15·4	10·0	10·8	12·3
Courtaulds	1939 or cost	59	12·0	9·9	10·4	15·2
Imperial Tobacco	Cost	27	17·8	17·6	17·3	16·9
Newton Chambers	1959 or cost	35	7·6	8·6	4·6	3·7
Lancashire Cotton Corpn.	See note 2	40	14·4	12·5	3·3	3·3
George Wimpey	Cost	19	25·4	23·0	23·5	23·5
Harland & Woolf	1936 or cost	40	2·3	1·8	5·3 (loss)	0·54
William Hancock	Cost	81	15·3	17·9	18·3	17·0

Notes:

1. In each case group figures are used, as it is not normally possible to ascertain profit before tax for the holding company alone. In any event the shareholder is obviously more immediately interested in the group.

2. Group fixed assets of the Lancashire Cotton Corpn. are at 1935 valuation for the holding company and at valuations between 1933 and 1950 as regards subsidiaries. In each case with additions at cost.

3. The gross profit before tax, as shown in the accounts, has been used and this has been related to capital employed. The latter figure is difficult to establish in as much as it would not be reasonable to take the figure as at the end of the year as this includes the profit itself. On the other hand, it would be equally unreal to take the opening capital, for not only is it being supplemented day by day by profit but may at some point in the year be increased by the acquisition of new capital. (Note that a scrip issue does not affect capital employed as it is merely a transfer from reserves to capital account.)

possible degree of variation in return that would arise were the fixed assets to be revalued.

What has been done, therefore, is to take an average of the capital at the beginning and end of the year. Similarly, with the fixed assets figure.

At this point, what deductions might be made? It is difficult to generalise from such a small sample. Experimenting a little, try putting the companies in order of apparent merit, as the accounts of 1963 might indicate. It gives an order of precedence:

1.	George Wimpey	23·5
2.	William Hancock	17·0
3.	Imperial Tobacco	16·9
4.	Courtaulds	15·2
5.	I.C.I.	12·3
6.	Newton Chambers	3·7
7.	Lancashire Cotton Corpn.	3·3
8.	Harland & Woolf	0.54

For the moment it is reasonable to discount the two at the foot of the list in view of the rather unusual record of each, and particularly as they are in what are today rather unstable lines of business.

The interesting point of this table is that the first three use the historical cost method of accounting; the fourth, Courtaulds, uses a 1939 valuation; the fifth, I.C.I., a 1958 valuation, and the sixth, Newton Chambers, a 1959 valuation.

In other words, it would seem that the apparent success of a company is in reverse proportion to the accuracy with which its assets are valued. This in itself is an extraordinary state of affairs, but will remain so until the State and the accounting profession can agree on some mutually acceptable method of accounting for inflation.

It appears then, from what we see here and from our previous arguments, that we must abandon hope of using rates of return on capital employed in comparing the investment potential of one company as against another, except by comparing the relative increase or decrease in each company over a certain period.

The absolute figures are in fact valueless; what must be considered is the movements in the ratios.

As an investor, what conclusions would be drawn from the figures shown in the table? For reasons we have previously discussed, any deduction we make is subject to very many qualifications. Nevertheless, the figures are not valueless, particularly within the individual company as the qualifications apply with equal force to each year.

In the first place, I.C.I. seems fairly secure. It is showing a fairly high rate of return, which though falling in 1961 is on the upturn once more. This high rate of return is, remember, all the more creditable considering the fact that the assets of the holding company (which represent about seven-eighths of the group) were revalued as recently as 1958.

Courtaulds seem to be showing a reasonable but unsteady return; falling in 1961, then in 1963 rising considerably, which does not tie up directly with turnover variations; however, there is insufficient information to comment further on this. In comparing Courtaulds and I.C.I. remember that

    (a) Courtaulds return is based on very low asset valuations.

    (b) The improvement shown by Courtaulds could be due to the influence of I.C.I. which in 1963 owned 37·5% of the ordinary stock of that company.

Imperial Tobacco are showing a high return — third to Wimpey's in fact — though it has been falling throughout the period; but both ratios are subject to the fact that assets are at cost — a revaluation could bring them down with a bump.

Newton Chambers seem to be going through a rather bad period since 1962. Their present rate of return is 3·7, which can hardly be considered satisfactory. According to the chairman's statement the main trouble lies in the continual heavy losses of one of the largest subsidiaries, Ransome & Rapier Limited.

The Lancashire Cotton Corpn. is as much the other side of the looking glass as it was in the previous chapter. Its ratio in 1960 and 1961 is out of all proportion to that in 1962 and 1963. Between October 1961 and October 1962 there was a big fall in trading profit, but no explanation of this is given in the annual report. As has been already said, the cotton industry is going through a difficult stage, though such empiricisms hardly explain the most remarkable change of fortunes shown by our figures, let alone the need for the abnormal liquidity ratio disclosed in the previous chapter.

George Wimpey seems on a fairly even keel. The high rate of return is probably partly due to undervaluation of fixed assets; but to what extent it is difficult to say, as in this case fixed assets represent only 19% of the total. One point to note about this type of company, i.e. large-scale contractors, is that a great deal of money is tied up in stocks and work-in-progress: in Wimpey's, 1963, 45% of total assets. It is obvious that an error in valuation of this figure in any year could considerably influence profits. However, when talking of trends it would be necessary to overvalue stocks and work-in-progress by an increasing amount each year to keep up a stable and high, though false, level of profit. This would soon end in disaster. The reason for making the point is that in considering one set of accounts in isolation it is worth bearing in mind. In the accounts which we are considering, a 5% error in valuation would mean a 22·5% error in profit.

The case of Harland & Woolf is rather exceptional. This is a company basically concerned with shipbuilding. We could apply similar comments here as with Wimpey's, so far as stock and work-in-progress are concerned. Actually, in 1963 a 5% error in the valuation of this item would affect profits by 450%. But then this is hardly fair comment, as the profit for the year was exceptionally low. It does, however, indicate that should such a company wish to show a profit, as against a previous loss, or a higher than normal profit in any one year, this is easily done by exaggerating the value of work-in-progress. It is true that the accounts are audited. Alas, it is also true that no auditor, or few at least, will vouch for the accuracy of work-in-progress of such a kind and quantity to anything near 5%, if at all. In fact, as with Wimpey's, they often rely on a director's valuation; though when this is so the fact should be stated. However, in discussing Harland & Woolf, all that can really be said, the only conclusion that can honestly be drawn from our figures, is the rather obvious one that the company is going through a bad period. Business reached its nadir in 1962 and showed some improvement in 1963. There is little else to be said without going into a detailed discussion of the economies of this particular kind of trade and the difficult conditions, both as regards staffing and competition, that apply.*

Last on the list is William Hancock. This is a company which at first sight seems to offer a very favourable rate of return, a rate which was in fact increasing up until 1962 and showed a slight fall in 1963. The essential point to remember here is, as was emphasised when considering Imperial Tobacco, that the fixed assets are at cost, and it is more than extremely likely that a revaluation would bring the ratios down with a bump. It is very much more so in the case of Hancock's than with Imperial Tobacco for whereas the latter has only 27% of its capital

---

*In fact, as pointed out earlier, it was soon necessary to put the business into the hands of a receiver and manager to protect the few assets that remained.

tied up in fixed assets, Hancock's has 81% so employed. A revaluation here could make a striking difference to the apparent prosperity of the company. It is, however, dangerous to be too dogmatic. Many of their houses are in valuable town sites; but on the other hand many are in country districts where either the value of the land or the pub itself may not have risen as much as might be expected. There are many imponderables.

The figures in Table C1 as has already been emphasised are of little value for absolute comparisons between the companies themselves. Each company in turn has been discussed and as it is suggested continually unless assets are valued on the same basis inter-company comparisons are of little worth — in the sense that Wimpey's 23·5% cannot be compared favourably or otherwise with I.C.I.'s 12·3% as both are not arrived at on the same basis.

It is possible, of course, to set one company against another in studying the movements of the ratios in each company. It is difficult with the figures as they stand because of the difference in dimension. The form of comparison can be clarified if the figures in Table C1 are translated into the same or equivalent terms by use of index numbers, taking 1960 as 100 — *this* will give the relative proportional changes in the figures for each company and absolute comparisons of variations in prosperity become possible.

Using this device the table will read as follows:

TABLE C2

RATE OF RETURN ON CAPITAL EMPLOYED

(1960 = 100)

Company	1960 %	1961 %	1962 %	1963 %
I.C.I.	100	65	68	80
Courtaulds	100	83	87	127
Imperial Tobacco	100	99	97	95
Newton Chambers	100	113	60	49
Lancashire Cotton Corpn.	100	87	23	23
George Wimpey	100	90	93	93
Harland & Woolf	100	55	−240	25
William Hancock	100	117	120	111

This table is in certain ways more instructive than Table C1 inasmuch as differences caused by variations in accounting methods are to a great extent eliminated.

The most noticeable fact is that 1960 was a bumper year for all except Hancock's in the sense that only Courtaulds in 1963 and Newton Chambers in 1961 topped the rate earned in that year. Hancock's have bettered it in each year.

Looking at 1963 we find that whereas I.C.I. is 20% down on the base year, Courtaulds are 27% up. This disparity in achievement is not immediately apparent from Table C1. Is it significant? No! For had we chosen 1959 as a base year, profits and ratios may have been such as to show a position in 1963 quite the reverse of the one that here appears.

In fact such a table, though useful for studying trends within a company and even for comparing trends from company to company, is still of little use for making absolute comparisons of rates of return, particularly when it tends to cover so short a period.

CHAPTER 5

Return on Ordinary Share Capital and Reserves

SO FAR, discussion has been centred on the rate of return on capital employed, having defined this as the ratio that profits before tax bear to total share capital and reserves.

Now when talking of shareholder's interests we are normally speaking of ordinary shareholders. Members holding preference shares or other shares of a similar nature usually have a prior but limited right to a share in profits. They are in most cases entitled to a fixed dividend which may be cumulative and nothing more. In some companies they have carefully defined rights to a further share in profits. This may be merely a right to participate in surpluses on a winding up or it may entitle them to a second dividend after the ordinary shareholders have received so much. These rights are not necessarily apparent in the accounts and are ignored for present purposes. In any event since the judgment in *Dimbula Valley (Ceylon) Tea Company* v. *Laurie* it seems that preference shareholders with rights to participate in surpluses on winding up have no present claim to any part of the reserves of the company be they capital or revenue.

It is now possible to construct a new table, this time excluding preference capital from the capital employed and deducting the gross preference dividend from the profit figure. Also included in this table is actual ordinary dividend paid, but expressed not, as is usual, as a percentage of nominal capital but as a percentage of the average total capital and reserves applicable to shareholders.

Table D seems at first sight quite a beanfeast for a statistician — one thinks immediately in terms of variations from means, standard deviations and correlations between dividend rate, and earnings rate among various companies. Such things will be left for the while. The present discussion is rather more simple.

RATE OF RETURN ON ORDINARY CAPITAL AND RESERVES

Company		1 Ordinary Capital and Reserves (see Appen- dix A) £000	2 Profit £000	3 Ratio of col. 2 to col. 1 %	4 Com- para- tive figure Table C %	5 Ord. div. (gross) col. 1 %	6 Ratio of div. to return %
I.C.I.	1960	538,594	86,308	16·0	15·4	6·6	41
	1961	579,460	60,116	10·4	10·0	6·3	60
	1962	616,295	68,633	11·1	10·8	6·0	54
	1963	655,399	83,173	12·7	12·3	6·3	50
Courtaulds	1960	157,515	20,074	12·7	12·0	4·7	37
	1961	171,543	17,727	10·4	9·9	4·6	44
	1962	154,949	16,716	10·7	10·2	6·4	60
	1963	136,961	22,657	16·5	15·2	9·0	55
Imperial	1960	144,345	27,181	18·9	17·8	9·4	50
Tobacco	1961	151,888	28,228	18·8	17·6	8·9	47
	1962	162,806	29,721	18·2	17·3	8·3	46
	1963	173,398	30,811	17·8	16·9	8·2	46
Newton	1960	12,465	943	7·5	7·6	4·5	60
Chambers	1961	13,261	1,139	8·6	8·6	4·0	47
	1962	13,302	627	4·7	4·6	3·8	81
	1963	13,232	494	3·7	3·7	3·8	103
Lancashire	1960	24,575	3,606	14·4	14·4	8·2	57
Cotton	1961	25,027	3,175	12·5	12·5	8·1	65
Corpn.	1962	24,682	805	3·3	3·3	5·7	173
	1963	24,015	794	3·3	3·3	5·9	179
George	1960	10,869	3,025	27·5	25·4	3·7	14
Wimpey	1961	12,683	3,108	23·9	23·0	3·2	13
	1962	14,200	3,178	22·7	21·1	2·9	13
	1963	15,997	4,016	25·1	23·6	3·8	15
Harland	1960	14,138	250	1·7	2·3	1·8	106
& Woolf	1961	14,294	185	1·3	1·8	0·9	69
	1962	14,356	1,036 (loss)	6·3 (loss)	5·3 (loss)	1·8	—
	1963	14,341	35 (loss)	0·27	0·54	0·9	—
William	1960	1,886	324	17·1	15·3	4·4	26
Hancock	1961	2,255	459	20·4	17·9	6·1	30
	1962	2,667	578	21·4	18·8	6·1	28
	1963	2,874	568	19·2	17·0	5·5	29

The first point to note is that the claims of the preference shareholders are, except in one case, Harland & Woolf, easily satisfied. In the companies analysed the proportion of ordinary to preference capital has been very high. It is a pity, but in fact is usually the case. For this reason there is little difference between column 3 and column 4. Column 3 usually has the edge, owing to the fact that whereas the preference capital is only entitled to a fixed percentage of profits, its real earnings are higher; and its exclusion, by taking a large slice of capital and a small slice of income from the figures in Table D, naturally boosts the return on ordinary share capital and reserves.

A second point of general interest is the way in which dividends that are paid compare with profits earned — there is often no apparent relation whatsoever. The apparently prosperous companies tend to pay over about half their earnings, the remainder being ploughed back. Wimpey's, however, pay over a very small portion indeed.

The actual proportions paid over are shown in the final column of Table E. Notice how companies in a weak position tend to pay out more than they earn, drawing on reserves. This is of course a state of affairs which cannot be but temporary. As a matter of interest we may take the average paid out over the four years.

TABLE E

DIVIDEND AS PERCENTAGE OF
RETURN

	%
I.C.I.	50
Courtaulds	49
Imperial Tobacco	47
Newton Chambers	64
Lancashire Cotton Corpn.	83
George Wimpey	13
Harland & Woolf	—
William Hancock	28

Note: In the case of Harland & Woolf, as the figures in column 3 of Table D for 1962 and 1963 are a minus quantity it is difficult to give a true comparative figure.

The one interesting fact about Table D is the fascinating similarity between the ratios shown by the first three companies, all large and each prosperous. The high rates of the fourth and fifth, i.e. Newton Chambers and Lancashire Cotton Corpn., are due to the fact that both have fallen on lean years and both for obvious reasons wish to keep up dividends. To do so, Newton Chambers has recently had to scrape the barrel of its profits, and the Lancashire Cotton Corpn. has had in the past two years to draw heavily on reserves. To make any assessment of the true dividend policy of both these companies it would be necessary to consider figures over a much longer period.

George Wimpey and, to a lesser extent, William Hancock are retaining a large part of their profits. In both cases the Chairman's Report indicates reasons for this. Wimpey's have a large construction programme ahead and are worried by rising costs. Hancock's are spending a great deal of money on improvements to licensed houses — apart from which their liquid position does not permit the payment of large dividends.

Harland & Woolf are in a rather difficult position, and in their case any dividend paid must, apart from being nominal in degree, come from any available reserves — a process which cannot continue indefinitely as subsequent events demonstrated.

With reference to the dividend column (Table F), it is interesting to compare the rate shown with the rate quoted by the companies in the financial press. The quoted rate is based on nominal capital only.

The obvious fact here is the total discordance between quoted and actual dividend rates.

The man on the Clapham omnibus reading his paper, whether he be a shareholder, an employee or a financially disinterested party, would on seeing the dividends quoted imagine that the members of the company were being rewarded handsomely for the money they had invested. Had he the information shown in the table just compiled he would be perhaps pleasantly surprised.

True, the investor when he purchases shares in the market is interested solely in the return he will make on the money he pays for these shares. However, as at any particular time the cost of the shares is principally determined by the dividend paid or expected to be paid, there would be little advantage at this point in prowling through the

TABLE F

		1960	1961	1962	1963
I.C.I.	quoted %	16·2	11·75*	13·7*	11·1*
	actual per Table D %	6·6	6·3	6·0	6·3
Courtaulds	quoted %	12·5	10·0	12·5	15·4
	actual %	4·7	4·6	6·4	9·0
Imperial Tobacco	quoted %	22·5	22·5	22·5	18·5*
	actual %	9·4	8·9	8·3	8·2
Newton Chambers	quoted %	17·0	18·0	13·0	13·0
	actual %	4·5	4·0	3·8	3·8
Lancashire Cotton Corpn.	quoted %	25·0	25·0	17·5	17·5
	actual %	8·2	8·1	5·7	5·9
George Wimpey	quoted %	10·0	10·0	10·0	7·5*
	actual %	3·7	3·2	2·9	3·8
Harland & Woolf	quoted %	5·0	2·5	5·0	2·5
	actual %	1·8	·09	1·8	·09
William Hancock	quoted %	17·5	17·5	20·0	20·0
	actual %	4·1	6·1	6·1	5·5

*Increased capital automatically lowering rate of dividend when quoted on nominal capital only. The total dividend in cash terms may be higher, as "actual" figure would indicate.

records of the past in order to include in the table the rate which the dividend paid bears to the current market price.

This would give the return which the public demands on that particular investment — taking into account various factors such as the risk element. This may make for interesting comparisons and it is intended to discuss the matter in more detail in a later chapter. At the moment concern is with the information that can be extracted from the balance sheet itself. It is only then, having done this, that it is planned to go on to use outside sources for comparative purposes.

To return to Table F. This emphasises, as has been already noted, the discordance between quoted and actual rates. What is of far greater interest is the level of the actual rates themselves.

Of the eight companies mentioned, two can possibly be considered as what are known as "blue chip" investments: i.e. I.C.I. and Imperial Tobacco. Now if it is assumed — and this is an arbitrary though conservative and reasonable assumption — that the gross yield on gilt-edge securities is expected to be in the region of $5\frac{1}{2}\%$, then it follows that the expected yields in public companies should be greater according, amongst other things, to the risk element prevalent at the time in the type of industry. Short of making a detailed statistical analysis of all firms within that industry, such yields would be difficult to ascertain. It is reasonable to say, however, that a company of long standing should show a yield above $5\frac{1}{2}\%$ (new and rapidly expanding companies are exceptional inasmuch as they often show unrepresentative and often highly fluctuating yields during the process of settling down).

Bearing those facts in mind, what of the figures shown in Table F? I.C.I., as might be expected, is showing a comfortable rate of return. Imperial Tobacco, the other blue chip investment, is also showing a fairly stable rate. It seems to be quite a deal more prosperous than I.C.I. but as has been seen, this is an illusion brought about by historical cost accounting.

Leaving aside the matter of asset revaluation for the moment, and considering the position of the other companies, Courtaulds seems in recent years to be pushing its head above water. Newton Chambers are, contrary to the picture given by the quoted dividend, passing a steadily lower return to ordinary shareholders: a return which is, and has been for four years, well below $5\frac{1}{2}\%$ (and this is a company that revalued its assets in 1959). Lancashire Cotton Corpn. is following the example of Newton Chambers, though at an apparently higher level again due to false asset valuation. George Wimpey appears to be paying a consistently inadequate dividend, falling till 1962 and picking up again in 1963. Harland & Woolf do not seem to merit much comment, their dividend return being virtually non-existent. Hancock's are paying a dividend which just about hovers around the blue chip $5\frac{1}{2}\%$ (which Hancock's, alas, is not).

So much for figures and conjectures. What is their relevance? Is the actual rate of dividend important? Is not the shareholder more interested in the return he makes on the money he pays for his share? And thirdly is it not true that though less than $5\frac{1}{2}\%$ is paid to shareholders a great deal more is, in many though not all cases, ploughed back in the form of forced savings?

All this may be true. But the purpose of ploughing money back is to enable the company either to exist or expand. In either case, if, although this process is repeated year by year, the rate paid on total shareholders' capital remains below the gilt-edged return, something is amiss. (One may wonder in many cases whether the nation's resources are being properly employed — this without particular reference to any of the companies which are being used for purely illustrative purposes.) It can happen for short periods while reorganisation or a large capital project is in process, but the purpose of this re-employment of profits is to increase the prosperity of the business and if this is not reflected in high and rising *real* dividend rates then where is it to be found?

So much for general remarks. There seems little point in discussing the position of each company separately at this point inasmuch as the information we have accumulated has not, except for the dividend position, given any further scope for comment than was possible in the previous chapter. It is best, then, to go on to the next problem, that being the incidence and proper treatment of depreciation reserves. It is a matter of some delicacy and the ideas used have no general acceptance at the present. Such a qualification must be made lest critics should claim the unwary are being led astray — which is quite opposed to the avowed purpose in writing this particular book.

CHAPTER 6

The Incidence of the Reserve for Depreciation

THIS is a difficult subject to tackle not because of its complex nature but because it is necessary to some extent to convince people away from the tradition of centuries.

The reserve for depreciation has always been shown in the balance sheet as a deduction from the fixed assets to which it applies. The present contention is that it should appear as a capital reserve on the liability side of the balance sheet.

The reason is quite easily demonstrated and simple to grasp — but to some perhaps difficult to accept. The point is, when depreciation is charged in the profit and loss account, no money is then spent. Consequently the working capital is increased by that amount. If the working capital is increased then so also is the effective capital employed. In fact, taking any balance sheet, the total of the depreciation reserve represents, or rather is represented by, additional working capital in whatever form it is held. Some of this "working capital" may of course have been turned into new fixed assets, but this does not affect the argument, which is that additional capital, to the extent of the total reserve for depreciation, has been retained in the business.

If the business has been in receipt of additional working capital then this is probably being used to earn additional profits, and it is unrealistic to compare these profits with the figure previously used as capital employed. The profits must be compared to the capital used in earning them, and this capital includes the reserve for depreciation.

It can, of course, be argued that the additional working capital in existence by virtue of the accumulated depreciation is swallowed up in maintenance charges on the ageing equipment and cannot therefore be considered productive. It could be argued further. Given a fairly stable non-expanding company it could be claimed that the continual scrapping and replacing of assets at different times keeps the accumulated depreciation figure at a fairly steady level. So does it stabilise maintenance charges. No one can possibly argue, however, that the total accumulated depreciation in, say, Newton Chambers case (amounting to over £2 million) is being used to finance the maintenance of plant and machinery while their trading profit in 1963 was less than £1 million.

A further point which might be mentioned here is that from a comparative point of view differing methods of dealing with depreciation can have a bedevilling effect both on the relative capital employed in two companies within an industry and the return which that capital earns.

The principal methods of charging depreciation are (a) on a straight line basis, and (b) on a diminishing value basis. There are two points to be made. Suppose two companies start business simultaneously, each with one asset costing £1,000 and working capital of £500. Suppose Company A writes off the asset (agreed life 10 years) on a straight line basis: i.e. at £100 per year. Company B uses a diminishing value basis, writing off say 40% of the written down value each year. Suppose each company earns profit before depreciation of £750. We then have the following position at the end of the year.

	Company A £	Company B £
Profit before depreciation	750	750
Depreciation	100	400
Net profit	£650	£350
Return on average capital of £1,125	57%	31%

This is obviously absurd. Both companies are in fact during this first year making the same return on capital employed. The difference is that Company B is putting a greater proportion aside for asset replacement, and as this is deducted from income appears to be making less profit.

It will be argued, quite truly, that as time progresses and both companies acquire more and more assets the respective annual depreciation charges may tend to equalise, inasmuch as A is putting equal amounts aside each year on all assets whereas B is putting aside large amounts on new, but very small amounts on old.

This is a fair comment and profits may, even after depreciation, be comparable *but*, and this is vitally important when considering rates of return, B's assets in total will always be at a lower net book figure than A's merely because B writes them down more rapidly, i.e. the initial difference will never be made up.

Consequently, one of a certain number of things must happen. If each company pays away all surplus (i.e. net profit, or equal proportions thereof), then B will have more working capital than A — in which case B's profits should be higher than A's and B will show a higher rate of return. Assuming equal efficiency this is quite misleading.

Secondly, if neither company pays away net profits, working capital will remain the same but the apparent capital employed in A will be greater than that in B, and again B will show — quite wrongly — a higher rate of return.

Thirdly, if dividend policies differ, the working capital to fixed capital ratio will vary accordingly but B will always show to an advantage.

The only solution lies, as has already been shown, in transferring Depreciation Reserve to Capital Reserves and thereby presenting a true picture of the real capital employed in the earning of profits. Only then does any comparison of rates of return become feasible — for in the case instanced, B's higher profit will then be balanced against a higher figure of capital employed.

So much for the incidence of varying depreciation policies. The second argument that will be developed is this. Depreciation Reserve is transferred to the Capital Reserves. What will happen when an asset is scrapped and replaced? Capital employed will fall by the depreciation written off. Yes, but so will working capital and therefore so should profits. The relation of the new profit to the new capital employed will remain the same as the old to the old — which is as it should be. Nothing has really changed.

This applies particularly in a large company. In a smaller business, where the quantity of plant is small, and in any organisation where the replacement is on a large scale, the fall in the level of maintenance costs may affect profits so as to increase the apparent return but this is merely a matter of increased efficiency which we shall be discussing later.

Where assets are replaced not out of working capital but out of new funds, then capital employed alters only by the difference between replacement cost and accumulated depreciation no longer required. Of course in a company which operates an historical cost system the amount may be considerable. It will, alas, further bedevil the study of movements in rates of return, but this is not the fault of the thesis being now put forward but further evidence (if such were needed) of the complete futility of an historical cost system.

If the old asset is replaced by something more elaborate and costly, then obviously the cost of the new machine will exceed the depreciation on the old — and capital employed will increase — as it should — for if new funds are introduced to buy better machines then obviously the assets of the business have increased. If the new purchase is made out of working capital then capital employed will fall by the accumulated depreciation, but profits may fall to an even greater degree due to the severe fall in working capital available for running the business.

Perhaps the point can be pressed home by a slightly absurd but nevertheless relevant example. Take the case of a man selling cabbages out of a wheelbarrow which he trundles round the town. As he sells and profits he puts money aside to replace the wheelbarrow when it wears out or when he wants something bigger. But these savings, though not spent on beer, are not left idle. They can be used to increase the stock of cabbages and perhaps branch out into cauliflowers. The savings for replacement in fact INCREASE THE CAPITAL EMPLOYED. They enable him to earn more profits till he is possibly in a position to buy a new wheelbarrow out of surplus moneys quite unconnected with the money originally put aside for the purpose.

True, the large and heavily mechanised business is in a slightly different position. However, remember that the rate of return on capital employed is a measure of the efficiency with which shareholders' capital is being used. Now if money is put aside and used in the business, profits will be affected, and where returns are increasing they should rise proportionately. If the reserve for depreciation is shown as a capital reserve then capital employed will increase with profits and tend to stabilise the return. As things are at present, when depreciation is shown as a deduction from the asset, capital employed remains stable and the rate of return will rise. This gives a completely false picture of the true state of affairs. There is no increase in the efficiency with which the capital is being used. There is merely more capital to employ.

It is true that as machinery ages maintenance costs increase, thus cutting profits. If the suggestions made are followed, then the rate of return will tend to show a decline depending on the proportion that maintenance bears to income. But this is reasonable. A business continuing to employ ageing assets can only preserve its efficiency at the cost of higher repair charges — profits must be affected and this should be reflected in the return on capital. It is not under the present system, except should the maintenance costs increase each year by the additional depreciation provided — which in practice is of course extremely unlikely, for if maintenance exceeds depreciation the asset had in many cases best be scrapped and replaced.

In any event, as has been pointed out already, in an established business where assets are continually being scrapped or replaced and, taken individually, are all of differing ages, maintenance will tend to level out, as also will the depreciation reserve (assuming stable prices and non-expansion). In such a case the whole of the depreciation reserve is in use as working capital; and as there is no material variation in maintenance, profits will not be affected thereby. Consequently, unless the reserve for depreciation is shown as part of capital employed the rate of return thereon is going to be overstated — sometimes considerably so where fixed capital investment is high.

At the risk of labouring the point too much: the amount put aside for depreciation each year is for the ultimate replacement of the asset. It is not for use in maintaining the asset. It is, until the asset is replaced, additional working capital and *increases effective capital employed*. The fact that the machinery is only kept at its original efficiency by increasing maintenance charges is not relevant to the argument. If it is costing more to run the plant, then the resulting lower profits should be reflected in a lower return on capital. The earning potential of the capital employed declines as the plant ages and this should not be denied by using a method of accounting which tends to suggest quite the opposite.

However, do not forget that in a fairly stable industry the rate of return does not normally fall each year, because the averaging out of plant age and maintenance tends to have a stabilising influence. What is relevant, though, is that the rate of return, though stable, will be at a

TABLE G

RETURN ON CAPITAL EMPLOYED INCLUDING DEPRECIATION RESERVE

Company		1 Total capital and reserves £000	2 Total depreciation reserve £000	3 1 and 2 £000	4 Col. 3 less preference capital £000	5 Profit to col. 3 %	6 Comparative figure Table C %	7 Profit to col. 4 %	8 Comparative figure Table D %	9 Dividend to Col. 4 %	10 Comparative figure Table F %
I.C.I.	1960	573,331	100,657	673,988	639,251	13·1	15·4	13·5	16·0	5·5	6·6
	1961	619,197	139,528	758,725	723,988	8·1	10·0	8·3	10·4	5·1	6·3
	1962	651,032	173,207	824,239	789,502	8·5	10·8	8·7	11·1	4·7	6·0
	1963	690,136	213,016	903,152	868,315	9·4	12·3	9·5	12·7	4·7	6·3
Courtaulds	1960	175,018	60,093	235,111	217,599	9·3	12·0	9·2	12·7	3·4	4·7
	1961	189,056	67,724	256,780	239,268	7·3	9·9	7·4	10·4	3·3	4·6
	1962	172,546	73,140	245,686	228,088	7·2	10·2	7·3	10·7	4·3	6·4
	1963	154,643	75,450	230,093	212,495	10·3	15·2	10·6	16·5	5·8	9·0
Imperial Tobacco	1960	157,203	28,961	186,164	173,306	15·1	17·8	15·8	18·9	7·8	9·4
	1961	165,171	31,335	196,566	183,463	14·5	17·6	15·7	18·8	7·4	8·9
	1962	176,164	31,777	207,941	194,893	14·7	17·3	15·3	18·2	6·9	8·3
	1963	186,268	33,335	219,603	206,733	14·4	16·9	14·9	17·8	6·9	8·2
Newton Chambers	1960	12,594	530	13,124	12,991	7·6	7·6	7·3	7·5	4·3	4·5
	1961	13,394	934	14,328	14,195	8·0	8·6	8·1	8·6	3·9	4·0
	1962	13,435	1,379	14,814	13,481	4·3	4·6	4·5	4·7	3·7	3·8
	1963	13,365	1,846	15,211	15,078	3·3	3·7	3·3	3·7	3·5	3·8
Lancashire Cotton Corpn.	1960	24,582	3,762	28,344	28,332	12·9	14·4	12·9	14·4	7·1	8·2
	1961	25,039	4,536	29,575	29,563	10·6	12·5	10·6	12·5	6·7	8·1
	1962	24,694	5,121	29,815	29,803	2·7	3·3	2·7	3·3	4·7	5·7
	1963	24,027	5,575	29,602	29,590	2·7	3·3	2·7	3·3	4·7	5·9
George Wimpey	1960	12,414	10,615	23,029	21,484	13·7	25·4	14·1	27·5	1·9	3·7
	1961	14,228	10,760	24,980	23,435	12·9	23·0	13·3	23·9	1·7	3·2
	1962	15,745	11,617	27,362	25,817	12·2	21·1	12·8	24·8	1·5	2·9
	1963	17,542	12,334	29,876	28,331	13·7	23·6	14·6	25·1	2·1	3·8
Harland & Woolf	1960	16,738	10,549	27,287	24,687	1·4	2·3	1·0	1·7	1·8	1·8
	1961	16,894	11,241	28,135	25,535	1·1	1·8	0·73	1·3	0·9	0·9
	1962	16,956	11,731	28,687	26,087	3·1	5·3	4·0	6·3	0·98	1·8
	1963	16,941	11,950	28,891	26,291	(loss) 0·32	(loss) 0·54	0·13 (loss)	(loss) 0·27	0·45	0·9
William Hancock	1960	2,336	740	3,076	2,626	11·3	15·3	12·5	17·1	3·2	4·4
	1961	2,847	852	3,699	3,106	13·6	17·9	14·8	20·4	4·4	6·1
	1962	3,402	891	4,293	3,558	14·5	18·8	16·2	21·4	4·5	6·1
	1963	3,609	942	4,551	3,816	13·4	17·0	14·9	19·2	4·2	5·5

lower and truer level if depreciation reserve is shown among capital reserves, where it belongs, than it is where conventional accounting methods are used.

At this point perhaps it is better to cut the verbiage and start once more to play with figures.

The quantity of figures contained in Table G is rather frightening. It is of course in intent informative. Is it in fact? Has the effort been justified (mine in calculating — yours in reading thus far) by making it possible to reach further and more useful conclusions? That something has been achieved is apparent by a quick glance at the considerable fall in the rates of return on shareholders' capital which is occasioned by the inclusion of depreciation reserve as part of that capital.

The trend in prosperity of course remains the same, for each company; but the amount they appear to be earning (see column 5) for their members does not impress quite so much as at the beginning of the investigation (more particularly in the case of Wimpey's). Of course the figures are still bedevilled by the historical cost convention and some attempt will later be made to eliminate this final barrier to a reasonable assessment. For the moment, note that I.C.I. and Newton Chambers, the two companies with a reasonably up-to-date valuation of fixed assets, are showing a return which is certainly a far sight from profiteering.

It might be useful to a proper appraisal of the figures just prepared to assemble one or two supplementary tables, each dealing with a separate aspect of the picture.

Firstly, consider the figures relating to the return on total shareholders' capital and reserves (Table H). Rather than take each year separately or, for that matter one year in particular (for no year can be considered truly representative), it is reasonable to take an average for the four years in both columns 5 and 6 and show also the proportion that the fixed assets of each company (before depreciation) bears to total assets employed.

This table certainly makes obvious the considerable effect on rates of return of including the depreciation reserve. As has been already said, it is impossible to make any valid intercompany comparisons because of the different bases of asset valuation. One or two comments may however be useful.

TABLE H

AVERAGE RATE OF RETURN ON TOTAL SHARE CAPITAL AND RESERVES

	1 Gross fixed assets to total assets 1963 %	2 Original rate of return per Table C %	3 New rate of return per Table G %	4 Reduction %
I.C.I.	74	12·1	9·8	19·0
Courtaulds	84	11·8	8·5	28·0
Imperial Tobacco	34	17·4	14·7	17·3
Newton Chambers	50	6·1	5·7	6·6
Lancashire Cotton Corpn.	43	8·4	7·2	14·5
George Wimpey	45	23·3	13·1	43·8
Harland & Woolf	58	0·54*	0·32	40·7
William Hancock	83	16·7	13·2	21·0

*In this case the 1963 figures have been used, as an average would have given a negative figure, which would have tended to confuse rather than instruct.

In the first place, note the enormous reduction in the return shown by Wimpey's. This is explained by the fact that fixed assets are almost completely written off and their reinstatement by transferring the depreciation reserve consequently has an abnormal effect on capital employed.

Imperial Tobacco's fairly low reduction, and that of Lancashire Cotton Corpn., is explained obviously by the relatively low proportion of fixed assets employed. Harland & Woolf have already been mentioned as being in a difficult position and any figures produced are likely to be abnormal.

The only other company that seems to deserve comment is Newton Chambers. The inclusion of the depreciation reserve here seems to make only a fairly small difference to the return. The reason here is the opposite to that given for Wimpey's. Newton Chambers' charge for depreciation is small and the aggregate is still fairly low when compared with total fixed assets. Much the same, though to a lesser extent, can be said for Lancashire Cotton Corpn.

The one remaining point is to note that in the majority of cases — the exceptions being Wimpey's and Harland & Woolf — there is a definite degree of correlation between the weight of fixed assets and the reduction in the rate of return. There is little point in establishing the degree of correlation by statistical methods, however, until such time as it is possible to revalue the assets of all companies on the same basis. It is interesting none the less to note that even without such a necessary step being taken there is a certain order to be seen if we ignore the two companies mentioned above.

The order of fixed asset importance and the fall in the rate of return can be shown thus:

	Fixed asset	Rate of fall
1.	Courtaulds	Courtaulds
2.	William Hancock	William Hancock
3.	I.C.I.	I.C.I.
4.	Newton Chambers	Imperial Tobacco
5.	Lancashire Cotton Corpn.	Lancashire Cotton Corpn.
6.	Imperial Tobacco	Newton Chambers

The reason for the reversal in order of Imperial Tobacco and Newton Chambers can be found above.

Table I shows the rate of return on ordinary capital and reserves, this time introducing the additional factor of dividends.

TABLE I

AVERAGE RATE OF RETURN ON ORDINARY CAPITAL AND RESERVES

	1 Fixed assets (gross) to total assets 1963 %	2 Rate of return per Table D %	3 Rate of return per Table G %	4 Fall in rate %	5 Dividend rate per Table D %	6 Dividend rate per Table G %
I.C.I.	74	12·6	10·0	20·6	6·3	5·0
Courtaulds	84	12·2	8·6	29·6	6·0	4·2
Imperial Tobacco	34	18·3	15·3	16·4	8·7	7·2
Newton Chambers	50	6·1	5·8	3·9	4·0	3·8
Lancashire Cotton Corpn.	43	8·4	7·2	14·5	7·0	5·8
George Wimpey	45	24·8	13·7	44·8	3·4	1·8
Harland & Woolf	58	—	—	—	1·3	1·0
William Hancock	83	19·5	14·6	25·1	5·5	4·0

Note. No figures are shown for Harland & Woolf where they would be misleading.

There is no need here for further comment as to the rate of fall except to draw attention once more to its extent. The correlation between this and the fixed assets is exactly as in Table H.

The ordinary dividend deserves comment. If you recall the discussion following Table D you will remember that it was decided that I.C.I. and Imperial Tobacco, being "blue chips", might fall to 5½% in normal times without an eyebrow raised. Other companies would be expected to do better. It seems, however, from Table I that Imperial Tobacco are the only company paying anything like a fair return. True, Lancashire Cotton Corpn. are paying 5·8%, but apart from the fact that they are not "gilts" their present rate is falling fast and at the moment, i.e. in 1963, they are paying 4·7%.

Looking at Table I again you will see that the average is a fairly true picture, trends apart, for no company except Imperial Tobacco, and, initially, I.C.I. and Lancashire Cotton Corpn., has paid anything like a reasonable dividend for four years. What is more, dividend rates in five of the companies have been steadily falling. True (as has been said before), profits are being "saved" on behalf of the members, but even so there is little point in saving continually to an extent that the member never receives a reasonable return on his real investment and merely lives on the consolation of there being large sums which he owns but apparently will never it seems receive.

As a last point: in Chapter 5, Table E, the relation between the ordinary dividend and the rate of return was discussed — on an average basis over four years. The experiment could be repeated with our new figures to note if there is any change (Table J).

The inclusion of depreciation reserve has not caused the figures in Table E to vary. This is obvious, as the only change is the denominator of the fraction. The slight differences are due to the necessary use of approximations in dealing with large figures. The only interesting fact that arises from Table J is the difference between average and 1963 rates of distribution.

Comparing column 3 with column 1, it appears that I.C.I., Imperial Tobacco and Hancock's are each this year keeping close to the average in the proportion of profit which they distribute. The very fact that they are in 1963 maintaining a four-year average is a reasonable sign of stability in distribution policy — though to the investor this may be of

TABLE J

	1 Average ord. div. as % of rate of return Table G	2 Comparative figure Table E %	3 Actual 1963 %
I.C.I.	50	49	49
Courtaulds	48	49	54
Imperial Tobacco	47	48	46
Newton Chambers	67	66	106
Lancashire Cotton Corpn.	84	83	174
George Wimpey	13	14	16
Harland & Woolf	—	—	—
William Hancock	27	28	28

little financial comfort in cases such as Imperial Tobacco, where profits are falling.

Courtaulds have stepped up the proportion distributed. There seems little point in seeking an answer — which in any event probably lies with I.C.I.

Newton Chambers and Lancashire Cotton Corpn. are going through lean years, as is apparent from the average proportion of profit distributed. In fact, in order to satisfy shareholders both have found it necessary in 1963 to draw upon reserves; Lancashire Cotton Corpn. considerably. Such a state of affairs obviously can be but temporary. Either profits must increase or dividends must fall. In both cases the trend is not very encouraging, though Lancashire Cotton Corpn., having cascaded suddenly in 1962 from a relatively high to an abnormally low return, does at least seem to have preserved stability in the last two years.

Wimpey's seem to have increased their distribution policy above average. Apart from the fact that it was low enough in any case — they have increased their share capital in 1963, which made an increase in actual dividend necessary if the published rate was to be preserved. As profits did not increase proportionately the distribution ratio naturally showed an increase.

So much for the influence of the depreciation reserve and the relation between dividends and profits. It is still not possible to compare company with company, due to the matter of varying asset valuations and the consequent unreliability of the figure of capital employed. The time has come now to examine this problem more closely — though in doing so it may be necessary to make some assumptions and hypotheses which will, because of their apparent arbitrariness, be rather suspect. It is, however, a problem that must be tackled, and the reader can but make his own decision as to whether to accept the manner in which the attempt to do so is made. No claim to particular ability in this matter is put forward other than the application of what appears to be common sense.

This "common sense" may or may not correspond to the state of thinking of the various professional accounting bodies on the matter of accounting for inflation at the time this book is read. A considerable amount of time and money has already been devoted both by the State and by committees representing the various professional organisations in the world of accounting with the object, so far unattained, of prescribing standards that could or should or must be adopted by members in practice. The arguments have been so diverse and the conclusions so consistently opposed that a parallel with the confusions within the Tower of Babel must inevitably be drawn. Until effective methods of accounting for inflation are both agreed and implemented by law then any serious student is advised to think the matter out for himself as we have attempted to do here.

CHAPTER 7

The Significance of Revaluation of Fixed Assets

Now it is patent that in any project to assess the return a man is making on his capital we must relate his profit which is measured in present time purchasing power to the capital figure stated in the same monetary terms.

For instance, suppose Fred Blogg buys a house for £1,000 in 1939 which he lets out at a net profit of £100. The return on his capital is 10%. Suppose that by 1964 he has managed, by increasing the rent, and in spite of higher maintenance costs, to increase his profit to £200. Is it reasonable (as present-day accounting methods suggest) to claim that Blogg is now making a net return on capital of 20%? Surely common sense knows that the value of money has fallen considerably since 1939 and prices have arisen accordingly.

The purchasing power of the £1,000 invested originally by Blogg will have fallen. In terms of present-day prices (not necessarily of houses but of goods and services for which that £1,000 could alternatively have been used) the value of the house would be say £3,000. In fact, if Blogg sold the house for £1,000 in 1964 he would be making a loss of £2,000. Now if the true value of money invested is now £3,000 the profit of £200 gives a return of only 6·7%, less than that earned originally. However, there is another factor to take into account — demand. If the demand for houses has risen disproportionately to the demand for other things, then the prices of houses will have risen more than the prices of other goods — supposing that supply has in each case remained constant. In fact due to a fall in supply, a rise in demand and an increasing scarcity of land, property values in most well populated parts of the country have risen very greatly indeed and it is not unusual to find a house selling at more than eight or nine times its 1939 price.

In the example given the accountant may argue, and often does, that for accounting purposes the selling price of assets is irrelevant for accounts are prepared on the assumption of continuation of business. However, when considering the capital employed the fact cannot be ignored that the fixed assets in question would cost, say, £7,500 to replace. Blogg could sell up at £7,500 and use this money for other purposes. His real rate of return is in fact only 2·7%, not the 20% that appeared in the annual accounts.

When applying these principles to companies operating on a much larger scale, it is wise of course to be a little careful. It is impossible to ignore the first point regarding the general effect of inflation on capital originally invested, i.e. the capital employed should be stated in terms of present-day purchasing power. (You may say, "Purchasing power of what?" — Well inasmuch as the capital belongs to members who could, had they retained it, have put it to alternative uses, then a fairly general index of prices would be a relevant measure.) The point being that profit in terms of today's prices cannot be valuably related to capital stated in what, in effect, is a foreign currency.

When coming to the second point, which was the exceptional increase in price caused by special conditions of demand or scarcity of the object, then it is necessary to tread a little more carefully. A company may have real property which they could sell for five times its original price, e.g. a warehouse in an area wanted for housing development. However, while the company continues in business unless it can sell this asset *and replace it at a lower price* with something of equal utility, then the saleable value is not relevant and cannot honestly be used to influence assessments of capital employed — unless the saleable value of all assets together exceeds the present book value in which case the total net surplus could be added to capital and reserves.

Taking up a point made in the previous paragraph, what exactly is the significance of "replacement cost"? Is it reasonable to revalue assets on this basis? What exactly is the end in view? An equitable method of measuring the real capital employed. There is a suspicion of approaching deep waters. Perhaps they could be evaded by tackling this seeming many faceted problem methodically and systematically.

In the first place, replacement cost can be relevant, as noted earlier, where it is less than saleable value of a particular asset (this is sometimes the case with land, buildings, etc.). It is relevant not in itself but in view of the fact that the realisable value of that asset is then a satisfactory measure of the actual capital invested and it can logically be considered apart from the other assets, provided that the asset could be sold and replaced at the lower price without noticeably affecting the operation of the business. This is a most important point. A company may have a factory in a site much more valuable in an alternative use (e.g. for housing development). The land may be shown in the books at £2,000. Its replacement cost may be £4,000 (i.e. the cost of a site of equal value to the company in an alternative area) but its sale price may be £10,000. Now this is a rather particular problem. We cannot rewrite the balance sheet of the company and revalue the land at £4,000, for replacement, though cheaper, would involve the complete dismantling of the factory and probably the effective abandonment of a certain part of the plant. It may even in some cases be necessary to sell up all fixed assets and, as it were, begin again. It is necessary, then, to modify previous conclusions to the extent that, where replacement of the particular asset would necessarily involve the replacement of some or all of the other fixed assets, then it cannot be revalued at sale price unless total sale price exceeds total replacement price of all as it were interrelated assets.

So far so good. But if sale price is, as will be found in most cases, below replacement cost — what then? On what basis is it fair to revalue? At replacement cost? If not, then how?

At this point it may be found that discussion becomes easier when returning to previous primitive examples.

Suppose Fred Blogg is in business again selling cabbages from a wheelbarrow. His balance sheet reads (ignoring irrelevant items).

Balance Sheet

	£		£
Capital	16	Wheelbarrow	10
		Cabbages	3
		Cash	3
	£16		£16

After Blogg has trundled his barrow around for 10 years his accountant decides (being a radical man) that the barrow should be revalued. Its sale value is about 50p (the years have taken their toll). Its replacement price is £25. *However*, barrows today are not what they were ten years before. In fact the actual barrow cannot be replaced, being no longer manufactured. All that is available is an improved model. The increase in price is partly due to the improvement but mostly due to inflation.

In these circumstances the replacement price is effectively no use for revaluation purposes, primarily because it is an unknown factor. All that is known is the price of an object which will do the same job but do it better. (In this example it is perhaps difficult to think in terms of superior wheelbarrows — say the new model has fins and independent suspension!) Anyway to be serious, how is a revaluation to be approached?

What must in fact be discovered is how much capital in terms of today's purchasing power Blogg has loaded up in his wheelbarrow.

If it is intended to follow the principles laid down in the previous chapter it is necessary to ignore the fact of depreciation of the barrow and assume that maintenance has preserved its utility value to Blogg, i.e. it performs its appointed task as well now as it did ten years before, even though its realisable value is negligible due to the fact that far more efficient barrows are now on the market.

On this premise, and for the moment ignoring changes in the value of money, then the barrow cannot be valued at less than it originally cost. It is true that if sold it would fetch a paltry 50p, but it must be emphasised now and for all time that the break up value of an asset is an entirely different quantity from its value in use, and is of no relevance (except in the exceptional cases hitherto described) when valuing the property of a business (which is, and intends to continue to be), a going concern. The point can be considerably clarified by taking the example already being used. In the first place, the value of the wheelbarrow to Blogg as an essential "tool of his trade" is far greater than its value to a purchaser in the open market who looks upon it as an antique accessory to his gardening equipment. Secondly, the value of the wheelbarrow to Blogg is necessarily influenced by the fact that if he is to remain in business *he must have a barrow* and (ignoring the fact that he may get one second-hand, which would merely beg the question) to obtain something of equivalent use would now cost him as much as, if not more than, the original cost of the old item.

It is therefore quite wrong to consider the sale price as a factor in a revaluation. How then does the argument proceed? Much depends on the particular circumstances. If Blogg's barrow was still being produced, and assuming again a stable currency, then the present price of replacing the barrow would be a fair figure at which to revalue. This price is not necessarily equal to the old, due to changing conditions of supply and demand. The principle can be applied generally.

However, as in Blogg's case so in all; neither of the necessary conditions seems ever to apply. In all industry, an asset, particularly a machine, is seldom replaced by the same thing: firstly, because of the desire of the company to move forward, and secondly, because of the fact that the supplier is continually improving (or at least altering) his product and a machine will in nine cases out of ten become unobtainable long before its useful life has ended.

Again, the value of money does not remain stable, and varies not only generally but at different speeds and in different markets.

Taking one aspect of the problem at a time. Suppose first that it is possible to ignore the second factor, i.e. changes in money values.

This leaves the problem of revaluing an asset which has no known replacement cost inasmuch as there is no identical machine on the market. Is it reasonable then to use the historical cost as being a constant? No; conditions of supply and demand vary continually and the cost of the same machine today, were it available, is not necessarily the same as it was ten years previously. Is there any way of gauging the hypothetical present-day cost? On the other hand, is this relevant? The issue seems to be becoming a little confused. Perhaps it would be better if we were to take up again our wheelbarrow.

Suppose the day after Blogg purchases his wheelbarrow at £10 the price rises to £15. Suppose also that the present premise of a stable currency still applies and that the prices of all other goods and services are constant. What should be policy regarding valuation in the accounts? Now Blogg has invested £10 as capital to acquire the barrow. The *general* purchasing power of this £10 has not altered: wheelbarrows apart he could make the same use of the £10 the second as he could the first day. *However*, and this is the critical point, Blogg is committed to the purchase of wheelbarrows. We are working on the premise of a continuing business, and in terms of wheelbarrows the purchasing power of his £10 capital is now very much less than previously. In order to obtain a true picture of the real capital employed it would be necessary to revalue the wheelbarrow in Blogg's accounts at £15; that is, at its replacement cost, which is in this case a known factor. The same argument would apply had the price fallen. It could then have been necessary to revalue downwards.

It has been supposed that the price rose immediately after purchase. Basically this was an unnecessary premise. The same rules must apply whenever the price increase occurs. The value of the barrow in the accounts should be the replacement price (assuming for the moment that this is known).

Having constructed this argument most carefully it can now be demolished. This does not make it superfluous, for in order to achieve a convincing solution to the problem in hand all avenues of approach must be explored carefully and either accepted as proper or rejected as irrelevant.

Now some time ago the purpose of the exercise was said to be that of measuring the real return on shareholders' capital invested. It was suggested this could only be achieved by measuring the profit and the capital employed in terms of the same units of purchasing power.

Now the basic purpose of profits is not to buy fixed assets. In the silly example Blogg does not seek profits to enable him to buy more and more wheelbarrows. He may in fact eventually decide to do so, with the ambition of expanding his business and thereby increasing his income. Nevertheless, this is a decision concerning what to do with the profit earned, whether to spend it on beer, bingo or wheelbarrow — into which many arbitrary factors creep. The basic point is surely — and it is even more obvious in a limited company — that the profits earned are available to the members to do with as they please.* They are not mortgaged to the purchase of fixed assets, i.e. assuming proper provision has been made for replacement in the accounts of each successive year. They belong to the members and can only be assessed in terms of their general purchasing power. Now if the profits are to be measured in these terms, so must also be the capital, i.e. the fixed assets must be valued according to the present general purchasing power of the

*Within limits prescribed by the State.

money originally invested therein. For the moment it is best to think in terms of valuing this change by reference to a basic retail price index.

What of the increased cost of replacement of particular assets both in the circumstances discussed earlier, and more generally where the value of money is constantly changing? In what way do such phenomena influence the argument? If the cost of replacing a machine has risen (assuming for the while that the machine can be replaced by another the same), then part of what are normally referred to as net profits must necessarily be detailed to supplement the replacement reserve where this is based on normal depreciation principles. It might be contended that the profits, or part thereof, are therefore measured in terms of their power of purchasing the machines and that capital should be valued accordingly. This is of course an interesting contention. It is of course invalid. The point is that throughout the life of the machine the provision for replacement (depreciation is an obsolete word) should be geared to the current cost of renewing the machine. Consequently the net profit will be stated after the fixed assets have been maintained intact.

The argument appears now to have run into a corner from whence there seems no immediate escape. It is intended to show a replacement reserve based on the cost of renewing assets; it seems logical that this should be supported by a revaluation of assets on the basis of replacement cost. It has previously been claimed that the assets must be revalued according to the movements in the general purchasing power of money. How are these two points of view to be reconciled?

Perhaps confusion arises from the way the argument has been framed. The idea that replacement cost was a proper basis for revaluing an asset whether it be above or below the historical cost was dismissed. Was this justified? Yes! The value of an asset to a business which is a going concern is something very nebulous and most difficult to define with any confidence.

Consider an everyday example, relevant to but quite unrelated to industry. You have a car, of reasonable performance. You purchased the car say five years previously for £500. Its present sale value is £40 (you've flogged it a little). To replace it with an identical model would cost £600. To obtain another vehicle which would be of equivalent utility would cost £450. Now state the present value *to you* of your car. It is suggested that none of these figures we have quoted is relevant to a proper revaluation, except perhaps the first — the original cost — which would need to be revised according to changes in general price levels over the period.

The replacement value (either of them) is *at the moment* irrelevant inasmuch as you do not intend (or cannot afford) to replace. The sale price is obviously of no interest as you do not intend to sell, the car having been maintained in running order. It is fully "depreciated" and besides the capital (and interest) involved in purchasing a new car the depreciation on such might not differ much from present maintenance costs.

You may actually, for reasons of price or persuasion, be saving for eventual replacement — but the amount you have saved, though keyed to the current price levels of the model in mind, bears no relation whatsoever to the present value to you of the car you at present possess.

Actually, to value the vehicle is a task which is best not attempted in so far as *personal* possessions have merits and advantages which are only apparent to the particular owner.

The purpose of the exercise was merely to illustrate the difficulties of valuation and to clarify the points already made with reference to replacement cost and sale price. It is now best to return to the sphere of commerce.

Taking up again the matter of the wheelbarrow, it seems that we must account for various basic situations. Firstly, where the price of all goods and services remains steady. Here there is no problem and no need for revaluation.

Secondly, the case already instanced, where the general price level remains steady but, due to say supply problems, the price of wheelbarrows rises. Here it is necessary to subdivide our discussion into cases — where the wheelbarrow is replaceable by an identical object and where it is not.

Suppose, as was previously suggested, that Blogg buys at £10 but some time later the price of an identical wheelbarrow rises to £15, other prices, as was assumed, being stable. What should Blogg do?

It has already been premised that the business must be looked upon as a going concern and therefore it is necessary to assume that replacement will *eventually* be essential. Consequently it can be insisted that Blogg provides for the replacement on the basis of a price of £15. The point that concerns us is does he also revalue the barrow on the same basis and if so, then why?

Turning to the concept of alternative use. The money that Blogg locked up in the barrow was £10. This money is worth no less now in terms of general purchasing power, only with respect to the buying of wheelbarrows. The fact that a replacement would cost £15 does not affect the fact that the capital invested and represented by the wheelbarrow was and is £10 in terms of its value in alternative uses. It might be argued that alternative uses become irrelevant once capital is committed to a *particular* use. This is a sound counter-point. Nevertheless, and even on the assumption of a going concern basis, the capital is not committed for all time and if when it is released (assuming no capital loss on dissolution), it is of the same value to the investor in terms of general purchasing power as it was when he first invested; and if this would be so whenever the release was effected, one cannot say that in the particular case the capital employed in terms of fixed assets has increased beyond the original cost of the wheelbarrow.

The same argument would apply in a situation where the replacement differed from the original due to improvements in styling, efficiency, etc., and where the original is in fact unobtainable. Provided the general value of money in terms of alternative uses remains fairly constant (i.e. where there is no general inflation or deflation) then price changes in the replacement cost of assets, although they should determine amounts put to replacement reserve, should not affect the valuation of the asset in the accounts.

The talk has been mainly of wheelbarrows but the same principle applies of course in industries of all sizes. There is only one qualification to make, and this is that where, as was mentioned pages previously, the replacement price has risen sharply, so that the current price at which the asset could be disposed of is greater than cost, then this is the value at which the asset should be shown. The contingency will arise very rarely, if at all, particularly when the qualifications previously made are introduced.

To continue. The way seems clearer now for having established one thesis the second flows naturally from it.

Where the replacement cost of an asset rises and the increase is due not to particular conditions of supply and demand as in the preceding case, but to a general fall in the value of money, then the previous argument is reversed. Here the value of the capital in alternative uses is altering and the stated capital employed must be varied, accordingly, by revaluing the fixed assets. How is this done?

In conditions where prices were rising proportionately for all products the answer would be simple: use the current replacement cost — though only in cases where actual replacement seems possible. Such conditions rarely exist. In the first place, prices do not rise proportionately; secondly, the asset is rarely replaced with a similar item. In such circumstances — which are the normal type — all that need be done is to revalue the assets on the basis of a very general index of prices. As the profits (and the capital) when invested belong (or belonged) to shareholders who would spend the money fairly widely otherwise, a consumer index is obviously indicated. (These are published in papers such as the *Monthly Digest of Statistics*, H.M.S.O.).

What of the mixed case, where the price rise is partly caused by inflation and partly by special market conditions? The answer flows obviously from what has already been discussed. There will never be any reason for revaluing an asset at less than its present equivalent cost determined by the price index chosen. The combination of the two factors just mentioned can only then refer to the possibility of a higher value being ascribed to an asset. As is stated below, this can only be considered when quoted shares are held as an investment other than a trade investment; for example, the temporary employment of otherwise idle funds in the Stock Market. In this instance it would be arguable that no harm would be done by showing that investment at its market value — if, and only if, that value is greater than the equivalent present worth of the moneys originally invested in those shares.

So much for the theory behind revaluation. It will apply to all fixed assets whatever their nature: to land, buildings, plant, machinery, vehicles, etc. Problems would arise, however, in the valuing of investments, both trade and other.

Trade investments are those investments in a supplying or associated company, for example, made for the purpose of furthering the aims of the business.

The method of valuation depends on the circumstances. If the company has a controlling interest, i.e. is a holding company, then the shares must be valued on the basis of a revaluation of that subsidiary's assets. This is because the holding company has literally power to force such revaluation and will then value the shares on the basis of the new capital employed figure revealed, i.e. on a capital basis rather than on a dividend (or earnings) yield or market price.

Where the trade investment consists of quoted shares and the calculation of value just outlined is less than the quoted price, this is no justification for using the higher market price. The fact that the shares are in the hands of the holding company may well give that company access to facts not available to the investing public.

Other trade investments, those where the investor does not hold a controlling interest, will be valued in the same way as other fixed assets. Investments other than trade investments will be treated likewise with the proviso, discussed above, as to the possibility of applying a higher value to quoted shares.

Having discussed the theory of revaluation in such detail it seems rather unfortunate that it is not possible now to go on to apply these principles to the companies we have taken for illustration purposes in previous chapters. Unfortunately this cannot be done without very much more information than is available to us. We cannot apply an index unless we know the year in which the asset was purchased, and assets are obviously being purchased continually. It is possible however to make some attempt, basing calculations partly on actual fact (i.e. where year of purchase is given) and partly on conjecture and the experience of other enterprises — though of course their methods may differ from those that have so far been laid down. It is possible at least to experiment and, provided the hypotheses are conservative, then although no fast conclusions can be drawn it may at least be possible to obtain some general pointers as to the possible effect of revaluation in particular cases. The best procedure will be to deal with each company systematically and make the assumptions quite clear so that the reader may judge for himself whether or not in the circumstances they are or are not reasonable. Accuracy is out; it is merely a question of drawing provisional conclusions from often unreliable hypotheses. Nevertheless, in the end it may be that the results are closer to the truth than was thought probable.

The deductions may be wrong, but on the conditions selected the errors will be most likely to tend towards putting too low a value on the assets and therefore towards giving a relatively generous impression of the return being made on the members' capital employed.

At all costs it is important to avoid being accused of gross exaggeration, and it is on this basic premise that evaluation will be primarily attempted.

After all these excuses and provisos it may be wondered whether the task is really worth the effort and imagination involved. This is a question that cannot be answered at this stage; it must await a closer examination of the actual figures and facts themselves.

Even then the reader may be left with tongue in cheek. But if nothing else is done except to show the direction in which the figures we have taken as our guides to progress and proficiency will move, and to what possible extent, in each particular company chosen, then at least some merit may be claimed.

In any event, the reader who has had the patience to come this far may be interested in the exercise even if it does little more in most cases than illustrate the futility of attempting something which perhaps not even Holmes could achieve.

Consider now each company in turn.

I.C.I.

Here the difficulties may at first seem less, for I.C.I. have revalued their assets more than once since 1945. However, two facts immediately come to the fore. Firstly, the basis of valuation is not known, nor whether it corresponds to the principles selected. Secondly the revaluation applied to the holding company only.

It will be necessary, for want of more information, to accept the revaluation up to December 1958. The fixed assets of the group at that date were valued at £493 million. At 31st December 1963, they were £570 million.

Now on the basis of the accounts for four years beginning with 1960, how is it possible to say how much of the £493 million just referred to applies to the "other" companies in the group? In 1960 the holding company's proportion was approximately 63%. If this is applied to the figure just given it is found that the holding company's share is £311 million leaving £182 million for the companies which have not revalued their assets. This figure is, however, the written down value. Again on the basis of the 1960 figures the cost would be approximately £218 million, i.e. the written down value increased by one-fifth. How now is it possible to revalue this figure? The problems are that

(a) We do not know the basis used by the parent company.

(b) We do not know the age of the assets.

(c) The parent company have revalued their assets more than once and so the percentage increase in 1958 is no guide.

Looking ahead at Newton Chambers, it seems that though their basis for revaluation is not the same as has been argued, the actual figures for the holding company show an increase of 75%. The group increase for Newton Chambers was 68%. Taking into account the proportion of assets attributable to the "other" companies, they show an increase of approximately 54%.

It is true that whereas Newton Chambers is an 1882 company, I.C.I. is a 1929 company. It could mean that the former has older subsidiaries. Again, I.C.I. may have formed a greater part of their subsidiaries themselves and fairly recently. This cannot be known without far more detailed investigation and going behind the accounts themselves. To be exact would actually, for reasons which it is unnecessary to explain, be impossible. Noting that Newton Chambers show a 54% increase for "other" companies, we might give I.C.I. the benefit of many doubts, and conservatively award them an increase of 40%. This brings us to a total fixed assets for these companies of £305 million, an increase of £87 million. This is the figure at 31st December 1958. Trade investments in 1958 were £126 million. If these were also increased by the same amounts it would mean a further £50 million, giving a total increase of £137 million. The approximate net book value of the assets of the holding company at that time was £311 million. The equivalent cost (based on the reserve for depreciation in 1960) would be approximately one-fifth above, that is, £373 million and excluding trade investments.

Total fixed assets revalued at cost, then, are £854 million at 31st December 1958. The price index at this time was 146·5; in 1963 it was 163·7, i.e. an increase of 11·6%. The increase in fixed asset values is therefore in the region of £99 million, to which must be added the £137 million above, giving a total estimated increase of £236 million.

Courtaulds

Courtaulds is a fairly old company born in 1913. It would be reasonable to base any revaluation on Newton Chambers and I.C.I.'s experience. However, Courtaulds' assets were revalued in 1939 and those of its subsidiaries are stated at cost or revaluation at an unspecified date.

The position here seems not a little difficult. It is necessary to know the portion of present fixed assets which existed in 1939 and the date at which the assets of subsidiaries were revalued. It would be better still were it possible to know the cost prior to revaluation — then we could work on the Newton Chambers hypothesis.

The only alternative, then, is to throw down the gauntlet and suggest that as I.C.I. showed an increase in company assets of 25% between 1950 and 1958 and group revaluations seem to be slightly lower, then it would be particularly conservative, considering the extraordinary increase in prices between 1939 and 1950, to assume that Courtaulds' assets on revaluation would show an increase of 50%.

This gives a figure to the nearest million of £75 million, including trade investments with other fixed assets.

Imperial Tobacco

The assets are at cost. The company was established round about the turn of the century. The proportion of land and buildings to plant is higher than with I.C.I., rather closer to Newton Chambers. The inclination would be to revalue group fixed assets by 68%, i.e. £52 million.

The trade investments show a surplus of £108 million on quoted investments. The surplus on the unquoted is comparatively negligible.

The total surplus is an amount of £160 million.

Newton Chambers

Little difficulty is presented assuming the revalued figures of 1st January 1959 are acceptable. All that is necessary is to increase the fixed assets by 11·6%, giving roughly speaking an increase of £1 million.

Lancashire Cotton Corpn.

This presents a well-nigh impossible task. The holding company's assets are at 1935 or subsequent cost. Subsidiary companies' assets are at valuations ranging from 1935 to 1950. What to do? The one important point seems to be that the major part of the fixed assets (around 80%) are owned by the holding company. There should be little danger of exaggeration in adding on 60%, which gives a figure of say £10 million. There is also a surplus on investments of £1 million. This is based on sale price, which is above revaluation on the basis being used. The total increase is therefore put conservatively at £11 million.

George Wimpey

The company is about the age of Courtaulds: 45 years old. Its assets are at cost. Its plant and buildings mix is fairly similar to I.C.I. As most of the assets are attributable to the holding company, and as it is an older company than I.C.I., it would probably be fair to increase assets by 75%; say £15 million conservatively.

Harland & Woolf

Here the fixed assets are based on a 1936 valuation. The usual problems occur, but as with Courtaulds and Lancashire Cotton Corpn. it is best to play safe and increase by say 60%. The reason for using 60% here and in the Lancashire Cotton Corpn. case, against 50% in the Courtaulds case, is that there was a considerable increase in prices between 1935/36 and 1939 (e.g. index rose by 8% between 1936 and 1939).

This would give an increase in asset values of £13 million.

William Hancock

The fixed assets are here split between those at net book value 1948 and those at cost.

The appreciation of those at cost must, by 1958, have been somewhat similar to the I.C.I. revaluation percentage in 1958, i.e. 25%; though in so far as I.C.I.'s revaluation was from 1950 and more important, inasmuch as so much of Hancock's assets are in property, the increase is probably far greater. It would be best however to be conservative and treat it as 30%, giving us a figure of £1,136,000. As for those at written down value 1948 (property dating from the nineteenth century) an increase of 100% would be reasonable in order to bring them back to cost and arrive at their appreciated value. This would mean adding £1,092,000.

As has been noted, here we are dealing with property and as was explained in the introductory essay the value of property usually exceeds the index adjusted cost — in which case the saleable value should probably be used — subject to the limitations given.

It is probably a case, then, of gross understatement in merely adding by way of total revaluation surplus £2,228,000; without detailed information which is not available, it is impossible to do more.*

General Notes

1. Goodwill has been ignored from the point of view of revaluation. Where it consists of trade marks, patents, "know how", etc., it can have a real value. However, it is a difficult asset to value even in such instances. Where it merely represents a surplus of capital over assets acquired then its value is far more nebulous and may actually be non-existent. This matter is discussed in greater detail at a later stage in the argument.

2. Comparative figures for years other than 1963 have been roughly computed on the basis of the retail price index of the Ministry of Labour statistics on incomes prices, employment and production. They are actually January figures but we have accepted them on the grounds that (a) the accounting dates of various companies differ, (b) it increases the conservatism of the figures of revaluation.

*See Appendix B, note 3.

3. As experience has indicated that return on ordinary capital is only slightly different (being a fraction higher) than return on total capital in Table K the latter is ignored as unimportant.

4. The profit figure has not in any way been adjusted to allow for the additional depreciation which would be necessary on the revaluing of the assets.

The initial sum would of course be a transfer from general reserve. The annual increment, though considerably smaller, would however be material and could affect adversely the ratios shown, sometimes to a considerable extent. It has, however, been decided to ignore this, and the reasons or rather the excuses for taking this step are:

(a) The relative impossibility of arriving at a supportable figure in any year. This is because the amount charged depends partly on the split between property and plant, the latter being more heavily depreciated, partly on the method of depreciation and finally on whether the revalued assets are those which tend to be no longer subject to depreciation, being mostly written right off.

(b) If the depreciation reserve is increased to a great extent, then obviously the increased funds are going to earn a return which must be set against the additional depreciation charge. As both these figures are incalculable and would require too much supposition to even estimate with any hope of precision, it has been decided to ignore each at present and merely suggest that they may tend to have a minor net effect — the tendency being toward a lowering of the ratio. Such a step is therefore consistent with a policy of excessive caution in the present stage of our argument. A policy which adds to the force of the various conclusions that are attempted.

What conclusions can be drawn from this table, accepting the fact that the new percentages are in this case hypothetical to the extent that they are based on figures arrived at by conjecture rather than fact? Correct figures would be relatively impossible to ascertain even were access possible to the books of the companies concerned — though in that event a far greater degree of accuracy would have been possible. Nevertheless, the figures selected were arrived at on the basis of experience and were most assuredly on the low side. Therefore any conclusions drawn, if wrong, will show the companies concerned in a better light than were the true figures available.

TABLE K

RETURN ON CAPITAL EMPLOYED
(after hypothetical revaluation of assets)

Company		1 Ordinary share capi- tal and reserves Table G £000	2 Revalu- ation surplus £000	3 (1 + 2) £000	4 Profit to col. 3 %	5 Com- parative Table G %	6 Divi- dend to col. 3 %	7 Com- parative Table G %
I.C.I.	1960	639,251	214,000	853,251	10·2	13·5	4·2	5·5
	1961	723,988	222,000	945,988	6·4	8·3	3·9	5·1
	1962	789,502	231,000	1,020,502	6·7	8·7	3·6	4·7
	1963	868,315	236,000	1,104,315	7·6	9·5	3·7	4·7
Courtaulds	1960	217,599	69,423	277,022	7·2	9·2	2·7	3·4
	1961	239,268	70,840	310,108	5·7	7·4	2·5	3·3
	1962	228,088	73,600	301,688	5·4	7·3	3·3	4·3
	1963	212,495	75,100	287,595	7·9	10·6	4·3	5·8
Imperial Tobacco	1960	173,306	148,000	321,306	8·5	15·8	4·2	7·8
	1961	183,463	151,000	334,463	8·4	15·4	4·0	7·4
	1962	194,893	157,000	351,893	8·4	15·3	3·9	6·9
	1963	206,733	160,000	366,733	8·4	14·9	3·9	6·9
Newton Chambers	1960	12,991	926	13,917	6·7	7·3	4·0	4·3
	1961	14,195	945	15,140	7·5	8·1	3·5	3·9
	1962	13,481	982	14,463	4·3	4·5	3·5	3·7
	1963	15,078	1,000	16,078	3·1	3·3	3·1	3·5
Lancashire Cotton Corpn.	1960	28,332	10,149	38,481	9·4	12·9	5·3	7·2
	1961	29,568	10,356	39,924	7·9	10·6	5·1	6·8
	1962	29,803	10,760	40,563	2·0	2·7	3·5	4·7
	1963	29,590	11,000	40,590	2·0	2·7	3·5	4·7
George Wimpey	1960	21,484	13,700	35,184	8·6	14·1	1·1	1·9
	1961	23,435	13,980	37,415	8·0	13·3	1·1	1·7
	1962	25,817	14,520	40,337	7·9	12·8	1·0	1·5
	1963	28,331	15,000	43,331	9·3	14·6	1·4	2·1
Harland & Woolf	1960	24,687	12,035	36,722	·68	1·0	0·7	1·8
	1961	25,535	12,280	37,815	·49	·73	0·34	0·9
	1962	27,087	12,760	39,847	2·6 (loss)	4·0 (loss)	0·64 (loss)	0·98 (loss)
	1963	26,291	13,000	39,291	·09 (loss)	·13 (loss)	0·33	0·45
William Hancock	1960	2,626	2,063	4,689	6·9	12·5	1·8	3·2
	1961	3,106	2,105	5,211	8·8	14·8	2·7	4·4
	1962	3,558	2,187	5,745	10·0	16·2	2·8	4·5
	1963	3,816	2,228	6,044	9·5	14·9	2·7	4·2

Looking first at I.C.I. and Imperial Tobacco. These are "blue chip" investments. They are the nearest thing to gilt-edged in industry. *Now* the point is that their value comes from the steady and stable (if not increasing) return they offer, *not*, as in the case of government bonds, in the certainty and fixed time of repayment and interest.

Because capital invested in the latter instance is "safe", a lower interest rate is generally accepted. In other words, "blue chip" industrials should carry a higher return to the investor than gilt edged.

Of course, the dividend is usually reckoned against the market price of the investment — from the point of view of the investor — and provided this remains steady and at a reasonable rate, then he is satisfied.

However, the dividend paid determines the market price of the investment; i.e. the public decide what return they require on a particular investment and the price drops or rises accordingly.

Now if the dividend varies, so will the market price. If the dividend falls the market price will also fall, but the capital loss will be greater than the fall in income. This can easily be illustrated. If the market price is £100 to give a return of 6%, this means the dividend is £6 p.a. If the dividend falls to £5 the market price will drop to £83 to keep the rate at 6%. The investor has therefore suffered a theoretical capital loss of £17. It may be argued that the same applies to gilt-edged. Here, however, the interest is fixed. If the price falls it is normally due to general variation in interest rates, and the lower capital sum has the same general earning power as the original investment. (Gilt-edged are also affected by maturity dates when the time element must be considered.)

"Blue chips" are equally prone to be influenced by general changes in the prevailing interest rates, but inasmuch as these are general they do not really concern us here.

A "blue chip" investment, if it is to be so, must therefore offer a stable or increasing dividend otherwise it can hardly be considered a safe buy.

Another factor must necessarily be the rate of return it is earning on equity capital. Dividends can be kept up out of reserves where profits are insufficient, but this cannot be continued indefinitely and does not exactly inspire confidence. A true "blue chip" should therefore show a reasonably steady or rising rate of return over a long period. Variations are often inevitable, but they should be not too frequent nor too abnormal. It might be reasonable, if figures are available for a long period, to study the "five-year" moving average.

Taking these considerations into account, what conclusions can be extracted from the figures in Table K? It might be best to consider each in turn. The first company on the list is one of the largest yet known here. It is looked upon with some respect and considered safe. It is in fact a "blue chip" from the point of view of the investor. Is this assessment justified from the figures? In the first place, inasmuch as the figures relate to a very short period, it is only possible to make provisional comments and statements which may be denied by longer-term analysis. However, the point of the exercise is to consider the situation from the point of view of the investor with a limited amount of information at his disposal. Also, who is to say what number of years is the ideal for a proper analysis? It could well be argued that recent years are of far more relevance to any realistic assessment and should be highly weighted in any statistical analysis. The interest centres, after all, in the potential of the business at present. The fact that it was enormously successful ten years ago is a rather pleasant historical observation but is no indication of present-day prosperity or prospects. The one value of figures for long periods is that the long-term trend can be observed, though again there are many points against the validity of any assessments of future profits made on this basis. The shape of the curve can vary enormously. A continual upward or downward movement is supposedly significant. When, however, the curve has no apparent trend in direction and resembles anything from a sine curve to a scenic railway it is wiser to consider the present results, or these over a period such as that chosen, when looking for signs of future prosperity.

Someone is certain to advise moving averages for the ironing out of annual variations and showing trends. These have a certain value, though there is some uncertainty as to its extent. In the first place it is necessary to eliminate the element of inflation: i.e. reduce all profits to an equal level, state all in the same terms. Secondly, there is something very unreliable in moving averages. This is a fine vehicle for illustrating that it is possible to prove anything with figures. In the present case, merely by taking the right numbers of years over which to calculate the average one can make a failing concern appear to progress. It is particularly so where the firm is declining more slowly than it once advanced. For instance, take a simple example of a company with profits over the past six years of 3, 4, 5, 10, 9 and 8. The company is on the down-grade yet the three-year trend would show rather differently and indicate continuing progress, being approximately 4, 6, 8 and 9. It

need not be said that any "inside" or "outside" information as to orders
and state of domestic or world markets is of course necesssarily taken
into account on occasions when investment decisions are made, but this
is by the way. The present problem is concerned with the assessments
that can be made from considering the figures published by the
companies for the information of the general public.

After this lengthy though not irrelevant digression it is necessary now
to return to the study of the figures so far produced. Referring, then, to
the results of I.C.I. What do the figures suggest?

In the first place, 1960 seems to have been an exceptionally good year.
1961 shows a fall in return of 38% approximately. Since then there has
been a gradual improvement. However, if the idea is to classify I.C.I. as
a "blue chip", it is normal to expect a steady or increasing return and
one which shows a rate consonant with the risk element involved. How
this is assessed is difficult to state, many factors being taken into
account: e.g. general financial strength and backing, long-term record,
type of end product, elasticity of demand. Generally speaking I.C.I. is
not considered, though this seems to beg the question, to be a very risky
investment, and a fairly low return would normally be acceptable. Here
we are dealing with return on capital employed, whereas the investor
thinks in terms of return on market price. However, as the market price
is, as has been already so many times insisted, determined principally by
dividends and prospects, and as these are determined by return on
capital and the trend thereof, then it is reasonable to consider the market
price as effectively determined by the return on capital.

Now general movements in interest rates apart, a "blue chip" should
have a fairly steady or increasing return on capital, leading (through
dividends) to a fairly steady or increasing market price, thus providing a
steady income and promising a possible capital gain on realisation.
Before going on to pass a provisional judgement on I.C.I. it might be
instructive to prepare one more table, this time bringing in what are
known as deviations from the mean (Table L). This is roughly the
average amount by which each figure in a group differs from the
arithmetic mean for the period and gives some standard for comparing
variations in the annual results tabulated for each of the various
businesses that are selected. By showing the deviation for both sets of
figures, i.e. those arising from Tables G and K respectively — those who

will not accept the revaluations of Table K may be convinced and even converted by the evaluations made of Table G and how they compare proportionately to those of the more "hypothetical" Table K.

TABLE L

AVERAGE RETURNS AND DEVIATIONS

Company	Table G		Table K		Fall in average return		Ratio of mean deviation to average %	
	average return	mean deviation	average return	mean deviation				
	%		%		Actual	%	Table G	Table K
I.C.I.	10·0	1·7	7·7	1·2	2·3	23	17	16
Courtaulds	8·6	1·3	6·5	1·0	2·3	28	15	15
Imperial Tobacco	15·4	0·25	8·4	nil	7·0	45	2	—
Newton Chambers	5·8	1·9	5·4	1·7	0·4	7	33	31
Lancashire Cotton Corpn.	7·2	4·5	5·3	3·4	1·9	26	62	64
George Wimpey	13·7	0·6	8·4	0·4	5·3	38	4	5
Harland & Woolf	0·6 (loss)	0·8	0·38 (loss)	0·6	0·22 (incr.)	4 (incr.)	—	—
William Hancock	14·6	1·0	8·8	0·9	5·8	37	7	10

In considering the claims of I.C.I. to be a "blue chip" and using the information contained in this table, the following points should be made:

(a) The average return in both Tables G and K is probably reasonable.

(b) The returns for the past three years have been below the average for the whole period.

(c) The mean deviation is 17% in Table G and 16% in Table K from the normal, which cannot be considered truly compatible with stability, particularly when compared with the other companies (excepting those in poor condition). A high deviation may be acceptable where the arithmetic mean is high, which in Table K it is not, at 7·7%.

(d) The return is slowly rising, and in any event 1960 may have been an abnormal year.

Taking these various points into consideration and noting that the dividend rate (Table G and K) has been until 1963 slowly falling, one must conclude something as follows.

This group has a good general record and is popularly thought of as a good risk. It is showing a fairly satisfactory return even on Table K, though insufficient to finance expansion on any scale and at the same time pay high or even merely modest dividends (in real terms — not as quoted). In support of this argument you are referred to the figures in Table I, which indicate the tendency to retain 50% of earnings thus leaving (per Table K) only 3·9% gross for dividend purposes. Also, as is apparent from both Table K and Table G, the dividend rate has been falling though now showing signs of levelling out. This business of a falling real dividend rate or a rate below, say, 5% may not seem frightfully relevant in this context — the link up with market price is difficult to grasp. However, if you consider yourself investing £1,000 which earns 8% but you find it necessary to plough back 4% annually and in doing so far from expanding merely stabilise your return — that is you only earn 8% by putting half back in immediately — then in fact you are only obtaining a return equal to the dividend of 4%, which at that level (apart from any tendency to fall) cannot be considered to be evidence of profiteering. Others may talk of the capital which you are amassing — this is a pipe dream. It is represented by assets (*things*) which have a value only in use and which if sold would make a rather sorry fool of your fortune. The value of the assets, as has been stressed often enough to bore, lies not in their realisable value but in their value in use — this refers of course to fixed assets not to items such as stock in trade — but even this could not be sold quickly and in bulk except at a loss.

On this count, together with the size of the mean deviation, it is difficult to accept on the information which is available I.C.I. as a "blue chip".

On the other hand, even in spite of the various and derogatory criticisms made, its fairly high average return and relatively low risk by size and type of business, when compared to the returns and risks in other companies in the list make it a fairly reasonable investment, particularly in view of the fact that both return and dividends per Table K are now on the upturn.

One further point, in conclusion, in relation to the accounts of 1960: the reason for a greater part of the criticisms levelled at these accounts lies in the high profit in 1960. Now sales in both years 1960 and 1961 were much the same; the difference lies in the "trading profit", which in accounts for 1960 was £24 million above 1961. If this could be explained away as abnormal then perhaps many of our conclusions would need revising. However, if the profit for that year contains abnormal income to that extent — which is certainly "material" — it would be stated in the accounts and could have been eliminated (or spread) in the analysis.

Courtaulds Limited

The second company on the list is Courtaulds. The progress of this company over the four years seems slightly erratic. The return fell from a high in 1960 to a point 25% below in 1962, and then in 1963 (perhaps due to the influence of I.C.I.) jumped again to a figure above the 1960 level.

The arithmetic mean for the four years was 8·6 per Table G. This, though not particularly high, is fairly reasonable and for a fairly well-established company not discouraging, particularly as the 1963 figure is 10·6. However, the mean deviation at 15% is sufficiently high to make the investor a little wary. Dividend returns are low but rising, though this must be suspect where it is only made possible by paying out a higher proportion of earnings (see Table D). All in all, the position shown by Table G is not such as to cause the shareholder any undue worry.

Looking at Table K, however, the position alters. The arithmetic mean return has dropped to 6·3, a fall of 28%, with a deviation of 15%. It is not a healthy state of affairs, particularly as Courtaulds is not generally considered to hold the whip hand in its trade — having to face strong competition from within and without this country.

The dividend position is not very encouraging either; for, though rising, it seems the company can still only afford to pay out 4·3% on capital employed, and then only at the cost of using up an increasing proportion of earnings.

True, 1963 shows improvement. The return has exceeded the 1960 high water mark and the dividend has been increased in spite of the fact that less of the profits were used for this purpose than in 1962.

Nevertheless, the picture that emerges from the figures as a whole is not one that arouses massive confidence.

Imperial Tobacco

It seems that here is at first glance the ideal "blue chip". Table G shows an average return of 15·4% with a mean deviation of only ¼%. The figure is obviously too high to be true, but Table K after revaluation (admittedly conservative) still shows a return averaging 8·4 with no effective deviation at all. How much more can one expect in the way of stability? A constant return exceeding 8% is certainly a sign of a safe investment.

There is one qualification concerning dividends. Table G is fine, but Table K gives a dividend which, from an unsatisfactory peak of 4·2% gross in 1960, has fallen to 3·9%. What is more the fall has been accompanied by a higher degree of reinvestment of income — which seems to suggest that the company is not wholly in easy street and is only able to stabilise its return on capital employed by continually reducing (though only gradually) the proportion of profit paid out in dividends.

It is a process which cannot be continued indefinitely and it will be interesting to observe the future record of the company.

Not that there is likely to be any real danger of decline and fall in an industry which supplies such a large part of the market, a market which is, whatever the sage may say as to the effect of the products, likely to endure.

Newton Chambers

There seems little doubt from any of the tables so far prepared of the present fortunes of the company. Because of the fact that assets were revalued in 1959, there is not a great difference between Tables G and K. The arithmetic mean return in Table G was 5·8% with a deviation of 33%; by 1963 the return had fallen to 3·3%, i.e. 43% below the arithmetic mean.

Much the same picture emerges from Table K. An arithmetic mean of 5·4%, a deviation of 31% and a fall by 1963 of 42%.

Not a very encouraging picture. There the fall has been only in the latter two years, but even so the return in the previous two years was not wonderful for a company of fluctuating fortunes. 1960 was inadequate, and 1961, though higher, was nothing to take much credit for. Apart from which, the dividend, low to start with, has fallen continually. It is now maintained at 3·1% only by drawing on reserves. This is to some extent illustrated in Table D.

The trouble is only exacerbated by the attempt to maintain a high quoted dividend. This involves drawing on a higher and higher proportion of profits, and eventually on reserves — meaning that the amount ploughed back is allowed to fall and thus reduce the possibility of retaining some form of equilibrium.

It is, of course, possible that the causes of the depression run deeper, and that even were the ploughing back increased at the expense of dividends the situation would not improve; this because the fall in return is not because of shortage of funds to maintain rate of profits and any extra funds put back would not even "earn their board".

This is mere conjecture. The Chairman's Statement indicates that the fall in profit is due to losses incurred by a particular subsidiary, and, with reference to the preceding paragraph, it is impossible to know whether the situation could be improved by ploughing group profits into that company.

There is little more to be said of this company; the figures speak for themselves.

On a point of general interest, Table K is rather interesting on the subject of dividends — assuming one accepts the premises on which it was prepared. Of the eight companies used only *one*, Lancashire Cotton Corpn., has topped 5% in dividend pay-out (that for two years only) — when 5% is the very minimum a normal man would tend to consider as worth investing for were he in business on his own. Even in Table G the only other companies to top this 5% were I.C.I. in two years (5½ maximum), Courtaulds in 1963, only at 5·1%, and Imperial Tobacco consistently. Not a very convincing record for a set of at least six notable companies. But proceeding with the catalogue of misfortunes.

Lancashire Cotton Corpn.

Here is a company suddenly fallen on bad times. The return (Table G) dropping from 12·9% to 2·7% in four years, or (Table K) from 9·4% to

2·0%. The arithmetic mean in Table G is 7·2% with a deviation of 62%, and in Table K 5·3% with a deviation of 62%. Deviations of this kind in fact make the arithmetic mean meaningless.

This is an odd company altogether. If you recall, when discussing solvency it was found possessed of considerable unused liquid funds. Without knowing more about the industry it is unwise to make too much of this, but the layman may be forgiven for wondering whether things may not have reached such a rock bottom had these funds been better used.

The dividend position is interesting. They have kept up a high quoted rate (Table F) — even though lower in 1962 and 1963 — but only at the expense of digging deeply into reserves (see Table D, col. 6). The real dividend rate (per Tables G and K) has fallen steadily by about 38% in each case, and as has been said it is now only being "artificially" maintained at 3·5% by drawing on what was previously treated as capital. All in all not a very promising picture, though perhaps the past two years are particularly unrepresentative! But then — the investor is more interested in present prospects than any previous conquests, glories, triumphs or spoils. The most interesting fact about the company is the sudden drop in 1962 from 7·9% to 2·0% in the rate of return.

George Wimpey

Contractors are often complex from an accounting viewpoint. The figures shown in the various tables are in some respects a little bewildering. The average rate of return is quite satisfactory even in Table K where it is 8·4% with a mean deviation of 5%. Table G showed 13·7% with a deviation of 4%; almost a "blue chip".

Two factors are interesting; one is the fall of nearly 40% on revaluation, which being based on fairly arbitrary hypotheses could well be challenged to the company's disadvantage. The other interesting thing is that the dividend is barely above 1% in Table K and below 2% in Table G. In fact, to keep a fairly steady rate of return it is necessary to plough back on average nearly 85% of profits. The quoted dividend has remained steady at 10%. However, and this point may have already been made before in our examination, a steady rate in a time of inflation is not the most welcome. But this will perhaps be discussed later.

Harland & Woolf

This is a difficult company to make any worthwhile or reliable statements or assessments about. It is obviously not very prosperous at present. The arithmetic mean is 0·6% (Table K) and 2·4% (Table G), both losses, a difference of almost 70%, this time to the advantage of the company. The trend led from a small profit of 1% in 1960 (Table G) to a loss of 4·0% in 1962 and then a slight improvement in the final year to a loss of 0·13%. The quoted dividend was kept at 5·0% in 1960 and 1962 and 2·5% in the other years. In order to do this it was of course necessary to draw heavily on reserves (except in 1961). The real dividend as a return on capital was of course extremely low, falling from 0·7% to 0·33% in Table K and from 1·0% to 0·45% in Table G.

The only encouraging aspect of the figures given is the slight upturn in 1963. Will it be maintained? Certain sources, not necessarily reliable, suggest that the fortunes of this company are on the mend. There is little to be done but watch and see whether the event confirms the suggestion. But this is really outside the chosen terms of reference and it is best to keep to the figures that have been abstracted and ignore the tendency to let hopes or good wishes override hard facts, however good the wishes or hard the facts.

William Hancock

The general picture here is a little mixed. The return is good in Table G and the mean deviation fairly reasonable. In Table K the return is again good at 8·8%, but not only has it fallen by 40% odd, which, remembering the conservative basis of the attempted revaluation, is very considerable, but the mean deviation of 10% is quite high for a return of that level.

Nevertheless, as shown the results seem reasonable. However, although quoted dividends have increased, real dividends have averaged only 4·1% in Table G and 2·5% in Table K. Again, as with the other companies already discussed, it seems that the return can only be kept up at the cost of keeping dividends down and ploughing the major part, in this case 72% (see Table D), of profits back into the business.

While this is necessary prosperity can only be said to be achieved at a premium.

CHAPTER 8

Profits, Dividends and Price Indices

WERE assets valued on the basis suggested originally, they would be stated more or less in the same terms as profits, and any increase in the rate of return would normally indicate an increase in profits in real terms. Where, however, the assets are not revalued, then, as profits rise due to a fall in the value of money and increased selling prices, the rate of return will rise. This presents a misleading picture which has been already effectively discussed in detail by watching the effect on the return of the revaluation of assets.

A further point that must be of interest to management and investor alike is whether the profits and dividends, though they appear to be rising, are actually keeping pace with inflation. The more so if part of the profit increase was due to causes other than the change in money values.

It may therefore be of interest to compare the movements in profits of the companies selected with the variations in the price index. In the present context it may be that little of value will be learnt, particularly in cases where companies have increased their capital from year to year, which is usually so, if for no other reason than the accumulation of reserves.

It would of course indicate where a company was earning less in real terms than the previous year whereas actual figures showed an increase; and to this extent it is useful, for, although in such a case the rate of return will presumably have fallen to an extent already discussed, this could have meant that profits were not keeping pace with increases in capital — which is not quite the same thing as failing to keep pace with a rise in the cost of living. The two tests would only produce the same effect were assets valued on exactly the same basis as profits — which in the tables and for practical reasons only is not so, though we have in fact advocated revaluation on this basis.

It is not suggested that this particular analysis is as valuable as those so far discussed but it is quick and in some cases extremely informative, i.e. where profits can be shown in real terms to be falling where in stated figures they appear to rise, and where at the same time capital employed is stable or increasing.

On this understanding it might be interesting to draw up a table showing the profit of 1960 as 100 and the profits for succeeding years in terms of this figure (Table M).

That is, taking 1960 as our base year it is possible to prepare a table showing the index numbers for the profits and dividends of the years succeeding. This can then be set alongside an official index of retail prices.

What, if anything, does the table convey? In the first place, what of the variations of capital, which have not been considered? Is it reasonable to discuss movements in profits and dividends irrespective of the level of capital that produces the profits? In this context possibly yes. The directors of the company have (with reservations) the job of maximising profits. To do so they raise capital from shareholders, banks, creditors, etc. This capital will, for various reasons, vary from year to year, but unless the profit earned keeps pace with the current inflationary rise in prices then, even though that profit appears to be rising, it may in reality be diminishing. Variations in capital are in such comparisons not relevant for to a certain extent the capital available is determined by the prosperity of the business. There are two exceptions. Firstly if capital is repaid to shareholders then obviously profits will be expected to fall, and in comparing these profits with an index it would be necessary to scale them up. This, however, has not happened in the case of the various companies being considered. Secondly, if the share capital has been increased by, say, a "rights" issue, then the profit would be expected to rise accordingly. In such an instance comparisons with the indices are no longer valid, except that if profit fails still to keep pace with prices then the position obviously merits inquiry. It might be said that no rights issue would be possible were not profits to come of it, but when the offer is made the future is inevitably in the category of the unknown and whatever present prosperity may promise, any number of supervening events could completely alter the anticipated, or perhaps calculated, results. In fact, though, pray that it be not often so, the money

TABLE M

PROFITS AND DIVIDENDS IN TERMS OF INDICES

Company		1 Gross profit	2 % increases on previous year	3 G.P. less preference dividends	4 % increase on previous year	5 Gross dividend (ordinary)	6 % increase on previous year	7 Retail price index	8 % increase on previous year	9 Ratio of dividend to profit
I.C.I.	1960	100	—	100	—	100	—	100	—	41
	1961	70·3	−29·7	69·7	−30·3	103·4	+3·4	104·4	+4·2	60
	1962	79·8	+13·5	79·5	+12·1	104·4	+0·97	106·1	+1·6	54
	1963	96·4	+20·8	96·4	+21·3	116·3	+11·4	106·6	+0·5	50
Courtaulds	1960	100	—	100	—	100	—	100	—	37
	1961	89·0	−11·0	88·6	−11·4	107·3	+7·3	103·6	+3·6	44
	1962	84·3	−5·3	83·6	−5·6	134·1	+24·0	108·5	+4·8	60
	1963	112·4	+33·3	113·3	+36·7	166·6	+24·2	110·4	+1·8	53
Imperial Tobacco	1960	100	—	100	—	100	—	100	—	50
	1961	103·8	+3·8	104·5	+4·5	100	—	104·4	+4·4	47
	1962	109·2	+5·2	110·1	+5·4	100	—	106·1	+1·6	46
	1963	113·3	+3·8	114·1	+3·6	105·2	5·2	105·5	−0·6	46
Newton Chambers	1960	100	—	100	—	100	—	100	—	60
	1961	120·6	+20·6	120·7	+20·7	94·1	−5·9	104·4	+4·2	47
	1962	66·3	−45%	66·5	−45·0	89·5	−4·9	106·6	+1·6	81
	1963	52·7	−20·4	62·4	−21·2	89·5	—	106·6	+0·5	103
Lancashire Cotton Corpn.	1960	100	—	100	—	100	—	100	—	57
	1961	88·1	−11·9	88·1	−11·9	100	—	104·4	+4·4	65
	1962	22·2	−75·7	22·2	−75·7	70·8	−29·2	106·1	+1·6	173
	1963	22·1	−0·5	22·1	−0·5	70·8	—	105·5	−0·6	179
George Wimpey	1960	100	—	100	—	100	—	100	—	14
	1961	102·2	+2·2	103·6	+3·6	100	—	104·4	+4·2	13
	1962	104·4	+2·1	105·9	+2·2	100	—	106·1	+1·6	13
	1963	131·0	+25·6	133·5	+26·0	150	+50·0	106·6	+0·5	15
Harland & Woolf	1960	100	—	100	—	100	—	100	—	106
	1961	82·8	−17·2	70·1	−29·6	50	−50·0	104·4	+4·2	69
	1962	−341·1	—	−512·1	—	100	+100·0	106·1	+1·6	—
	1963	24·4	—	−114	—	50	−50·0	106·6	+0·5	139
William Hancock	1960	100	—	100	—	100	—	100	—	26
	1961	143·7	+43·7	143·3	+43·3	168·5	+68·5	103·6	+3·6	30
	1962	177·7	+23·7	177·2	+23·9	192·7	+14·3	108·5	+4·8	28
	1963	174·9	−1·6	175·3	−1·1	192·7	—	110·4	+1·8	29

Notes

(a) Profits indices are shown both before and after preference dividend. The profits are of course before tax.

(b) The index for dividends is based on the gross dividend paid.

(c) The index used is the Index of Retail Prices taken from the *Board of Trade Journal*. The figures vary from firm to firm because of the varying balance sheet dates. The index numbers are calculated as at balance sheet date.

may have been raised to prevent a foreseen calamitous reversal of fortunes rather than increase an already profitable investment. Alas in the present state of the law, the directors retain a great deal of knowledge which might well have been made available to the members. True, in the case just mentioned the directors may be accused of "breach of trust", but who is to prove that they were aware of the prospect, and were not genuinely raising the capital for new ventures in which they genuinely believed lay the foundations of some commercial Eldorado?

But this is to digress a little. The excuse for the exercise was to note how profits and dividends were showing up against inflation. Perhaps it is best now to consider each company in turn.

I.C.I.

Unfortunately the year selected as a base year was a year when profits were particularly high. This can be seen from the statistical record shown in the report — this indicates that 1960 profits were the highest for the ten-year period. The subsequent fall was attributed to falls in world prices and increase in competition. Nevertheless, the fact remains that profits fell sharply in 1961 and then rose gradually to 1963, when they were still almost four points down. That is, the profits fell by 3·6%, whereas over the period the general price index rose by 6·6%. Of course by considering figures over a longer period different results may be shown. It might be proved that over twenty years profits capped prices. This is not the object of the exercise. As a matter of fact going back to 1959, when profits were considerably lower, there was a rise in profits to 1963 of approximately 6·3%, but a rise in prices again of a greater degree, this time 10·3% — agreed, it is proper to keep to our four-year period and the information conveyed by the accounts for that period. What's more the shareholder is more interested in present trends rather than long-term records. I.C.I. do give a ten-year financial statistical summary. This shows that between 1950 and 1963 profits rose by approximately 177% whereas prices increased by a mere 37%. But

(a) There was a continuous increase in capital and the shareholder is not told whether any *new* captial was raised.

(b) Is this long-term record of more value than the present short-term trend?

However, to return to the figures and an important aspect which has been ignored. Although the profits fell against the index over the complete term, in the latter two years the rise in profits was proportionately far greater than that in the index. What is more, in 1963 the increase was almost twice that of 1962. These are obviously factors in favour of a hope of good days to come.

The ordinary capital of the company did increase considerably in 1963 but this was due to a scrip issue, which does not involve the acquisition of new and permanent funds.

What of dividends? Here the position is interesting. The increase in dividend, both in 1961 and 1962, failed to keep pace with the index. 1963, however, showed a jump of fourteen points — quite considerable and way ahead of the price index. The amount paid out rose by over 11%. This was necessary to keep the quoted dividend high on the capital which had been increased by the scrip issue from £269 million to £416 million. It was made possible by the considerable increase in profits that year — in fact the proportion of profits used was only 50%, which was very close to the arithmetic mean for the four years. Note that the dividends, unlike the profits, showed a continual increase over 1960. This was because although profits were particularly high in that year dividends were not raised to the same degree. In fact, as can be seen from the table, only 41% of the profits were paid out in that year.

As far as the percentage change in dividends goes, 1960 and 1961 were, as earlier implied, below the rate of increase in prices, 1963 showed 11·4% dividend jump against 0·5% increase in prices. This was discussed in the preceding paragraph. The interest will lie in the figures for 1964. The dividend index will inevitably be far ahead of the price index, but the relevant factor will be the rise in the rate of increase in each case. If that for dividends does not keep pace with that for prices then the shareholders will be to that extent the losers. In fact 1964 was a good year in which both profits and dividends increased at a rate considerably greater than the price index.

A final footnote. Having shown the very unusual increase in total dividend for 1963, when we refer to Table G we find the rate for that year to be at an all time low (it rises slightly in Table K) for the period being examined. It is easily explained inasmuch as the amount paid out, though greater, is still less than the previous year in terms of the relation it bears to the funds owned by the shareholders.

Courtaulds

Here the profit index fell in 1961 and again in 1962. It then jumped some 30 points in 1963 so that the final year showed a profit, 13 points up on the base year and 2½ points ahead of the index. The reason for the sudden upturn in prosperity in 1963 is not identifiable, though from the accounts it appears that quantitatively the greatest contribution to the increase was made by the viscose division. The index of profits rose by 36·7% in 1963 whilst that of prices rose by only 1·8%. It was a sudden and drastic reversal of previous trends and is not a reliable guide in itself. It would be necessary to await at least the results for 1964. The year 1964 was another good year, as it happened, both for profits and dividends. The favourable trend was maintained until 1965 when it was modified by the deal with I.C.I. Ltd. involving the acquisition by the latter of Courtaulds' interest in British Nylon Spinners.

The dividend index showed a continual increase throughout the period and well ahead of the price index, 66 points against 10 being the final result. However this was made possible only by the fact that whereas only 37% of 1960 profits were paid out, a continually higher proportion was distributed in 1961 and 1962 — up to 60%. It dropped with the high income for 1963 to 53% which compares with an artithmetic mean of 48%.

A point relatively in favour is that Table K shows a tendency for dividends to increase, though even by 1963 they were little to be proud of — nevertheless a continual upward trend is always an encouraging phenomenon. A further point of interest is that the table also shows that the return on capital jumped suddenly in 1963 this again being an encouraging sign inasmuch as the rise in income was due not so much to an increase in capital but to a more satisfactory employment of the capital then employed.

Imperial Tobacco

There is nothing breathtaking in the results of this company. This might have been expected from our previous experience. Equity profits (and the rate of increase thereof) exceeded the price index over the period and in each year.

The dividend, on the other hand, remained constant up until 1962, lagging 6 points behind prices. It then increased by 5·2% in 1963. This was to prevent a sharp fall in the quoted rate due to the scrip issue in that year. The quantitative increase was made possible by the increase in profits — the proportion distributed remaining constant at 46%. However the dividend index still remained below the price index at the end of the period even though in October 1963 the price index fell by 0·6%. Generally speaking it must be said that over the period profits have beaten prices by 9 points and that dividends, though slow to move, are more or less up now with prices. Another sign of a safe investment — were it not for the irritating fact that Table K shows a real rate of dividend that is continually falling. That is, even though a higher proportion of rising income is ploughed back each year, the real return received by the shareholder is steadily becoming less. In fact, and in real terms, the return on capital is only maintained at a stable level by reducing the return to the shareholder.

Newton Chambers

The condition here is apparently not too satisfactory. Profits have fallen 48 points, dividends have fallen 10 points, prices have risen 6·6 points. The rates of increase or decrease are no more encouraging. Profits rose in 1961 but have fallen each year since, though some may take comfort in the fact that the rate of fall has dropped from 45% to 21%. Dividends fell in 1961 and 1962 but were maintained in 1963 by drawing on reserves. Not a happy state of affairs, and one confirmed by Table K. There seems little more to be said except to express hope that the years 1962 and 1963 are in a sense exceptional and that the prospects of 1961 will soon be recovered and multiplied.

Lancashire Cotton Corpn.

This company does not present an encouraging record. Profits have slumped by 78 points in three years from 1960 to 1962. They have levelled out in 1963, but not at a point that could be considered satisfactory. The only, and alas hardly breathtaking, sign of possible improvement lies in the fact that the profits fell by 0·1% less than the index in 1963. Dividends were kept reasonably high (though 29 points down in 1962 and 1963) compared with profits but this has only been made possible by drawing heavily on reserves. This is corroborated by the evidence of Table K. Actually, in a company which is in a difficult situation price indices are rather irrelevant quantitatively, though relatively they may be of academic interest, e.g. in 1963 dividends were maintained while the index fell by 0·6 point. However such incidental observations are not likely to bring much comfort, being fairly meaningless when facing the hard facts previously set down.

As far as this company is concerned this table has in fact added little to our appreciation. There is naught to do but wait and watch for auguries of a better future in the accounts for the period to come. As a matter of general interest the Chairman's Report contains a note of optimism — though perhaps this is inevitable.

To digress for a moment. Chairman's reports are of various kinds — from those that merely summarise the results of the year to those which attempt a detailed disquisition on the past, present and future prosperity of the company. They should be read but the tongue should not be too far removed from the cheek. This is no disrespect to the integrity of the chairman and with no relevance to any particular set of accounts discussed — but the chairman is the leader and the job of the leader is to encourage, which necessarily involves introducing optimism into the most dismal circumstances. Nevertheless, the report can contain useful supplementary information and can give the reasons for the results shown up in an analysis of the figures — reasons which may give cause to believe that present conditions, if bad, are merely transient and outside the control of the board, and if good, are likely to improve beyond the dreams of the most avaricious of members or Inspectors of Taxes.

Seriously, the report should not be ignored, and it is not so difficult to sum up its relevance fairly quickly. It does not take long to decide if it was written in the style of a Dr. Pangloss on the one side or a Mr. Micawber on the other.

George Wimpey

The results shown for this company are quite interesting. Profits lagged behind prices in 1961 and even though they showed a greater relative increase in 1962 they were still a little behind. Suddenly in 1963 they rocket to a point 27 points ahead. This seems to demand a little research. The share capital was increased by a one for one scrip issue but this would make no difference to profits, being a mere book transfer from reserve to capital account. Total assets increased, but to say this begs rather than answers the question. In fact, on examination of the accounts, the Chairman's Report gives little clue to the sudden jump in income — which seems to be merely the result of better trading conditions. However, it might be as well here to make a general point that, though it applies to all companies, has particular relevance to contractors. It concerns the valuation of work-in-progress. This is a difficult matter and inevitably involves a great deal of nebulous estimation — estimation which cannot always be supported convincingly. This is not necessarily the fault of the accountant but arises from the difficulty, or complexity rather, of the calculations involved. It also involves the problem of whether profit should be taken on uncompleted contracts, and if so then to what extent. In view of this the figure shown in the accounts could well be wrong and in so far as it is so then profits must be affected. Needless to say, a continually wrong basis of valuation will only affect the profits of the first and last year during which the error continues.

However, and when considering the profit for a particular year, it must be remembered, that the stock or work-in-progress figure may be incorrect. The error may be at the beginning or close of the year; in either case profits will obviously be affected. Now often the stock figure is not high enough for a relatively small error in appraisal to have a material effect on net profit — much depends on the relation of stocks to turnover and to the size of the profit. In contractor's accounts the work-in-progress figure is usually high — in the case in question it was £19 million at 31st December 1963; this compared with a net profit of £4 million. Now obviously a 5% error in valuation can have a material effect on the profit and a 5% error would not be considered unusual in this case; the profits would be reduced by almost £1 million, i.e. by 25%. An error of this dimension would in fact bring Wimpey's profit index back from 131 to about 100, quite a serious reduction in the circumstances. It is not suggested that the reason for the profit increase lay in a stock error but we are merely pointing out the possibility, and the effect that a quite marginal error could have.

As a matter of general interest the relative effect on profits of a 5% error in stocks and work-in-progress of the other companies in our schedule would be approximately: *

I.C.I.	8%
Courtaulds	9%
Imperial Tobacco	27%
Newton Chambers	60%
Lancashire Cotton Corpn.	53%
George Wimpey	24%
Harland & Woolf	960%
William Hancock	5%

Newton Chambers and Lancashire Cotton Corpn. show unusually high figures purely because they are at the moment earning low profits. In each case the relevant figure for 1960 would be much lower, 25% in the case of Newton Chambers and 17% in the case of Lancashire Cotton Corpn. Even these figures are on the high side, Newton Chambers even exceeding Wimpey's. The important distinction is that in the case of contractors such as Wimpey's errors in stock or work-in-progress valuation are far more likely to occur, due to the particular difficulties involved in valuing contracts in course of completion.

It might be added that in talking of errors the term is being used in a very wide sense — not only to mean miscalculation or application of wrong principles but to include differences that can arise when proper principles are correctly applied, yet where the nature of the task is such that even on these conditions two men working separately could arrive at quite different conclusions.

*It is a fact worth remembering, even if it is disturbing in its implications, that few auditors would be prepared to vouch for the arithmetical accuracy of the stock figure except granted a margin of error of 5% in either direction.

Referring again to the list, now if profit varies then the return on capital will vary to precisely the same degree. In those cases then, where the percentage variation in profits is high the effect on the return shown in Table K and the conclusions drawn therefrom could be quite important — whichever direction the error may take — for remember it may be in either direction. (Stocks are more likely to be over-stated due to a desire to maximise profits in lean years.) In fact, in the cases of Newton Chambers and Lancashire Cotton Corpn., even an inevitable 1% error could in 1963 have a noticeable effect.

Harland & Woolf is a special case. Its profits are abnormally low — a 1% error would eliminate them completely. It might be deduced from this that the profit shown is fairly meaningless. In the case of the other companies in the list the effect of a 5% error would be fairly slight and anything as low as 1% would not be significant at all.

A final point — an error in year 1 is generally corrected automatically in year 2 in the opposite direction, provided stocks are valued on a consistent basis. That is, it is not possible to continually push up profit by overvaluing each year, except to a small extent and for a limited period.

Basically the point is that the profit shown in any particular year can be considerably influenced in some cases by the value put on stocks and work in progress.

This digression commenced from the consideration of the jump in Wimpey's profits in 1963. It is not suggested that it is due to wrong value of stocks and work in progress — but it must nevertheless be pointed out that this could be so.

However, to return to Table M. Profits are now way up on prices, though in 1962 the rate of increase fell behind. After the sudden leap forward it will be interesting to watch future trends.

Dividends failed to keep pace with the index in 1961 and 1962, but in 1963, due to the scrip issue and the desire (presumably) to bolster the quoted rate, the index rose 50 points, pulling well ahead of the price index.

Because of the increase in profits this was done without noticeably decreasing the proportion ploughed back. Summing up one could say that 1963 has played havoc with the trends and it will be from the point of view of Table M necessary to watch future results in order to draw any final, or even provisional conclusions as to the true direction in which the company is moving. The story from Table K is, however, rather more detailed and encouraging, apart from being more precise. Here it was possible to paint a picture of a fairly steady organisation.

Harland & Woolf

Little comment seems needed here, everything relevant has already been said that could be. Table M adds little to our knowledge. The figures speak for themselves.

The points to note are the upturn in profits in 1963 and the behaviour of dividends, which have been kept at alternating levels, principally by drawing on reserves. Any comparisons with prices would be pointless. Apart from the fact that profits and dividends lag far behind, the figures prevent even the consideration of rates of increase, in the sense that though dividends increased by 100 points in 1962, against a 16 leap in prices, this is a mere statistical illusion and cannot be considered of any importance. In this case it is the general trend that matters and this is far from being encouraging. As has been mentioned earlier, this company was put into the hands of a receiver and manager shortly after this date. It continued in business on what can only be described as an extremely erratic course and was taken over by the State in 1978.

William Hancock

Profits here seem to be racing away from prices, having gained 64 points in four years; though note that in 1963 the percentage increase in profits was negative, against a positive 1·8 movement in prices. In addition to this the rate of increase in profits, though particularly high originally, has fallen each year. The same appies to dividends: the index is 80 points ahead but the rate of increase has been falling and in 1963 was below that for prices.

Looking a little more carefully at the accounts, capital was increased by a share issue in 1961 which, with premium, brought in approximately £500,000. This would account for quite a considerable part of the increase in profits in that year. Generally speaking, Table M is not here a very reliable guide — much more information and a longer period would be essential. It is best in this case to concentrate on the information contained in Table K, though even here conclusions were somewhat qualified.

The general trend seemed to be upward until 1962 then to drop slightly in that year. However, inasmuch as the upward movement was less each year, the real trend seems to be fairly unfavourable. However, this is a highly competitive industry and the capital outlay on alterations to premises is bound to have an initial dragging effect on profits.

This, however, has been discussed already and there seems little point in labouring the matter any further. To sum up, the best to say is that the trend may be downward but that the general picture drawn from the various analyses made is not entirely unfavourable. After all, provided it moves with the times it is difficult to imagine a brewery of any size being a poor investment — especially taking into account the amount of property that they tend to hold, so often in the most valuable of town sites, and so often grossly undervalued in the balance sheet. It was attempted to correct this in the previous chapter; but without detailed knowledge any assessment of real value is difficult even to estimate with any degree of confidence.

CHAPTER 9

The Search for a Standard of Efficiency

HAVING dealt with the solvency of a company and having discussed at some length the process of calculating the return on the moneys belonging to the members, and the various problems involved, an analysis of the figures of certain companies has been attempted and provisional conclusions drawn.

Now comes the question of what must be termed for lack of a more precise word, "efficiency". The fact that the company is paying members a certain dividend or making a certain return on their capital is very important to them but it does not tell the full story. The company may be earning 6% on the member's capital as calculated, but to do this they may be borrowing at 8% from debenture holders or at 10% from a bank.

Take an example.

Capital	£
Shares	100
12% debentures	100
10% loan	100
Profit before interest	30

If the capital all were in shares then members would earn 10%. At present they earn only 8%. It would therefore be to their advantage to subscribe for shares in place of the loans, etc.

This is but one aspect and will be dealt with in a later chapter. The second and more important is that the real worth and movement of the company can only be gauged by the amount it earns set beside the total assets used in earning the income. Now when referring to total assets, what is meant is not total net assets, i.e. capital employed as previously defined, plus loan capital. Total assets mean one thing only and this was simply illustrated in the first chapter. They are all the *things* owned by or owed to the company on the basis of which they operate. A debtor is an asset as much as is a wheelbarrow — in fact the debt can be sold if money is needed. Again, the debtor can be seen as one to whom the business has temporarily lent money — usually at an interest represented by the discount lost if payment is delayed.

Looking at the position from the opposite angle, the liability side of a balance sheet represents money invested, voluntarily or not, in the business. The creditor is an investor as much as is the shareholder and the capital he provides by, as it were, lending money to buy his own goods must earn a return with any other investment. True, the creditor does not receive payment for his loan except in the sense that he demands additional moneys for late settlement in the form of denial of discount or the imposition of a surcharge.

Viewing the position slightly differently and postulating that in as much as the "creditors" figure is, or tends to be, relatively steady, then it represents a permanent though to a certain extent involuntary interest free investment in the business.

Are there any exceptions to this generalisation? Are there any assets which should be excluded from our concept of "total assets" or any liabilities which must be ignored? There are in fact certain borderline cases which merit some detailed discussion and which might lead to differences in opinion.

The first example that might be relevant is the sinking fund investment. Often for purposes, say, of providing funds for renewing a lease a company will invest a definite amount each year which with interest will supply the required amount at the correct date. In the balance sheet will be two equal and opposite entries: a sinking fund account and a sinking fund investment account. In a paper recently published I suggested that this latter "asset" should be excluded from the concept of total assets. Now I am inclined to the other point of view. The fund account is basically a reserve. The fact that it is invested particularly is irrelevant. The moneys could have been used in the business and may in fact have earned a greater profit in this way. It could also be argued that, if a sinking fund investment account is to be excluded, so then should all other investment accounts relating to moneys invested outside the business. This would be absurd.

A second type of asset that might claim exclusion is the fixed asset not in use, this might often apply where a building, etc., is in course of construction. The fact that such an asset is obviously not income earning is irrelevant. The company has moneys at its disposal and if it wishes to use them to purchase useless assets or to construct assets which will not be usable for some time this is their business, and presumably inasmuch as they assume that the money will amply be repaid then it would be absurd to exclude such assets. The money need not have been spent in this way (unless, say, the factory was on the verge of disintegration): it could have been spent on additional stocks.

The third type of asset that might put forward a convincing case for being excluded is cash which is held for a particular purpose and which must be disposed of fairly quickly and finally. A particular example often occurs at balance sheet date when this is the 31st December. Large sums are often held for tax which must be paid over on the following day. Is it fair to include these amounts in total assets? This is a nice problem. Very often substantial amounts of money are involved. It might be usefully argued that there are always amounts payable immediately after balance sheet date — or at any time — often large amounts. Dividends due might almost be put in the same category. The point with all these items is that they represent cash in a continual process of accumulation. The dividends or tax due are paid out of near liquid resources which are made available at the due date by the normal processes of budgeting. These funds are not lying idle up to the time they are needed and if they are excluded then this understates the true total assets employed.

A final item of interest is goodwill. Should this be excluded? The short answer is no! The subject is discussed at length in a later chapter. The difficulty lies in the various ways in which the item can arise. Normally, however, it finds its way into a company balance sheet due to the purchase of a business at a price higher than the sum of the net assets purchased. The difference is known as goodwill, and is in truth an asset in the sense that it is, though intangible, an income-earning item. It consists of nebulous factors such as "the good name" of the vendor or some kind of particular "know-how" or competitive advantage which is sold with the business. In many cases it can even have a value in itself — it is possible to sell "know-how" — and though intangible, it is real in the sense that it attaches to the asset purchased and enhances its value to the business. It should therefore not be excluded.

The one practical difficulty lies not in the presence of goodwill in a balance sheet but in its absence. It is, for some illogical reason, often written off very quickly. In other cases it never existed as a purchase but is present in the name and reputation the company itself has created. Should an attempt be made then to assess the true goodwill and include it in the total? On what basis could a valuation be made? Is the task so beyond the realms of reason as the question suggests? The point is that the fairest basis of valuation lies in the surplus of the value of the business as a going concern over the total value of the individual assets as they have been valued. The value of the business as a going concern depends on the return on capital in the sense that the risk is assessed and the return relevant to this; that figure is then subtracted from the return earned. The capitalised figure of the result is in fact the value of the goodwill (the rate of discount being the "risk rate"). It would of course be necessary in the process to eliminate any goodwill figure in the accounts already.

However to do this would be somehow to work outside our terms of reference. For in fact the return on capital shown for each company would be equal to the risk, which in fact would say nothing of relative prosperity, and only of relative risk. The true comparative "efficiency" or prosperity of the company would be indicated by the size of the goodwill figure related to the other assets and it would be movements in goodwill that would show the present trend in results and in return on capital. It would be necessary indeed to approach the whole analysis from quite a separate point of view.

What then is the answer? To include goodwill at its full value would not only alter the method of analysis; it would involve estimating the "risk return". This could possibly be done by studying market quotations, but results are likely to be unreliable. The obvious solution is to exclude goodwill altogether. That is the true goodwill. Is it possible to distinguish between the "true goodwill" and say the goodwill of a business purchased? Perhaps so. As has been hitherto argued, this goodwill is part of the cost of the tangible assets purchased. It actually was paid for in cash and must then be treated as any other asset. Does this represent a hurdle? Many companies have written off this goodwill. In order to make fair comparisons it should be reinstated — but this is not possible for in many cases the outsider does not know what it was. Consequently the fact must be accepted that to this extent comparisons may be invalidated.

It might be suggested that the problem could be compromised by eliminating all goodwill. This would be both difficult and pointless. Difficult because it is often included in a collective item, e.g. "goodwill, patents, trademarks, copyrights", etc. — some parts of which are of a rather different character; pointless because there is little value in comparing two things both of which are incorrect and not necessarily in the same proportion.

Consequently for the time being goodwill will be left as we find it.

The next problem to be tackled, having defined and excused the concept of "total assets", is to decide upon the profit figure that must be used for calculating the return. This will not be the figure shown in Appendix A. For in addition to adding back preference dividends it is necessary to also add back all interest paid on moneys borrowed. The adding back of discounts lost, which was referred to earlier, is not feasible for reasons which it would be foolish to discuss.

What other adjustments are necessary? The question of non-recurring items of income or expense must be considered. Three points may be made. Firstly, non-recurring items have a fascinating habit of recurring continually in different guises. Secondly, exceptional items of expenditure or income should be spread over the period to which they properly apply. Thirdly, material and particularly unusual items should be added back or deducted as necessary. Those three points will be borne in mind as the chapter continues.

A final point concerns a matter which goes rather to the root of the whole argument. It concerns the very terms we are using. It is intended to discuss this in more detail in a further chapter, for the moment it is necessary to make one or two lesser points. Suppose of two companies, A and B, A shows the higher return. But suppose B paid out far more to employees in the form of bonuses, additional incentive moneys, sick pay, pensions, share ownership projects, etc. Should these be eliminated, so that labour charges were on equal basis with A, then B might show a far greater return than A. Which company is in fact the more "efficient"? What in fact is meant by efficiency? Is it a matter of which company adds most to the national product, or which company is making best use of that part of the country's resources at its disposal? These are not the same questions in differing terms. The problem is, can either be answered in terms of profit — if not then are we wasting our time?

The first question — Which company is adding most to the national product? — is complex. The term product is rather material, and if it is preferable to speak in strictly quantitative terms then the profit is a vital part of the product, and if two companies with equal wage policies are earning unequal profits in terms of return on capital then presumably the company showing the higher return is adding most to the national product. This term "product" is not only vague, it is useless, in the sense that it tells nothing of value. The point is to discover the increase not in the quantity of matter which is produced but in the wealth of the nation. Now increases in wealth cannot be arrived at merely by watching the progress of profits and wages and interest, etc. It must be seen in terms of *what* is produced, where and why, under what working conditions and at what expense in the sense that Eliot uses the idea when he speaks (in *The Idea of a Christian Society*) of ". . . the steady influence which operates silently in any mass society organised for profit and the depression of standards of art and culture . . .".

It is impossible that we should increase the real wealth of the nation by producing, at however little cost, quantities of inessential goods at the expense of items more necessary to the protection of the general standards both of living and of culture.

Many a company in the early nineteenth century made tremendous contributions to the national output, which may make modern returns look rather feeble; but if the policy is to judge increases in wealth by counting gold and ignoring the plight of the man who indirectly made it, the misery of the machine shop and the poverty of the pits, then it is time to change the terms of reference.

Wealth is more than money; fairy gold does not make a man's fortune nor a country's. No more is it goods and services alone. Two countries may have the same gross national product in terms of goods and services but it is the country in which these are best distributed that is the one with the greater claim to real wealth.

The essential lesson to be drawn from this sermon is that it is difficult to compare two companies at random and assess their relative efficiency in terms of return on capital. In certain industries prices are deliberately controlled by the State for defined reasons, companies within this industry may be consequently showing a lower return even though in fact they are operating just as expertly as companies in non-controlled industries.

Again it may be State policy to develop certain depressed areas. It may offer monetary incentives, free factories, etc. The companies here may be equally efficient as those in healthy regions, that is they are making the best use of resources available. However, where the loan is a substitute for fixed interest capital, which the company in the depressed area cannot obtain, or service, then the results in terms of the yield on equity or capital and reserves as shown so far, are no guide to relative efficiency, for the one company is able to show profit that does not bear the cost of raising capital. This assumes that the other company is paying loan interest, for if neither is doing so then the problem does not arise.

In such instances the solution is to eliminate the loan interest altogether by adding it back to profit, the returns of both companies then become compatible. Or do they? If Company B in the depressed area shows a lower return than Company A in a prosperous region, does this then mean that Company A is the more efficient? Much depends on what is meant by efficiency. In one sense Company A is adding more to the national product inasmuch as it is able to use resources to greater advantage and increase capital in money terms at a greater pace than B.

However B is providing work and even possibly attracting subsidiary or ancillary companies to a depressed area. It is offering society something above the nominal profit it is making. This intangible contribution to the welfare of the country is not easily thought of in money terms. Were this possible, then it may be shown that the contribution made to the national welfare in terms of the improvement of social conditions is greater than the actual profit made by A, or at least greater than the difference between the two figures shown in the original calculation.

This is well enough, but even if B is saving the lives and homes of countless voters, is this any comment on its efficiency? Coming to brass tacks, the management of B on taking the site in the poor area would take into account the additional costs and greater risks and would demand implicitly a grant to remove these disadvantages. They would not accept the site voluntarily, unless they could be confident of paying sufficient salaries and promising an adequate return to shareholders. They expect a lower profit per pound of capital but allow for it by relying less on outside finance. As part of capital is free, less of the profit will be needed for dividends, and the business may prosper to the satisfaction of all concerned.

Efficiency in the only adequate definition must be the sign not of accidental advantage in location or capital supply but an indication of effective management, i.e. the more efficient company is that company employing its assets most advantageously as a result of deliberate decision on the side of those responsible for managing the company.

How is this efficiency to be discovered? Only by reducing each company to the same basis, i.e. eliminating all uncontrollable elements. The type of capital advantage referred to can be eliminated by the ignoring of interest charges. Here however care must be taken. When the question of free aid does arise there is a certain element of controllable variation in the manner of raising capital. This requires skill and judgement and is a matter dealt with in the chapter on gearing. Capital raising then deserves consideration as well as asset employment. It is not sufficient to earn a better return if one is paying very much more for the capital necessary to earn it.

This being so it may be more informative to study the return on equity rather than on total assets when comparing two companies in an industry. This is for comparative study not for absolute evaluations or for the study of movements in one company, when both methods are used together if the more effective results are desired.

Apart from the capital advantages there are the differences springing from labour policy, i.e. social considerations. On one side it may be claimed that expenses incurred in providing comforts or benefits for work people are at any level incurred with the hope of thereby raising efficiency and profit. This may be so in some instances but not always.

There are many companies that either through philanthropy engendered by a natural prosperity or better by a sense of social obligation afford employee benefits quite gratuitously and without apparent self-seeking. These companies accept a lower return than competitors by such policy though the image produced, even accidentally, may more than compensate for the sacrifice. True many such companies may be earning a high return already and the additional cost is not very material in its effect. Nevertheless, these items must be eliminated and extra benefits added back if profit returns are to be valid in inter-firm comparisons. Whether this is feasible in practice is doubtful unless sufficient information is given in published reports.

Another and more relevant factor is what may be referred to as locational advantage. Company A may be showing a higher return than Company B merely because it enjoys a more advantageous location, e.g. a cafe on the promenade may be far more sought after than the same cafe on the outskirts of the town.

Again a company with cheap access to raw materials and sales outlets has natural advantages, no thanks to itself in the most part, over one that does not enjoy equal facilities. In order to gauge efficiency in such instances it is necessary to eliminate these uncontrollable and continually changing factors. The means that could be employed are discussed in outline in a later chapter, that on company law reform.

When this is done we may essay to claim some possibility of assessing efficiency in company comparisons. Would we be justified?

Is the skill of the management anything more than a talent that may be employed for personal gain or to the advantage of a group against the society that gives it the opportunity to do so? Is efficiency in the manner defined a concept of real value? Can we acclaim Company A for showing itself more efficient than Company B when the former produces fruit machines and the latter medical aid. This is a question that will be discussed in the following chapter. Suffice it to say for now that it is valid to say that Company A is the more efficient in so far as it is using its resources more economically. Whether it should be allowed to do so is another matter.

Any comparisons made between industries rather than companies within an industry are subject to the introduction of considerations that are not entirely matters of economics, but bring in questions of politics, value judgements and ethics.

Is there any point in proceeding? Yes. It is still possible to assess the return each of the companies is earning on capital employed — and then go on to criticise on the basis of the figures supplied and the influence of known tangible factors already discussed, but do not forget that there may be other facts behind the scenes which if known would influence conclusions.

It is better to proceed with the analysis and deal with difficulties as they arise though keeping them constantly in mind.

One thing that must be said at this point is that, and this qualifies a previous remark, if A is paying employees pensions and providing other additional benefits over and above those provided by B it is not necessarily necessary to add back the additional benefits if it can be shown that these are only apparent in the sense that they either compensate for a low standard wage or are the only means of retaining staff.

The problem arises immediately with the first of the companies in the list. I.C.I. show profit before tax after deducting a very substantial amount as provision for employees' profit-sharing scheme. Should this be added back? It represents in 1963 8% of net profits which must be considered to be material. The reason this was not done previously was that concern was then with profits available to shareholders. An even larger amount is shown as "pension fund contributions, pensions and gratuities". Should those be added back? With the exception of Wimpey's no other company showed an equivalent item. Wimpey's paid in the region of 6% (after charging pensions) to staff pension schemes. However, the fact that such items are not shown in no way indicates that they do not exist and are not lost somewhere in trading profit. For present purposes pension contributions will be ignored as normal and profit-sharing scheme appropriations will be added back as not — even though theoretically they could be mere perks to keep employees *happy on relatively low salaries.* Generally speaking, however, profit-sharing schemes tend to be genuine — in the sense of being an extra rather than a substitute.

Considering now each company in turn the first point is to deal with any adjustments to profits which on the premises put forward appear necessary to a proper calculation of a meaningful (with reservations) rate of return on total capital. As the adjustments may come under such a variety of headings tabulation is not feasible — except for one company at a time. As is the nature of things it is wisest to begin at the beginning with the first company on our list, this being I.C.I. It is proposed to commence in each case with profit before tax and make the necessary adjustments to this figure giving where necessary the reason for these adjustments, i.e. where they have not already been fully explained in the preceding paragraphs either explicitly or by implication. Where figures cannot be accurately determined this will be stated. The basis of any estimate will be made quite clear — this will be common to such items as interest on bank overdraft and amounts paid on short term borrowings from other sources — though where the debt is repaid prior to the year end the problem becomes a little complex and it may be necessary to ignore such items. These problems can be dealt with as they may arise rather than anticipate more difficulties than may actually be found. The first stage then is to adjust the profits shown in Appendix A for each year and for each company individually.

I.C.I.

	1960 £000	1961 £000	1962 £000	1963 £000
Profits before tax per Appendix A	88,044	61,852	70,369	84,909
Debenture and fixed loan interest	3,740	2,738	6,506	7,958}
Other loan interest	687	930		
Provision in respect of employees' profit-sharing scheme (see text)	8,564	8,734	6,719	6,880
Interest payable*	300	300	1,222	981
Adjusted profit	101,335	74,554	84,716	100,728

*This may include interest on bank overdraft and has been treated as such. Where bank overdraft interest is added back the rate taken is low, at 3%, because of not knowing (a) the average level and whether the end of year figure is representative, (b) if creditors are paid on cheques dated at end of financial year (inflating the overdraft figure in the accounts).

Courtaulds

	1960 £000	1961 £000	1962 £000	1963 £000
Profit before tax (Appendix A)	21,044	18,697	17,707	23,648
Interest on debenture stocks and other secured loans	267	363	685	2,771 } 903 }
Bank overdraft, approx.	30	39	50	51
Provision toward copartnership benefit	94	127	146	22
Adjusted profit	21,435	19,226	18,588	27,395

Imperial Tobacco

	1960 £000	1961 £000	1962 £000	1963 £000
Profit before tax (Appendix A)	28,032	29,079	30,572	31,664
Interest on notes	563	563	563	553
Interest on unsecured loan stocks	1,600	1,600	1,600	1,608
Bank and other interest	1,553	2,187	1,759	1,324
Special provision for obsolescence*	—	—	—	407
Amount provided re previous years for retirement benefits for African workpeople*	—	—	—	200
Profit of non-consolidated subsidiary†	93	389		
Adjusted profit	31,841	33,818	34,494	35,756

*These figures should theoretically be spread, but without necessary information this is not possible.

†No figures are given for 1962 or 1963 — presumably in those years the accounts of the Canadian subsidiaries were consolidated with the others.

Newton Chambers

	1960 £000	1961 £000	1962 £000	1963 £000
Profit before tax (Appendix A)	950	1,146	630	501
Debenture interest	38	37	37	37
Interest on bank overdraft	21	53	90	82
Adjusted profit	1,009	1,236	757	620

Lancashire Cotton Corpn.

	1960 £000	1961 £000	1962 £000	1963 £000
Profit before tax (Appendix A)	3,606	3,175	805	794
Debenture interest	48	47	46	46
Adjusted profit	3,654	3,222	851	840

George Wimpey

	1960 £000	1961 £000	1962 £000	1963 £000
Profit before tax (Appendix A)	3,151	3,220	3,290	4,128
Interest on bank and other loans*	162	217	284	246
Discount on issue of loan, stock, etc.	42	—	—	—
Adjusted profit	3,355	3,437	3,574	4,374

*It is not possible to discover whether interest on overdraft is included in this item. It is presumed that it is.

Harland & Woolf

	1960 £000	1961 £000	1962 £000	1963 £000
Profit before tax (Appendix A)	377	312	(909)	92
Interest on bank overdraft, approx.	—	59	95	53
Adjusted profit	377	371	(814)	145

William Hancock

	1960 £000	1961 £000	1962 £000	1963 £000
Profit before tax (Appendix A)	351	503	622	612
Debenture interest	14	14	13	13
Other interest*	6	9	12	22
Adjusted profit	371	524	645	647

*It is assumed that interest on overdraft is included in this item, there being no evidence to the contrary.

Before going on to evaluate Table N, it might be as well for the reader to prepare one more table summarising the results so far — in terms only of returns and deviation from the arithmetic mean. This will help compare the results from Table N with the figures from Tables D and G, which concern the return on ordinary capital employed. It is wisest to ignore the return on total share capital and reserves as it was found that the inclusion of preference share capital only introduced additional complication of detail without affording any useful and additional information. It is intended to refer to the interest paid on preference capital in the course of this chapter — the word interest is used, rather than dividends, as preference shareholders have few effective rights which give them advantages above the ordinary "lender" — particularly since the recent Dimbula Valley judgement: but this has been fully discussed elsewhere and there is no purpose served in labouring the

TABLE N

RETURN ON TOTAL ASSETS EMPLOYED

Company		1 Total share capital and reserves per appendix £000	2 Minority interests £000	3 Debentures and other long-term loans £000	4 Current liabilities £000	5 Total £000	6 Total 5 + depreciation £000	7 Total 6 + revaluation surplus £000	8 Profit as adjusted £000	9 Return on capital 5 %	10 Return on capital 6 %	11 Return on capital 7 %
I.C.I.	1960	573,331	31,160	73,109	128,000	805,600	906,257	1,120,257	101,335	12·6	11·3	9·0
	1961	619,197	38,111	59,430	136,601	853,339	992,867	1,214,867	74,554	8·7	7·5	6·1
	1962	651,032	40,143	99,506	135,699	926,380	1,099,587	1,230,587	84,716	9·2	7·7	6·8
	1963	690,136	41,417	136,498	141,189	1,009,240	1,222,256	1,458,256	100,728	9·9	8·4	6·9
Average %		71	4	10	15	100	100	100	mean M.D. M.D. as %	10·1 1·2 11·9	8·9 1·3 14·6	7·2 0·9 12·6
Courtaulds	1960	175,018	—	—	23,045	198,063	258,156	327,579	21,435	10·7	8·2	6·5
	1961	189,056	4,501	3,265	29,008	225,830	293,554	364,394	19,226	8·5	6·6	5·3
	1962	172,546	9,145	26,659	33,652	242,002	315,142	388,742	18,588	7·7	5·9	4·8
	1963	154,644	9,529	46,901	39,050	250,124	325,576	400,676	27,395	11·0	8·4	6·8
Average %		76	2	8	14	100	100	100	mean M.D. M.D. as %	9·5 1·4 14·7	7·3 1·0 13·7	5·8 0·8 13·8
Imperial Tobacco	1960	157,203*	30*	93,000*	32,000*	282,233	311,194	459,194	31,841	11·4	10·3	6·9
	1961	165,171	75	93,490	33,407	292,143	323,478	474,478	33,818	11·7	10·6	7·1
	1962	176,164	95	94,066	35,969	306,294	338,071	495,071	34,494	11·4	10·1	6·9
	1963	186,268	83	93,050	37,378	316,779	350,114	510,114	35,756	11·2	10·2	7·0
Average %		57	—	31	12	100	100	100	mean M.D. M.D. as %	11·4 0·1 0·9	10·3 0·1 1·0	7·0 0·1 1·4

	Year											
Newton Chambers	1960	12,594	—	704	2,953	16,251	16,781	17,707	1,009	6·3	6·0	5·7
	1961	13,394	—	694	4,118	18,206	19,140	20,085	1,236	6·8	6·5	6·2
	1962	13,435	85	682	5,160	19,362	21,741	22,723	757	3·9	3·5	3·3
	1963	13,365	164	672	5,200	19,401	21,247	22,247	620	3·2	3·0	2·6
	Average %	73	—	4	23	100	100	100	mean / M.D. / M.D. as %	5·1 / 1·5 / 29·4	4·8 / 1·5 / 31·2	4·4 / 1·5 / 34·1
Lancashire Cotton Corpn.	1960	24,582	—	2,300*	3,300*	30,182	33,944	44,093	3,654	12·2	10·7	8·3
	1961	25,039	—	2,128	3,214	30,381	34,917	45,273	3,222	10·7	9·2	7·2
	1962	24,694	—	1,918	3,127	29,739	34,260	45,020	851	2·8	2·5	1·9
	1963	24,027	—	1,735	2,333	28,095	33,670	44,670	840	3·0	2·5	1·8
	Average %	83	—	7	10	100	100	100	mean / M.D. / M.D. as %	7·2 / 4·3 / 59·7	6·2 / 3·7 / 59·7	4·8 / 2·9 / 60·4
George Wimpey	1960	12,414	—	2,214	11,431	26,059	36,674	50,374	3,355	12·4	9·1	6·7
	1961	14,228	—	2,627	14,877	31,732	42,492	56,472	3,437	10·7	8·1	6·1
	1962	15,745	—	3,029	16,447	35,221	46,838	61,358	3,574	10·2	7·6	5·8
	1963	17,542	—	3,226	18,170	38,938	51,262	66,262	4,374	11·2	8·6	6·6
	Average %	45	—	8	47	100	100	100	mean / M.D. / M.D. as %	11·1 / 0·7 / 6·3	8·3 / 0·5 / 6·0	6·3 / 0·35 / 5·5
Harland & Woolf	1960	16,738	147	—	9,353	26,238	37,479	49,514	377	1·4	1·0	0·75
	1961	16,894	165	—	9,150	26,209	37,940	50,220	371	1·4	0·98	0·74
	1962	16,956	180	—	10,274	27,410	39,360	52,120	814	2·9	2·06	1·5
	1963	16,941	—	—	9,698	26,731	37,280	50,280	loss 145	loss 0·54	0·39	loss 0·29
	Average %	64	92	—	35	100	100	100	mean / M.D. / M.D. as %	0·15 / —	0·08 / —	0·7 / —
William Hancock	1960	2,336	—	453	734	3,523	4,263	6,326	371	10·5	8·7	5·9
	1961	2,847	—	416	925	4,188	5,040	7,145	524	12·5	10·4	7·3
	1962	3,402	—	383	1,130	4,915	5,806	7,993	645	13·1	11·1	8·1
	1963	3,609	—	369	1,469	5,447	6,389	10,221	647	11·9	10·1	6·3
	Average %	68	—	9	23	100	100	100	mean / M.D. / M.D. as %	12·0 / 0·8 / 7·0	10·3 / 0·7 / 7·0	6·9 / 1·0 / 12·0

*Estimated figure only.

point here except to mention that the remarks are not confined to preference shares with no preference as to capital.

There is a serious danger that a multiplicity of tables will tend to confuse more than instruct. It has been attempted throughout to keep them to a minimum and many are merely of the nature of summaries.

Nevertheless, the problem which was set to be solved seemed to be one of mathematics, and to any satisfactory answer a certain quantity of figures must be essential.

As far as the assessment of return on capital is concerned most of the relevant analysis is contained in Table O. The next task is to attempt a complete summary, and from there, both criticise the results we have shown and deduce the conclusions, useful or otherwise, to be drawn from them.

In the first place, the return shown on total capital in Table N will tend to be less than the return in Table K. Were it not so it would indicate that the company was paying a higher rate to lenders, i.e. debenture holders and banks, than was being earned by ordinary shareholders.

As explained above, preference shareholders are "lenders" in this sense. The extent of the difference in the respective rates will depend on the rate of interest paid on loans and other liabilities. Where this is low and where those which carry no interest are quantitatively large then the rate earned on ordinary capital employed is likely to appear high.

A point to note, however, is that although the fact that the return per Table N is lower than Table K indicates that lower rates are paid on loans than on ordinary capital employed, it refers only to average rates. The fact that current trade creditors are high could cloak a high interest rate being paid on a loan, e.g. earnings rate Table K 5% — earnings rate Table N 3%. This 3% could be made up by averaging £100 at 10% with £233 interest-free current liabilities. It is therefore essential to look at the individual accounts on which the tables are based a little more closely to see whether in fact any company is actually paying interest charges in excess of the return on total assets. If so, then this is necessarily to the disadvantage of the shareholder and the loan should be eliminated as soon as possible, either by raising fresh funds from members or by retaining more in the way of profits.

The main interest rates concern debenture and other long-term loans, of a similar nature, bank loans and bank overdrafts. The stumbling

		Return on capital per balance sheet		Return on capital incl. depreciation		Return on capital incl. depreciation and surplus on revaluation	
		1 Total capital employed Table N %	2 Ordinary capital employed Table D %	3 Total capital employed Table N %	4 Ordinary capital employed Table G %	5 Total capital employed Table N %	6 Ordinary capital employed Table K %
I.C.I.	1960	12·6	16·0	11·3	13·5	9·0	10·2
	1961	8·7	10·4	8·3	8·3	6·1	6·4
	1962	9·2	11·1	7·7	8·7	6·8	6·7
	1963	9·9	12·7	8·4	9·5	6·9	7·6
	mean	10·1	12·5	8·9	10·0	7·2	7·7
	%D.	11·9	15·0	14·6	17·0	12·6	16·0
Courtaulds	1960	10·7	12·7	8·2	9·2	6·5	7·2
	1961	8·5	10·4	6·6	7·4	5·3	5·7
	1962	7·7	10·7	5·9	7·3	4·8	5·4
	1963	11·0	16·5	8·4	10·6	6·8	7·9
	mean	9·5	12·6	7·3	8·6	5·8	6·6
	%D.	15·0	16·0	14·0	13·0	14·0	15·0
Imperial Tobacco	1960	11·4	18·9	10·3	15·8	6·9	8·5
	1961	11·7	18·8	10·6	15·4	7·1	8·4
	1962	11·4	18·2	10·1	15·3	6·9	8·4
	1963	11·2	17·8	10·2	14·9	7·0	8·4
	mean	11·4	18·4	10·3	15·4	7·0	8·4
	%D.	1·0	2·0	1·0	2·0	1·0	—
Newton Chambers	1960	6·3	7·5	6·0	7·3	5·7	6·7
	1961	6·8	8·6	6·5	8·1	6·2	7·5
	1962	3·9	4·7	3·5	4·5	3·3	4·3
	1963	3·2	3·7	3·0	3·3	2·6	3·1
	mean	5·1	6·1	4·8	5·8	4·4	5·4
	%D.	29·0	31·0	31·0	33·0	34·0	31·0
Lancashire Cotton Corpn.	1960	12·2	14·4	10·7	12·9	8·3	9·4
	1961	10·7	12·5	9·2	10·6	7·2	7·9
	1962	2·8	3·3	2·5	2·7	1·9	2·0
	1963	3·0	3·3	2·5	2·7	1·8	2·0
	mean	7·2	8·4	6·2	7·2	4·8	5·3
	%D.	60·0	62·0	60·0	62·0	60·0	64·0
George Wimpey	1960	12·4	27·5	9·1	14·1	6·7	8·6
	1961	10·7	23·9	8·1	13·3	6·1	8·0
	1962	10·2	24·8	7·6	12·8	5·8	7·9
	1963	11·2	25·1	8·6	14·6	6·6	9·3
	mean	11·1	25·3	8·3	13·7	6·3	8·4
	%D.	6·0	4·0	6·0	6·0	6·0	6·0
Harland & Woolf	1960	1·4	1·7	1·0	1·0	0·75	0·68
	1961	1·4	1·3	0·98	0·73	0·74	0·49
	1962	2·9	6·3	2·06	4·0	1·5	2·6
		loss	loss	loss	loss	loss	loss
	1963	0·54	0·27	0·39	0·13	0·29	0·9
					loss		loss
	mean	0·15	0·76	0·08	0·6	0·7	0·13
	%D.	—	—	—	—	—	—
William Hancock	1960	10·5	17·7	8·7	12·5	5·9	6·9
	1961	12·5	20·4	10·4	14·8	7·3	8·8
	1962	13·1	21·4	11·1	16·2	8·1	10·0
	1963	11·9	19·2	10·1	14·9	6·3	9·5
	mean	12·0	19·5	10·1	14·6	6·9	8·8
	%D.	7·0	7·0	7·0	7·0	12·0	11·0

block is the latter. The average rate paid thereon can vary greatly and the accounts do not indicate it. Generally speaking however it tends to be low when averaged throughout the accounting period being analysed. It is usually cheaper to run an overdraft (where security is available) than raise a loan from a bank or from other sources, be they private or public, in the sense of picking pivate pockets or borrowing from the State in one form or another. The reason being that the interest rate paid on the overdraft is on a day-to-day basis and may be negligible during the more liquid parts of the year. (This should be qualified by pointing out that in years of escalating inflation a fixed loan could be preferable to a varying overdraft. This is because of the monetary profit accruing from the fall in the real value of a fixed sum borrowed. This fall in value may actually be in excess of the actual cash paid over in interest, when the period of the loan is taken as a whole.)

This could be true, say, of Hancock's where the accounts are at 31st December. Trade is probably much heavier in summer months and the cash position easier. December may show the overdraft at its peak.

Perhaps the next step is to follow the usual practice of considering each company in turn.

I.C.I.

There is little to say in this case; neither Table N nor O adds much to the discussion in the previous chapter, and in no way modifies our conclusions, except to the extent that the mean deviation in Table N, column 9 seems slightly more favourable — but this advantage has almost disappeared in column 10.

The total return is an average ranging from 10·1 in column 9 to 7·2 in column 11. The fact that the latter figure would appear fairly reasonable in normal circumstances is marred by the high deviation of 12·6%. The return was as low as 6·1% in 1961. However, this begs the question of what is a reasonable rate of return on total assets. Instead of, as in the past, speaking in terms of how much the investor should expect, the emphasis is now on what return society should demand, or even insist on, on that part of its limited resources acquired by one business unit. The question is of some complexity. It is hoped to attempt some sort of settlement in a later chapter. A low of 6·1% does not seem unreasonable by general standards, but how are these standards determined? And an income of £6 per cent must be looked at in terms of the security of the capital used to produce it.

As for interest payments, the highest paid is 6·5% — dangerously near the borderline; and on a large amount, in fact, more than 50% of the total of Table N, column 3. However, two favourable points. Firstly, in 1961, when the return fell to 6·1%, this loan may not have existed (the accounts do not give a break up of the loan figure in that year) because total loans were less than half the 1963 figure. Secondly, the loan has been reduced from £76 million in 1962 to £56 million in 1963. No further comment seems necessary.

Courtaulds

Here again there is little by way of additional information to dissuade us from the position adopted on studying Table K. A return of 9·5% seems reasonable but, adopting the figures in Table K, then there is nothing impressive about 5·8% with a deviation of 13·8%. The only encouragement is drawn from the fact that the 1963 figures are slightly above the arithmetic mean.

Although the loan stock is only 8% of total capital the greater part of it carries an interest rate of 7%, which is about equal to the average earnings rate on a Table G basis and above it on a Table K basis. There are limited signs of improvement in the fact that 1963 figures show a noticeable increase over those of the previous year. Whether this is a sign of good times ahead or merely a temporary improvement can only be seen by awaiting the results of years to come.

Of course it still imperative to decide what is a satisfactory interest rate. This was to be left to another chapter — but it must be emphasised that whatever rate is earned it *must* be lower than the rate paid to acquire the capital on which the return is made (except perhaps in those cases where funds must be acquired for short periods to overcome temporary embarrassments and they can only be acquired quickly by paying what is in effect a surcharge). It might be argued that concern should be with average rates paid for capital. That is hardly a defensible position. There is no point in obtaining long-term funds at an interest rate that will exceed the money that these funds will earn. There can surely be no argument on this point. It is true that earnings will vary from year to year, and from that point of view an average might be acceptable; but the principle cannot in any way be denied in any business which is to remain viable. It is a matter of elementary economics. Of course it will be asked what happens if the profit rate drops below the interest rate. The answer depends on the various factors that may be involved. Many questions must be asked. What is the possibility of repaying the loan? Are there any funds available for this purpose? Can they be acquired by raising fresh capital from the members — or by raising a new loan at a lower rate? What are the conditions attaching to the old loan? Can it be repaid at will? Is there a premium on repayment?

In the case of Courtaulds the loan is unsecured and is repayable in 1982/87, i.e. at any time between those dates. This is some way ahead. If the prospects of earning a higher return than 7% in the future are not certain (it is true that in Table G terms 8·4% was earned in 1963, but the deviation was 14%; on a Table K basis, which is more relevant, the position is even less promising, the return being 6·8% with a deviation of 14% from a 5·8% arithmetic mean) the company could of course buy in the loan — as opposed to redeeming it. It is, however, a substantial sum, £40 million. This compares with a working capital of nearly £50 million and an annual profit after tax of but £14 million in 1963. Assuming the dividend is to be maintained, this leaves £7 million p.a. At the moment it seems that this is needed entirely, merely to maintain profits, and is hardly available for use in buying in the loan. Even were part of it put to this purpose it would take a sizeable part of the life of the loan to complete the process — particularly if, as is likely, the price exceeds the nominal value.

Apart from earning profits there are of course other possibilities of balancing the position. Members may be prepared to supply the necessary funds by means, say, of a rights issue. On the other hand, it may be possible to raise an alternative loan at a lower rate. This is doubtful as no one is likely to lend money on a risk investment at less than 6½% which is the present approximate level of earning per column 5, plus a mean deviation of 14%. It seems, then, that the only solution is to raise further funds from members. To do so would involve paying out a greater proportion of profits in dividends — if the dividend rate quoted is to be maintained —and this may be impossible without endangering future income. If on the other hand the dividend is dropped then the rights issue may not succeed.

It would therefore appear that the loan must probably be retained. It was in fact issued in 1962 gratis to members, out of reserves. It was a move in the battle at the time with I.C.I. Nevertheless the loan is now a real liability (it is possibly no longer in the hands of members) and the circumstances of its issue are irrelevant.

As for judging future prospects the trading profit rose by about 50% in 1963, yet the turnover only increased by 7%. The answer to the problem then posed, lies in facts which are not available. The greater part of the increase arose from profits from viscose fibres — these jumped from £8 million to £13 million — accounting for over two-thirds of the difference. Much would seem to depend then on the maintaining of this improvement in the fibres division — though perhaps in a company of such varied activities a similar leap forward in some other division cannot be discounted. As with I.C.I., the size of the deviation is a fair indication of the difficulties underlying accurate forecasting of the profits of future years. One point relating to Courtaulds' accounts which is worthy of commendation (to digress a little) is the quantity of additional information that is provided, particularly as to the contribution toward total profit made by each individual department or activity. The use of this and other information will be discussed later.

Imperial Tobacco

Here again the consistency of results speaks for itself. The size of the figures is not great, but then with an almost non-existent deviation this is perhaps not so important. The difference between the return on total assets and that on capital employed is quite considerable, due to the fact that only 57% of assets belong to members (as opposed to 76% in Courtaulds and 71% in I.C.I.). The balance is mainly in loans, the rates on which (according to the accounts) are well below the lowest rate shown in Table O. However, various facts must be taken into account. Firstly, when the loans have to be renewed higher rates may be demanded. Secondly, the method of revaluation adopted in Table K may be quite wrong, and in fact total value of assets may be very much higher than surmised in the text. This however applies to all companies and it cannot be denied that Imperial Tobacco show a fairly consistent and apparently reasonable return, a return lower on average than that of I.C.I., but more satisfactory inasmuch as it never strays beyond 1% of the arithmetic mean, whereas that of I.C.I. varies around 13%. A third factor is the possibility of government interference — higher excise duty — reducing sales and profits and therefore lowering the return. So far no attempt has, of course, been made to state what a "reasonable" return on total assets might be. Up to the moment the tendency has been to use the figures to show the amount that could be paid on borrowed moneys and to help assess the stability of the company. It has also been shown how it can differ from the return on members' capital employed according to the proportion this contributes to total funds. There has again been a temptation to compare one company with another — but this is very dangerous ground — for it effectively assumes that the contribution to the economy and the efficiency of the company are both indicated by the size of the return and that one company can be compared to another irrespective of the fact that each is producing a separate product. These are very questionable and, in fact, quite unwarranted assumptions. They ignore so many different factors and are based on premises which far from being stated have not even been formed. This it is intended to discuss in the next chapter, though the subject is one on which any sound conclusions are quite unlikely to be reached — so many controversial matters standing in face of a satisfactory or even merely feasible solution. But to continue.

Newton Chambers

Again little can be added to the general comment given in the last chapter. The majority of the assets are employed in members' funds — a mere 4% being in loans. The greater part of these are at 6%, which is higher than the arithmetic mean return in table N in each of the three columns. However, with a mean deviation of over 34% in column 11 it is fairly apparent that any short-term assessment on this basis is fairly pointless. The fact is that the return has fallen from a bare 6·2% in 1961 to an extreme low of 2·6% in 1963. The company is seeing difficult times and there is little more to be said.

Lancashire Cotton Corpn.

The same remarks apply in this instance as to Newton Chambers: a low arithmetic mean in column 11, but an extremely high mean deviation of approximately 60%. In circumstances such as these a short-term analysis gives no more information than do the figures themselves. The profits have dropped considerably from an average of 7·8% for the first two years to 1·8% in the latter years.

Luckily the interest rate on loans, which in any event represents 7% of total funds, is as low as 3½% — which, though not covered by the present return, is comfortably within reach, assuming the present trend is reversed — or rather, provided the return, now almost stable, increases; if not, there is little to look forward to but eventual disintegration. One point peculiar to this company is its high liquidity, which may afford an opportunity to quickly take the current when it serves. It will be interesting to observe the results of coming years.*

George Wimpey

Loans are only 8% of total funds and the only rate shown is 6%, which is below the lowest rate shown in Table N. No rate is given for the unsecured loan.

One of the interesting facts about the company is the size of the figure of current liabilities, most of which consist of "sundry creditors". The total current liabilities represents 47% of total funds, higher than those attributable to shareholders. This is common in this type of concern — where the length of time for completion of contracts leads to high figures of work-in-progress and debtors. As a result there is a time lag in receipts which unless financed permanently by members (which would be unwise because of necessary variations), must be reflected in a correspondingly high figure of creditors.

The arithmetic mean return in column 11 is just above 6%. The figure is not particularly high and cannot be said to inspire great confidence, particularly as the low mean deviation indicates that it varies little from this level.

*See Appendix B, note 1.

The low relative level of members' funds accounts for the noticeable difference between return on total assets and return attributable to members — much in the members' favour.

Harland & Woolf

The only new fact of any pertinency arising from Table N is that in this instance, as opposed to all others, the profit expressed in relation to total assets is (with one exception) greater than the return on equity. This is due to the abnormally low profit figures and the fact that the share capital includes £2·6 million preference shares which is 19% of the total shown. As has been said before, the abnormal situation of this company makes any useful analysis impossible.

William Hancock

This company's record is reasonable. The arithmetic mean return is 6·9% with a deviation of 12%. Results were in fact improving from 1960 to 1962 but fell back slightly in 1963.

In quoting the figures based on an arbitrary revaluation there may of course be errors either way. The company is a fine example of the difference revaluation may make.

The original Table G figures were 10·1% with a deviation of only 7%. If the revaluation erred to the company's disadvantage, then in fact it may be far more prosperous than the Table K based figures in Table O would indicate. If the revaluation was too conservative, however, the arithmetic mean may well be forced below what level might be desired, and this together with the liquidity position would put things in quite a different perspective.

The equity return is again quite high, due to the relatively low figure of members' funds employed.

In any event, whatever the figures at present indicate reasons are given (good reasons) for the low liquidity and variance in return. In addition to this, no indication of links with other more well-known breweries is suggested in the accounts. That these exist is obvious to anyone living in the area in which this brewery principally operates.

So much for the figures for each company. Having examined in this chapter the earnings of each company in relation to total assets employed, of what real significance are the answers which have been obtained?

CHAPTER 10

The Economic and Social Significance of the Analysis

THE preceding chapter attempted to illustrate the movements, over a short period, in the return on total assets presently employed. The method has been to limit the analysis to the results of the individual company — comparing one year with another and noting deviations and trends. What we must now query is whether the return itself has any quantitative significance and whether it can be validly used for inter-company comparisons.

Take the instance of Imperial Tobacco shown in Table N as earning a return of around 7·0% p.a. That is to say, for each £100 of capital invested, the company earns £7 in each calendar year. This is represented by an increase in assets (and therefore in capital) of the amount. As already noted a certain proportion is paid over to shareholders and the remainder is retained in the business.

Now it is not the intention of this book to look for justification of profits as such (the value of profit as a basis on which to rest an economy is something quite separate). The term profit merely describes the amount by which the price paid for an object exceeds the cost of putting it into a condition and place for sale to a consumer (using this word in its widest sense) in an open or private market. Is the amount of profit or its relationship to capital, that is the rate of return, of any significance when considering the contribution made by that company to society as in itself or compared to other producers in different fields? This is the important question. How can one assess the value of a contribution? It is all very well for Adam Smith to state that "labour is the only true measure of value" this but begs the vital question of how one is to value labour. It also ignores the fact that any single working person has at his or her disposal an international heritage of ideas, methods and implements assembled over the centuries. To value it in quantitative or qualitative terms is absurd. To say that one hour's work well done in one field is equivalent in value to an hour in the next, is unsupportable. So also is any system which relates value to work units whatever their type — be they measured in terms of human energy lost or tonnage produced. Similarly to relate value to ability — say based on an I.Q. rating or on the relative quality of output is again quite ridiculous. What has to be assessed is the social utility, in the particular environment, of the goods or services produced.

The question of whether there is justification for paying unequal wages for unequal work is not for the moment being discussed. The value of work done can be separated from the amount paid for it.

Even this is an insufficient yardstick in itself for a man may produce an article of great value to society to the detriment of his own health. The perfect example could be in the coal industry. From the social value of the article, i.e. coal, must be deducted the human and social cost of the prevalence of pneumoconiosis and rather higher mortality rates.

So in considering the value of the product the cost in human terms must be remembered. This might represent something tangible, such as the cost of clinics or treatment in our example, but more often it is something which can hardly be given a fixed value inasmuch as it consists of such elements as reduction in expectation of life or just physical or mental pain. If a man does a brilliant year's work and then breaks down under the strain, the loss of his services for the future may be far greater than the contribution he has made in that particular year. It is merely the old question of deducting decreases in capital from increases in income.

The wealth of a country or (*pace* the economist) national income cannot be sensibly measured in any other manner, one man may work to the limits of his ability for 8 hours a day producing imitation period furniture for suburban villas, another in the same town may work an equal day on cancer research, production of surgical instruments, or even slum clearance or waste disposal. Now there are various points to be made here. Inasmuch as both men may quantitatively and qualitatively (in the sense of using an equal degree of skill) be expending equal effort, any just society which demands all these products should afford each an equal wage — for if work is to be the measure of value, then equal units of work should demand equal reward. This of course ignores the fact that society may wish to measure work units according to the social value of the product. It would be possible perhaps to devise a system of α, β, γ units with a price attached to each. This hardly affects the argument — being that the wages of each worker, in the example taken, must be determined not by the price the product controls but by some independent and previously determined standard rate of payment for the particular work done. Otherwise then each man must take what the consumer will pay for his product or service, and value then becomes completely unrelated to labour but depends solely on factors of supply and demand.

This brings the question of whether the true value of labour lies in the price the third party will pay for it. If this is so, then the question of profit, right or wrong, needs no answer in the pure sense, inasmuch as profit, by logical definition, must be the surplus of an income over the figure for which the recipient is prepared to work — assuming conditions of free movement of labour.

The point needs little elaboration — it applies to the workman as to the sole trader, the sole trader as to the public company. In the latter case the question of dividends arises. Here the profit is not that stated in the accounts, it is the balance of this figure remaining after shareholders have received a fair return on their capital — a return consonant with the prevailing interest rates and with the risk of losing any part of that capital.

If anyone is to say that there is an assumption of the social justification of the payment of interest the only answer must surely be that no assumption is necessary. If A wishes to hire B's machine, which B could profitably use, he will ask A to pay for it. So also, if A asks B to advance him £1,000 to buy such an item, B must surely feel equally entitled to compensation.

In the case of the company, the real profit is the "surplus" dividend paid to shareholders, plus the balance remaining to the company after it has retained (or deducted) such an amount as is necessary to maintain the prevailing return on capital. To this must be added the profit earned by employees in the form of wages, and benefits over and above the minimum (assuming full employment) for which they were prepared to work. It is necessary to assume full employment to eliminate situations where men will work for next to nothing in order to live.

It is possible, where full employment does not apply, that the unemployment benefit could be taken as a minimum, though as this takes no account of differences in skill, then perhaps minimum union rates would be a fair guide, or even the average rate prevailing in the trade, assuming some men to be paid less and some more than their marginal wage in free market conditions.

The question then arises as to how this profit should be distributed, whether to employees and/or shareholders, or whether it should rather be repaid to the public in the form of reduced prices. On the other hand if it were retained by the company — for unless it can increase its asset wealth it cannot expand — this is equivalent theoretically to allocating it totally to the shareholders. The solution seems to be to retain that which is necessary to expansion plans in the form of reserves, but to allocate these reserves between employees and members either by the establishment of special trusts or by the issue of additional shares.

It must be realised that at present the word profit is being used in a very precise sense — not quite as it was defined in preceding chapters. There it was the net income after tax before any distributions to shareholders, though some attempt was made to discuss the advisability of adding back additional benefits paid to employees. It is possible that if the principles and premises we have just established were accepted, and a realistic rate of interest on members' capital employed were treated as a charge in arriving at profits, then the return on total assets of the majority of companies today would be severely depleted — which would indicate on a national scale, and in monetary terms, that the country was in danger of losing rather than gaining wealth. Perhaps this would account for the current poor state of the U.K. economy.

On the other hand, if society is not to allow labour the price its product controls, but to devise a system of payment according to numbers of work units, as discussed, then of course we reach eventually a completely intolerable economic position. Either prices are left to find their own level, in which case you have a system fitted only for chaos, with unallocated profits in abundance on one side and losses and failures on the other, irrespective of national value.

It may be found, for example, that industry is producing far too much reproduction furniture and far too few surgical instruments. It is possible that houses will be full of gadgets of doubtful utility and the streets full of litter. Is the alternative a system of price controls. This may discourage the production of inessentials but without subsidy it would not affect sales of the other class of goods mentioned. No, the solution would lie in heavy taxation on one side and equivalent subsidies on the other (accompanied perhaps by price controls) in order to ensure the production of the right quantity of essential goods and services. Would this ensure an expanding economy? Is this the easiest way to increase the nation's wealth? It is one thing to be ensuring the production of essentials but unless the subsidies are sufficient not only to balance the budget but also to provide a "profit" margin for expansion, the wealth of the nation will be unlikely to increase.*

The other factor is necessarily that such a system may well lead to inefficiency in the use of resources. The company assured of its subsidy will not be so anxious to minimise its expenses and the man labouring under the load of a devastating tax system will be somewhat discouraged from giving of his best.

The fact is that once the profit motive is removed then unless the idea is accepted of a completely authoritarian system then some other motivating force should be found to take its place. At present nothing resembling such a force exists and never will until the individual member of society is more concerned with what he can put into the national kitty than with what he can take out.

Digressions seem to abound. The subject being discussed was the value of quantitative assessments. How for example it is possible to judge whether £7 per cent is a good return for Imperial Tobacco, or a poor one, or whether it has any significance whatsoever. Is it necessary to consider the interest rates prevailing at the time? This immediately raises the question of how these rates are determined and on what premises or for what reasons.

In the first place interest rates vary considerably. In one project it is possible that the investor is prepared to accept 3% or even less perhaps in the hope of halcyon days ahead. Another lender in different

---

*The present plight of B.S.C., British Leyland and the public transport systems is not irrelevant here.

circumstances may demand an apparently usurious rate of 50%. The point here is that he possibly considers that the chances of losing his capital in the first year are in the region of 2-1 against.

If one analysed the Stock Exchange prices of securities and shares at any time the variance in interest rates demanded would soon be apparent. The amount required depends basically on the risk taken. There are, of course, other factors, such as the availability of credit. A borrower wishing to raise funds when, due say to a credit squeeze, money is in short supply, may have to pay a premium. Again however this is often the risk element in reverse. A credit squeeze means a clamping down on production and makes risk projects even more "risky" due to the lack of cash available for purchasing the products. Consequently the borrower pays high rates, because the lender demands such rates. From another point of view the amount a manufacturer is prepared to pay for funds depends on his profit expectancy. If he anticipates a return on capital of 10% he will be prepared to borrow up to a limit of that amount. However, it is not sufficient to consider the borrower's assessment. He must persuade the lender of the profit prospect and the safety of his capital — so again it is a matter of coming back to the lender's assessment of the risk.

The risk is naturally three sided. There is the risk that the dividend rate promised, or interest rate assured, may not be maintained. There is the normal risk that the capital invested may be lost by failure of the business or depleted on a realisation in the open market — due to the inability of the company to keep to its promise. Thirdly there is the risk of loss of capital through a general fall in interest rates. Suppose interest rates change throughout the country — suppose the general rates demanded rise, due perhaps to a credit squeeze, or an increase in economic activity, bringing about a greater demand for a limited supply of funds and higher payments therefore. If then X has invested £1,000 at 6% and the rate expected on that type of investment rose to $7\frac{1}{2}$%, then the market price of the investment would drop to £800. This loss of £200, assuming a stable currency, would be equivalent to over three years' interest. In present conditions, where government policy is not always calculable, then the danger of a loss on sudden realisation is a factor that must be taken seriously into account, particularly by the smaller investor.

It is this element of risk — the change in expected rates — that influences the price of relatively "risk free" investments in the market. Government bonds are issued at different times and at varying interest rates — depending on economic conditions at time of issue. There may, for instance, be two series of defence bonds in existence, one at 5%, another at 6%. The price of these will differ on the market by such an amount as will equalise the expected yield. When expected rates change the prices will alter disproportionately.

When, then, considering the return made by a company in quantitative terms, it is not the yield quoted on gilt-edged that must be a starting point but the effective rate paid on the basis of their market price. This should then be adjusted according to the risk element as discussed previously. This brings two questions. How is the expected yield fixed, and secondly, how can one measure the incidence of the risk element?

In the first place the expected yield varies — but normally only between fairly narrow limits. It tends to a certain extent to be governed by bank rate* — the rate charged by the Bank of England as the lender of the last resort. This rate is again determined partly by government policy and partly by international economic policies. The basic question of why the rate moves around the 5½% level is unanswerable in brief. Why should it not hover around 50%? The answer probably brings us back to economics' own giant of fiction — their man on the Clapham omnibus — their Richard Roe. That is to say to Robinson Crusoe, and the argument would probably run back to such basic terms as the yields from an acre of wheat increasing in an arithmetical progression amounting roughly to 5 units per year — the original output being 100 units.

As for the risk element this is something which cannot be assessed objectively except in the broadest terms. It is a matter of opinion and experience. Stability of profit return is obviously a determining factor in the sense that the more stable the return and the longer the period, the less the risk. General trends are also important, as is the experience of other firms in the same industry. The question of trends may be dealt with in the following chapter but it is well to remember the warning given earlier that trends based on, say, moving averages, can be deceptive. It may be necessary in some cases to find some method of

*Now Minimum Lending Rate.

eliminating cyclical variations more satisfactorily than by the simple four- or five-year average.

So far a stable currency has been assumed — in periods of inflation the problems are even more difficult. The figures studied must be such as those shown in Table K, i.e. the capital must be stated in the same terms as the profit, if any satisfactory comparisons are to be made.

Finally, whatever the results of a particular company analysis are shown to be, there is the basic danger in any industrial enterprise of the bottom falling out of the market, or the emergence of a competitive product that on the basis of some new research is able to price the other out of the market.

The risk can work both ways of course where market prices are concerned. The effective rate on an industrial may drop to 2% because of expected future returns and capital appreciation. The important point to remember is that this cannot apply to government bonds, where the interest is fixed, and the eventual capital return stated in advance.

Stability or trends are, as has been so often said, important. Another factor that is generally taken into account is the average return. In the case of I.C.I. this is in the region of 7%. True the mean deviation is as high as 12·6% but assuming the arithmetic mean to be 7·2% this indicates a fairly safe investment. There is of course the risk element. The return may fall as low as 6% which by any standards, when we are considering a "risk investment", is low. Nevertheless, an arithmetic mean of 7·2% is reasonably encouraging. Not so in the case of, say, Courtaulds, where Table N shows an arithmetic mean of only 5·8% with a deviation of nearly 14%, when 8% of the capital demands an interest rate of 7%. There are in fact many aspects of funding which must be taken into account when assessing the risk.

However, for the moment, forget I.C.I. and Courtaulds and return to Imperial Tobacco. A regular return of 7% (per Table N) with a relatively non-existent deviation somehow smacks of stability.

This is fair enough. Imagine then a company in which the risk is apparently non-existent (*pace* government policy). Can it then be said that this company with a return of 7% on total assets and 8·4% on net assets is earning a return that in view of its quantity, indicates a sound investment from the point of view both of the shareholder and the nation.

Suppose for the while the question of benefits to employees is eliminated. Is it feasible then to argue that this is a company of value to society in the sense that it is earning a return above the expected yield? This brings the inquiry out of the nebulous field of economics into the arena of ethics. Is there good reason for entering this sphere?

The answer must be yes! This chapter has attempted to evaluate the significance of return on total assets. The economist may say that this company is contributing considerably and steadily toward national income. It is stable and is returning a figure above the national average. Is this sufficient grounds for applauding its results?

What does the economist understand by income? Is it the total of income earned in wages, profits, interest, etc. If so then such an evaluation has no sound foundation. A bingo hall may be earning 50% on capital employed. For every £100 invested therein it shows an annual increment of £50. The national income will necessarily increase. If this is so then the term "national income" is meaningless. Concern should be centred far more on national weath.

Looking again at *The Idea of a Christian Society* by the late T. S. Eliot, many relevant remarks could be quoted. The book, from the point of view here, could be renamed *The Idea of Any Properly Constructed Society*, christian or humanist.

Take these two quotations at random from this particular book. "We are being made aware that the organisation of society on the principle of private profit, as well as public destruction, is leading both to the deformation of humanity by unregulated industrialism and to the exhaustion of national resources and that a good deal of our material progress is a progress for which succeeding generations may have to pay dearly." And again ". . . was our society which had always been assured of its superiority and rectitude, so confident of its unexamined premises, assembled round anything more permanent than a congeries of banks, insurance companies and industries, and had it any more beliefs more essential than a belief in compound interest and the maintenance of dividends".*

The point is surely that it is not possible to make any quantitative assessment of a company's success without taking into account the products upon which this assessment is based.

*T. S. Eliot, *The Idea of a Christian Society*, Faber & Faber.

It is not suggested that Imperial Tobacco is producing a valueless product but, in social terms, it is an interesting point whether tobacco has any real value.

However, argument or not, it is necessary to weigh the theoretical contribution of this company against the potential harm it does both towards what Eliot refers to as the "Depression of standards of art and culture" and towards the physical and economic wealth of the nation.

It may or may not be true, the point is not proved, that tobacco is a considerably potent force influencing the incidence of cancer. If this were so, and it is a fact that anyone who wishes to make a point can use statistics, that most flexible of subjects, to prove most things, then one must weigh the apparent contribution this company makes towards social wealth against the negative effect its products have, in the sense of debilitating the very force that makes the forward movement of this society possible.

There is no question of indicting Imperial Tobacco in particular. The point at issue is that in judging the return made by one company against the return made by another one must inevitably take into account the social value of the product which they are supplying. This may be impossible of attainment in real terms, but the impossibility does not deny the necessity, and unless some such assessment is attempted, any statement as to the increase in the wealth of the nation, in terms of increasing the national income, is meaningless. In other words National Income cannot be measured in terms of the reward for labour, it can only truly be measured in terms of the social value of the goods and services produced, from which must be deducted the damage done in producing them.

You may well say that such a measurement is impossible of realisation; very well; this is unimportant; the inability of man to assess his wealth in real terms is no excuse for the employment of standards of value which cannot be supported by any premises whatsoever.

It will be argued that the discussion has now moved to ethics, perhaps this is so, but any rationally based society must be founded on some ethos. Unless this is true, that is, until some precisely stated premises are available, any quantitative assessments have no value whatsoever.

The only possible conclusion therefore is that, although the amount of the return on capital is relevant to the investor, from the social standpoint, it is, in isolation, no indication whatsoever of the contribution that enterprise is making towards the national good.

It is surely true that any society, whatever the size of its national product in monetary terms, is fundamentally a sick society unless it has some generally accepted ethic on which to base a real valuation of the actual goods and services produced.

It has already been remarked that the return on total assets has a very limited value in inter-industry comparisons. It is certainly no indication of the contribution each is making to society but, what is more, is little help in settling relative efficiency when this term is narrowly defined, as in the chapter on company reform, as the contribution made by management when factors outside their control are eliminated; e.g. allowance having been made for locational advantage.

A producer of baby foods, or anaesthetics, may show a return of 1% but may be maximising the possible profit. On the other hand a proprietor of fruit machines may show a return of 20%. What has this to do with efficiency? That man is content with his 20%. A sensible consultant could possibly increase his return to 30%. He is therefore not running at maximum efficiency. Even if he were, is not the term "efficiency" in this context, socially valueless. Because a monopoly is able to exploit the public by charging extraordinary prices for non-essential products and thereby earn a return of 50% on capital, can it be then said this is an efficient company?

If we stay by the literal meaning of the term and assume the company to be maximising possible profits, we must come down on its side. In this case the term efficiency may have a nominal value, but in real terms is no criterion on which to judge the value of one business against that of another, except in the sense that persons managing or manufacturing juke boxes, or other accessories to a poverty stricken culture, are apparently more successful in business than those whose vocation it is to improve the human condition in one way or another.

Profit being high does not indicate an increase in national wealth, but merely that, in certain areas of economic activity, wealth moves at a phenomenal speed from one pocket to another, the increase in the income of the entrepreneur, or rather the return on his original moneys, being recorded as an increment to the national wealth, regardless of the manner in which it was accumulated, i.e. by an unproductive method of employing limited resources. All that happens is that the sixpences kindly donated by the many are collected in the purses of the few. To count the profit without the loss may be comprehensible but is hardly consonant with economic good sense.

The only occasion when this guide to efficiency is meaningful is when two firms in the same industry are being compared. Even here it is necessary to postulate, if not perfect competition, something akin to it. Suppose then we have two firms each producing pin tables. If firm A shows a higher return, there might be some justification in claiming that firm A is more efficient at producing pin tables. This presupposes, if the information is to have anything faintly resembling real value, that pin tables are a necessary good. It in no way demonstrates that the management of firm A are an efficient team that can be separated from the product and applied with success to a completely new venture.

Again, whatever the return, the question recurs, would not the resources employed in the firm referred to be of more benefit to society if reinvested elsewhere, irrespective of the comparative return?

The point is reached where the profit a business earns is quite unimportant from a social point of view when compared with the product which the business provides.

Any society which, in fact, bases its sense of achievement on the profit shown, or is, in other words, organised on the profit motive, must look to its premises, and unless it does so it cannot claim superiority either in wealth or achievement. Until Western Civilisation (as it is so called) accepts some such argument it must eventually decline and decay as have so many societies which preceded it. There is no other way. Where this fundamental ethic is to come from none can say. Christianity tried to provide it but seems to have failed. Communism sought it but shows no noticeable signs of achievement. Perhaps after all the fault lies not in the ethic itself but in the inability of man (or his unwillingness) to accept and apply it. As Jefferson said in his letter on democracy: "Palacios may be great, others may be great, but it is the multitude that possesses force, and wisdom must yield to that. . . ." And the ethic of the mob is synthetic in the worst possible sense of the word—it is, in its collective mood, the epitome of the organisation of which Sydney Smith claimed one could never expect justice for it has no body to be kicked and no soul to be damned.

It is not only in the mob that man has shown his inadequacy. The fault lies within. There are few who have shown themselves able to subordinate emotion and instinct to the intellect. Until man can do this there will be no order, and without order continued existence, or even healthy evolution, is impossible. All civilisations seem to pass through the same process of growth, fruition and decay, the natural scheme of things from which man, with his self-knowledge, may have been expected to escape. As the trees shed their leaves in autumn, so one generation of men passes and another comes to take its place and each is as the old.

Certain men with sound motives have attempted to solve the problem by forcing society to conform to a pattern by the use of force, sometimes coupled with example, and so we find states which, having reached the decay level, are stopped in process of natural evolution or rather revolution. The phoenix fails to arise and so, scattered about the world, are these odd relics of the past, any progress being the result of external forces. Like so many white dwarfs they merely exist in a state of balance until they eventually disintegrate or are assimilated into more active units.

The pattern can only be changed by the will of the individual. Laws can be passed and enforced, but instinctive patterns of behaviour are not thereby changed in any set direction. Education can play its part but the final movement must and will emanate from the individual when the day comes when reason prevails. As Robert Owen said in his address to the County of Lanark, "Men surely cannot with truth be termed rational beings until they shall discover and put in practice the principles which shall enable them to conduct their affairs without war."

By war we need not think only of military campaigns, equal damage is done by companies brawling on the economic level and by man's natural reluctance to put anything before self-interest.

There is a great statement associated with Socialism. "To each according to his need, from each according to his means."

It is interesting to note how much emphasis is placed upon the first part of this slogan and how little on the second. Too many must be forced to give, too many profess to need too much. Happy the time, should it come, when men demand to give and must be persuaded that they are in need.

CHAPTER 11

A Note on the Significance of Capital Gearing

CAPITAL gearing refers to the manner in which funds are raised. Moneys may be raised at varying prices, i.e. rates of interest, and for different periods. At one end of the scale is the ordinary share and the reserves attaching to it. These reserves are not moneys raised in the normal sense, but being undistributed profits, in the case of revenue reserves, they are effectively a re-investment by shareholders. At the other end of the scale is the bank overdraft, and perhaps the bill payable at sight. In between are preference capital and *inter alia*, debenture and long-term loans, with or without security and repayable at a specific time or on demand, deposits, trade bills, and state grants, gratis or repayable, etc.

A company is said to be highly geared when its capital is spread over many types of funds. It is low geared when the greater part of its capital is concentrated in share capital and reserves.

At first sight, it might seem that self-financing by the accumulation of reserves is preferable. This, however, is not always so. Ordinary shareholders may expect a higher return on total equity than a debenture holder, particularly where the debentures were issued at a favourable rate of interest.

Again there is no point in accumulating reserves unless they can be employed. Better to wait until the time comes and raise money at the most convenient rate or of the appropriate kind. This applies particularly where more money is needed at one time than at another, due perhaps to the seasonal nature of sales, or the necessity to buy raw material at particular times and in large amounts. The point made is that there is little point in maintaining permanent capital at the level needed only at certain peak intervals during a financial year or years.

Take an example. Suppose a company is promoted — the object

135

being the manufacture and sale of Christmas crackers. It may be found that average costs can be kept low by working throughout the year with a limited amount of labour, rather than flat out towards the peak selling period. In a business such as this, we are assuming that sales occur at one period only.

Suppose total cost to be £20,000, being labour, materials and administration expenses. No income is earned until this sum of money leaves the bank. It would appear, then, that the company needs £20,000 to set up in business.

If it raises this sum in shares it will have a permanent capital — with annual increments as reserves are accumulated. Is this sensible? It must, presumably, pay a satisfactory dividend on the total amount. In the first year of business this money is only needed at the rate of £1,666 per month. If a bank overdraft is used (and is available) the average borrowing would be £10,000. The interest paid may be less than the anticipated dividend. This would obviously be advantageous to the promoter.

Again, at the end of the financial period the income will be received. Suppose this to be £25,000. Assuming the £5,000 represents super-profit before payment of interest then it is possible that within a year or two the company could be self-financing. Bank overdraft would be less each year as would be interest payments. Eventually no interest would be payable and all profits would come to the shareholders.

Of course they now have £20,000 permanently invested and would expect interest. Whether this is satisfactory would depend on whether the interest demanded is greater than that paid to the bank. If so then it would be wise to split the resources. The obvious solution would seem to continue to use the bank. However, in practice the bank is not likely to be too willing to be sole provider unless the company can offer sufficient security. It would also be distrustful of an organisation which was not prepared to invest in itself.

The same would be true of other sources of short-term credit, e.g. merchant banks which may lend on bills of exchange renewable as occasion requires.

Much depends on the risk element. Where the enterprise is relatively risk free then no difficulties would arise in finding support from the sources mentioned. On the other hand it would be equally easy to raise share capital on promise of a moderate rate of dividend. But it must be remembered that in the latter event interest is being paid on twice the average moneys required. If the dividend payable is 5% then obviously it is pointless to borrow permanently £20,000 when £10,000 on average could be obtained at less than twice this figure — allowing perhaps for the fact that security may be needed.

On the other hand we must remember that interest rates vary and to rely on short-term credit entirely could be dangerous. At times of economic crisis the total necessary to continue the business may not be available or only at prohibitive rates.

There are in fact many aspects to consider, from the safety of permanent capital on which even if no dividend is paid one can depend, to the economy of raising cash as and when necessary and at the cheapest rates ruling.

Where the risk is high, capital is going to be expensive in any shape and the tendency will be to concentrate as far as possible on short finance leaving the raising of more permanent capital to a time when the business has proved itself and the market is in a mood for accepting low returns.

When the risk is low, capital will be cheaper and it may be wiser to take the advantage of long-term finance at an economic rate thus guarding against future troubles or the risk of interest charges moving to levels which are to say the least unattractive.

Seldom is it sensible to assume the future prosperity of a business. Any investment must contain an element of risk. The financial columnist is no oracle nor is the accountant a prophet. The history of any enterprise must surely contain in some prominent place these words of Euripides: "Zeus in Olympus disposes of many things. What the gods ordain, no man foresaw. What we looked for is not fulfilled: the gods bring unlooked for things to pass. Thus befell this strange event."

Consequently although a particular venture may appear to guarantee many palmy days to come, there is ever the possibility that some unhappy fate in the form perhaps of an impecunious government will interfere with the flow of cash. In such an event the milk may well turn sour and the honey cease to flow from the hive.

Assuming the business remains solvent, and profits can be earned even though they be not so great as before with the risk element more noticeable, then the promoter may be thankful to have found permanent capital at the commencement. This, if share capital cannot be withdrawn except on a reorganisation. Had he relied on short-term resources it might be expensive to renew them when times are hard. Not only will this increase the cost side but at a time when income is falling. It should be remembered that shareholders can never demand a dividend even if they have preferential rights — dividends are payable at the discrection of the directors and they need give no reason should they decide not to declare a dividend in any particular year.

This does not apply to fixed interest. This is payable irrespective of results or wishes. It is an expense rather than an appropriation of income. That is to say it would appear in the profit and loss account and not in the appropriation account. The preference which this interest enjoys as an item payable, depends entirely on the nature of the capital itself, i.e. whether it be secured or not and if secured then the terms of the agreement with the person supplying the particular moneys borrowed.

Where capital is secured it is normally in the form of a debenture. This is a loan supported by a deed giving the lender recourse to particular assets should default be made in payment of capital or interest. The actual conditions written into the contract vary. The security may be fixed or floating. A fixed charge is a charge upon specified assets. A floating charge attaches to the assets generally.

Debentures will be paid before other liabilities on winding up the company and the holders normally have the right to enforce such winding up in defined circumstances.

It might be supposed that debentures would be the most attractive form of investment both from the point of view of the lender and the borrower.

The lender may consider accepting a low return in being given a sound security. The borrower may find this an economic manner of raising money particularly at shortish notice.

There is however another side to the coin. The lender although secured must consider the risk in the sense that even though he has recourse to property can he be sure despite assurances that the property will be valuable or even existing when the time for payment has arrived? Can he bank on regular payments of interest (he will not wish to risk the fuss and bother of court proceedings)? Again does he wish to tie his money up for the time specified?

True he can sell on the market but the general level of interest rates being impossible to forecast there is the danger of a loss on a hurried sale.

The rate at which the debenture and any other loan stock is issued depends on the state of credit. If the average rate on that type of investment is 8% then £100 purchased at that rate will earn £8 each year.

Suppose some years hence the holder wishes to sell quickly. Suppose the interest rate is then on that type of security 10%. The debenture will only fetch £80 in the market. He will have suffered a capital loss of £20, nearly three years' earnings. This is a risk that each purchaser of loan stock takes and the confidence in the stability of interest rates will determine the ease of raising cash by such means and the interest rate that will need to be paid.

Accordingly in a period of confidence in the stability of the economy a security will sell more easily and this may well be a more important factor than an estimate of the risk element in the project, that is, where this is not dangerously high.

It may be that a low risk concern will not attract this form of capital at least not at an ideal rate where the state of general content is tending towards the low and the possibility of some coming economic depression is not discounted.

So much for the lender. The borrower is also prone to doubts in taking money from these sources. In the first place no business man wishes to have the millstone of fixed payments about him, particularly when these must be paid at times when the earning power does not justify the expense. There is no apparent reason why money should be borrowed at 10% when the business earns only 6% and the careful entrepreneur will guard against such possibilities. In borrowing at a high rate he must be sure that the money can earn a rate that is even higher.

Another factor which the borrower must consider is the state of credit generally and his in particular. In raising cash on securities he is mortgaging assets. Where the charge is fixed this will normally be in land and buildings — these having a more permanent value. However, it is labouring the obvious to remark that this is a once only affair. Having mortgaged the property there is no longer any opportunity to raise money on this asset should the need suddenly arise. Consequently wisdom suggests that some valuable asset should be retained for inevitable troubled times.

Another factor is that property rarely comprises more than a relatively small section of the total assets. Consequently the amount raised is possibly not great compared to the amount needed particularly as few will lend very much more than half of the estimated value of the asset except at very high interest charges.

An additional difficulty springs from the fact that once valuable assets are highly mortgaged, other forms of credit may be more difficult to obtain and higher interest may once more be the price.

There is the alternative of a floating charge — this is a charge on all assets, giving the lender priority in a winding up. However, similar objections are likely to apply here.

Returning now to more general aspects of the problem, it was said a little earlier that no man will pay 10% to earn 6%. This needs perhaps a slight qualification or at least some cautionary phrases. In the first place as was pointed out at the time, we are concerned with expectations. It may be that the business is earning 6% but that one of the reasons for this low rate is lack of capital for necessary expansion. The additional capital may increase the rate earned on total moneys employed, thus making it worth paying more than 6% for this capital. The amount that should be paid will depend on the optimism of the management. This should be based on serious examination of market conditions and prevailing movements in demand. This again involves discussion not only of economic matters but also of such possibilities as change of government and international relations. Warfare in another area can have serious repercussions on demand for products.

Secondly there is the occasion of raising capital not for general purposes but for particular projects. Here various considerations quite different may arise. The general earnings rate, i.e. profit to capital employed, may be 6%. It may be expected to remain at this level or thereabouts. However, if in one division there is the opportunity for say five years of earning 15% then it is obviously worth while raising money at a high rate to work this scheme. The money may be borrowed for the expected term of the venture, where this is known, so that when the project is completed the money can be repaid and high interest need not be paid out of general earnings. This type of venture is fairly common and will often explain the reason for loans at different rates in the balance sheet.

From another point of view it is patent that although 6 or 12% is paid on new capital the average rate may still remain below 6% and even in the instance given it is even then essential that the average earnings on total capital should remain above the average paid even over the short period else the new project is, *ceteris paribus*, a waste of time and money. However, some qualification is demanded by the fact that although the short-term effect may be uneconomic there may be other factors some intangible which must be brought into account. The new project may by increasing goodwill or "selling the company's name" have a positive and benefiting effect on the following periods.

Putting these intangibles aside and returning to the general thesis the facts can be illustrated mathematically and quite shortly. Suppose present capital to be £500 for which interest is payable. Suppose the general earnings rate to be 10% on capital employed and the rate paid for capital to be 6%. The position is then as follows:

$$
\begin{array}{lll}
\text{Income} & \text{£500 at } 10\% = & \text{£50} \\
\text{Interest} & \text{£500 at } 6\% = & \text{£30} \\
\hline
& \text{Profit} & \text{£20} \\
\hline
\end{array}
$$

If a new project is anticipated at what point does it become non-viable. Take some figures at random. Assume a yield of 15% for which money can be raised at not less than 9%. The cost of the project is £100.

$$
\begin{array}{ll}
\text{£100 at } 15\% = & \text{£15} \\
\text{£100 at } 9\% = & \text{£9} \\
\hline
\text{Profit} & \text{£6} \\
\hline
\end{array}
$$

Assuming the earnings rate in each case to be before interest, the true return on capital is 4% for the general and 6% for the special investment. Average return is 4·3%.

Suppose now the earnings rate on the new project was 12½%. This would give a profit of £3·5 and a return on capital of 3·5%. The return is below the average and the new project cannot, again barring some special advantage, be considered economical as it will lower the average earnings rate. This is bound to happen whenever the net return on the new capital is lower than on the old.

It may be argued then that the new project is only attractive if the expected net return on the additional capital is greater than or equal to the ruling percentage.

Is the argument entirely good? Could it not be argued that the amount payable depends not on the relative change but on the new level of the average return? If the new average though lower is still higher than the general level in the industry, then it may be worth investing the additional capital, as total profit is greater than otherwise obtainable.

The logic of the theory would be that assuming the adequacy of the present return then should the new project show a net return less than would be acceptable for the business in its entirety it is worth developing even though the total profit now shows a lower rate on total capital employed. In other words it is worth continuing to put money into a business whilst the net result is a return which is above the return expected in that type of business or the rate ruling in the industry. Where the rate drops below this figure then further investment is not recommended unless the new project is essential to the maintenance of the profitability of the concern.

This may appear an oversimplification. Perhaps it is. Nevertheless it points to the important factors. It also gives reasons why it may be found that a company has raised various loans at various rates for different periods.

The tendency so far has been to speak of fixed interest as opposed to share capital. Different forms of the former have been mentioned but not of the other. There are in fact any number of shades of shares with all types of combination with regard to voting and dividend rights.

The principal forms are the ordinary share and the preference share. The latter is entitled to a fixed dividend before anything is paid to the ordinary shareholder. Neither can demand a dividend in any one year, payment being at the whim of the directors of the company.

There are variations of both type of share. There is the participating preference — the holder being entitled to a further partaking of profit once ordinary shareholders have received a stated amount. Again preference shares may be cumulative or not as regard to dividend. Both participating and cumulative shares are issued where something slightly more attractive than a plain preference is required but ordinary shares are to be kept to a minimum.

From the point of view of the borrower the preference share has the disadvantage, especially where cumulative, of demanding dividends and mortgaging future profits — for assuming profits are made then although no dividend need be paid in the one year the debt may remain and in any event should a dividend be declared, as it must be sometime to keep ordinary shareholders contented, then the rights of the preferential shareholders must be respected. Here again we have the problem of preference dividend rates being perhaps higher than current return on capital.

Ordinary shares are often referred to as equity interest. Holders are in fact the true owners inasmuch as they take the ultimate risk and the ultimate profit or loss. Variations occur. There are "A" ordinary shares, "B" ordinary shares — the qualification referring to restricted rights usually with reference to voting — and such things as deferred ordinary shares. These latter are normally the perks of the promoters. They would not rank for dividend until X% was paid on other shares, after this they would take a large proportion of any balance.

Ordinary shares with restricted voting rights are frowned upon by authority and are tending to become slightly more infrequent. The argument is that the members who take the risk should also have the control and any restriction on the control should not be countenanced particularly as the shareholder may not when purchasing the shares realise the degree of the limitations imposed. Such shares have little to do with capital gearing and rather more with financial juggling

For an example of the variations of capital that exist and in one company, it is instructive to consider the accounts of a well-known catering and manufacturing company, J. Lyons & Company Limited (these are shown overleaf).

Issued Share Capital reads (1964)	£000
5% Cumulative Preference Shares of £1	647
7% Cumulative Preference Shares of £1	5,207
8% Cumulative Preference Shares of £1	1,000
6% Preferred Ordinary Shares of £1	650
Ordinary Shares of £1	400
A. Non-voting Shares of £1	5,758
Proportional Profit Shares of £1	500
B. Proportional Profit Shares of 50p	225
	£14,387

Debentures and Loans	£000
4% 1st Mortgage Redeemable Debenture Stock 1963/73	1,700
Deduct proceeds of sale — secured properties	1,062
	638
4% 1st Mortgage Debenture Stock 1975	582
6% 1st Mortgage Debenture Stock 1983/88	3,000
Mortgages	1,722
Loans	960
	6,902

Total Funds	
Share Capital	14,387
Share Premium Account	1,309
Capital Reserves	10,806
Revenue Reserves and Unappropriate Profit	2,280
Total	28,782
Debentures and Loans	6,902
	35,684
Bank overdraft	3,643
	£39,327

Far more detailed information would be necessary in order that any really valuable comment be made on these figures. Suffice it to note certain general observations. Total capital can be analysed as

Self-finance	33%
Share Capital	40%
Loan Capital	27%

There seems little remarkable about this at first glance except perhaps the fact that share capital exceeds by a material amount the item of self-finance. In a company of seventy-odd years' standing one might expect a greater dependence on accumulated reserves. Keeping to the resolution not to delve too deeply into this company when necessary information is scarce it might yet be instructive to compare these ratios to those relating to other companies (Table P).

The figures appearing in the table show that in this limited sample there is very little correspondence between the various companies. Rather than indulge in research which would considerably lengthen the chapter and which is not necessarily relevant to the purpose of the book it is wisest to draw attention to one or two facts and the implications these might suggest.

(a) There seems no correlation between the age of the company and the degree to which it is self-financing i.e. the tendency does not seem to be to replace borrowings by savings and become relatively independent.

This must be qualified by the fact that it is not easy to repay ordinary shares or non-redeemable preference shares, nevertheless Spillers, 78 years old, has yet a surplus of loans over self-finance. So also has Bowaters, whose age is not given but exceeds 27 years.

(b) The proportion of share capital is high in the greater number of companies. All companies rely on share capital for 40% or more of total moneys. The average is 56% with a mean deviation of about 23%. If Scottish Television is excluded on grounds of being unusual, then the average becomes 54% with a deviation of only 18%.

The deviation is however too large to claim consistency and the important point is merely that the average share capital seems to represent over half of net assets where the sample, though not large, nevertheless seems fairly wide with reference to the type of industry.

(c) When the analysis is confined to ordinary shares the average, Scottish Television being irrelevant, falls to 49% in the first instance with 44% in the second.

If the true equity alone is considered then the average falls to 39% for almost all of the ordinary shares of Lyons & Company and all of Scottish Television ordinary shares are non-voting.

(d) J. Lyons & Company, Scottish Television and the Thomson organisation are peculiar in the sense that they are what may be referred to as owner occupied.* As the Walrus and the Carpenter they are not typical of their kind. Looking at the report of the Thomson group there

TABLE P

CAPITAL GEARING — RELATIONSHIP BETWEEN SOURCES OF CAPITAL

Company	Age years	Share Capital			Self-finance	Loans	Bank over-draft
		Equity	Non-voting ordinary	Other			
		%	%	%	%	%	%
Tate & Lyle	62	70	—	3	7	20	18
British Petroleum	57	41	—	1	50	8	—
Bowaters	pre-1939	59	—	8	14	17	2
Thomson	41	21	—	28	28	23	—
British Motor	14	56	—	12	25	7	—
Pressed Steel	38	42	—	3	24	31	—
Spillers	78	52	—	5	26	17	8
Hall Thermo-tank	66	35	—	14	28	23	3
United Steel	pre-1939	33	—	8	49	10	3
G.K.N.	65	51	—	5	44	—	—
Scottish Television	1	—	98	1	1	—	—
Lyons	70	1	16	23	33	27	9
Boots	76	56	—	3	28	4	—

Notes

1. The figures are for the financial period ending within 1964, with the exception of Scottish Television which is to 1965 and for six months only.
2. Share premiums have been treated as share capital owing to the fact that they are not strictly a method of self-financing.
3. Each figure is a percentage of the total except for bank overdraft which though also a percentage of the total is not included in the total.
4. The figures are for the holding company only.
5. Scottish Television is a subsidiary of the Thomson organisation, but whereas it was initially wholly owned 45% of the non-voting shares have been sold to the public.*
6. The second column shows the age of the company, the figure being taken from the notice of the general meeting or the directors' report. Neither United Steel nor Bowaters indicate their age but both are pre-1939 companies.

* See Appendix B, note 4.

can be little doubt of the true ownership and control. The list of directors and other officers of J. Lyons & Company gives a similar impression. The low figure of equity in these instances is almost certainly a function of these characteristics.

Scottish Television is an even more remarkable illustration of a closely controlled company or so it would appear from the Annual Report where the initial summons to a general meeting ends with a notice pointing out that only preference shareholders are allowed to vote. These comprise less than 2% of the total share capital. This announcement is followed by a smiling picture of Lord Thomson.

The accounts of the holding company in 1965 contained the announcement that the company were making 45% of the non-voting shares available to the general public. This was according to the wish of authority in the shape of the Independent Television Authority that ownership or rather shareholding should be more widespread. The report comments that a great number of the new members were resident in Scotland. This apparently gives the Chairman much pleasure. He states that he finds this "a particular source of gratification in that it not only demonstrates the high esteem in which Scottish people hold Scottish Television but also justifies our decision to share with them this essentially Scottish activity, a decision arising . . . from our recognition that local Scottish participation would be desirable in a number of respects".

In the report attached to the television company's results the Chairman points out that 25% of the staff had elected to become members: presumably these are part of the 45% and partly Scottish. It would be interesting to know whether the word "staff" signifies higher executives or lower paid work people. In any event it is difficult to see how the noble band of Scottish members are going to participate in any respect except as receivers of dividend when they have no power to vote and being so, no part in the management or policy making of the organisation.

It seems quite contrary to the traditional Scottish temperament to lend savings in such a manner to a gently smiling English peer.

As has been remarked at an earlier stage non-voting shares are unpopular with those concerned with the public image of the limited company and are normally a device for keeping control in few hands. It is a pity that organisations of the size of the company referred to should create such a poor example.

So far as our particular analysis is concerned it might be reasonable to exclude both Lyons and Thomson from the list (together with the television company) and note the result.

The average ordinary share capital now becomes approximately 49·7% which is particularly high considering it is all equity capital. Nevertheless, while there is a deviation of 20% it is safe to say merely that whereas the share capital content, 56% as a whole and 49.7% in equity, is high in many companies there seems little ground again for seeking any correlation between the distribution of available moneys.

Looking at the figures recorded in the loans and overdraft section there seems little to be made in the way of wisdom or general comment.

Attention has already been drawn to the fact that the overdraft figures at year end are far from reliable in the sense of being a guide to financial policy. There is a tendency for the balance sheet to be looked at as a show piece and the overdraft is kept low at the particular date either by juggling debtors and creditors, that is, calling in the former and delaying the latter, or in the instance of the holding company calling in available cash from subsidiaries.

As an illustration of this latter factor (Table Q), the companies are listed again showing the bank overdraft of the holding company and then following this the equivalent comparative figure for the group. The third column shows the relationship between net assets. The figures are in millions.

No suggestion is made that these figures prove anything. It is interesting to note though that out of the ten companies having overdrafts, six show amounts for the group very much more than those for the holding company. What is more the difference seems to have no relation to net asset variances. That is, the subsidiaries do not appear to be the major part of the group so as to claim the greater part of the overdraft. It appears that the borrowing on overdraft basis is done mostly by subsidiaries or else cash is handed over by them at the end of the financial period in order to present a prettier picture in the holding company's accounts.

It is true that holding companies tend to make charges to subsidiaries for administrative costs and that these would probably or possibly be

TABLE Q

	Overdraft of holding company	Overdraft of group	Ratio between net assets of the group and net assets of the holding company
		£ million	
Tate & Lyle	7·6	9·4	1·9
British Petroleum	—	15·3	1·1
Bowaters	1·9	5·0	2·0
Thomson	—	0·7	1·3
British Motor	—	—	1·5
Pressed Steel	—	—	1·0
Spillers	3·9	3·7	1·2
Hall Thermotank	0·3	0·3	1·0
United Steel	4·7	4·7	1·0
G.K.N.	—	17·0	1·7
Boots	—	0·1	1·0
Lyons	3·6	6·0	1·3

agreed at year end. It may be that they are then paid in cash rather than left in credit. Or if they are to be paid it may be more convenient that they be paid at the close of the period rather than at any other time. What appears a device to impress the unwary investor may indeed be part of the customary pattern of business. If things seem otherwise perhaps as Lord Sands said of a certain decision of the House of Lords. "it is our frail vision that is at fault".

Does all this matter anyway? Perhaps not so much to the members of the holding company but what of the members of the subsidiary who do not see the holding company's accounts? Apart from this is it not essential that a tradition of honesty free from equivocation should be established? Surely the protection the public is entitled to demands that what is displayed in the window should in some way resemble both in price and quality what is sold in the shop.

So much for the general nature of gearing. How far is this relevant to the accounts we have been analysing in the greater part of the book? Does it influence in its application to these companies the conclusions drawn?

It is relevant to the return on capital, very much so, but this has

TABLE R

Company	Year	Preference Shares						Loans								Bank overdraft		Rate of return Table N
		% total cap.	Rate paid	% total cap.	Rate paid	% total cap.	Rate paid	% total cap.	Rate paid	% total cap.	Rate paid	% total cap.	Rate paid	% total cap.	Rate paid	% total cap.	Rate paid	
I.C.I.	1960	3·1	5·0	—	—	—	—	2·3	N/A	2·7	4·5	—	—	1·5	3·75 to 5·75	0·73	N/A	9·0
	1961	2·8	5·0	—	—	—	—	2·5	N/A	2·4	4·5	—	—	0·38		0·80	N/A	6·1
	1962	2·8	5·0	—	—	—	—	1·3	N/A	2·4	4·5	4·6	6·5	2·1		0·87	N/A	6·5
	1963	2·4	5·0	—	—	—	—	0·58	N/A	2·1	4·5	5·3	6·5	2·9		1·0	N/A	6·8
	mean																	7·1
Courtaulds	1960	2·4	5·0	2·9	6·0	—	—	—	—	1·8	3·5 to 4·5	—	—	—	—	0·18	N/A	6·5
	1961	2·2	5·0	2·7	6·0	—	—	—	—	1·9		—	—	—	—	0·37	N/A	5·3
	1962	2·0	5·0	2·4	6·0	—	—	—	—	1·7		—	—	—	—	0·40	N/A	4·6
	1963	1·9	5·0	2·5	6·0	—	—	9·2	7·0	1·7		—	—	—	—	0·38	N/A	6·4
	mean																	5·7
Imperial Tobacco	1960	1·1	5·5	1·1	6·0	0·6	10·0	3·3	3·75	4·3	4·0	2·3	4·0	—	—	7·1	N/A	6·9
	1961	1·1	5·5	1·1	6·0	0·6	10·0	3·2	3·75	4·3	4·0	4·3	4·0	—	—	8·2	N/A	7·1
	1962	1·0	5·5	1·1	6·0	0·5	10·0	3·0	3·75	4·1	4·0	4·1	4·0	—	—	7·9	N/A	6·9
	1963	0·8	5·5		6·0	0·5	10·0	2·9	3·75	4·1	4·0	4·1	4·0	—	—	8·1	N/A	7·0
	mean																	7·0
Newton Chambers	1960	0·7	5·0	—	—	—	—	3·0	6·0	0·8	3·5	—	—	—	—	9·9	N/A	5·7
	1961	0·6	5·0	—	—	—	—	2·8	6·0	0·8	3·5	—	—	—	—	8·7	N/A	6·2
	1962	0·7	5·0	—	—	—	—	2·3	6·0	0·6	3·5	—	—	—	—	12·4	N/A	3·3
	1963	0·6	5·0	—	—	—	—	2·4	6·0	3·5	—	—	—	—	—	7·3	N/A	2·6
	mean																	4·4
Lancashire Cotton Corpn.	1960	0·3	5·0	—	—	—	—	3·0	3·5	—	—	—	—	—	—	—	—	8·3
	1961	0·3	5·0	—	—	—	—	3·0	3·5	—	—	—	—	—	—	—	—	7·2
	1962	0·3	5·0	—	—	—	—	2·9	3·5	—	—	—	—	—	—	—	—	1·9
	1963	0·3	5·0	—	—	—	—	2·9	3·5	—	—	—	—	—	—	—	—	1·8
	mean																	4·8

Company	Year	Preference Shares				Loans						Bank overdraft		Rate of return Table N
		% total cap.	Rate paid	% total cap.	Rate paid	% total cap.	Rate paid	% total cap.	Rate paid	% total cap.	Rate paid	% total cap.	Rate paid	
George Wimpey	1960	2·3	6·0	0·7	5·0	4·0	6·0	2·4	N/A	—	—	2·5	N/A	6·7
	1961	2·1	6·0	0·7	5·0	3·6	6·0	1·1	N/A	—	—	5·8	N/A	6·1
	1962	1·9	6·0	0·6	5·0	3·3	6·0	1·7	N/A	—	—	4·9	N/A	5·8
	1963	1·7	6·0	0·6	5·0	3·0	6·0	1·9	N/A	—	—	3·2	N/A	6·6
	mean													6·3
Harland & Woolf	1960	5·2	4·5	—	—	—	—	—	—	—	—	—	—	0·75
	1961	5·2	4·5	—	—	—	—	—	—	—	—	3·9	N/A	0·74
	1962	5·2	4·5	—	—	—	—	—	—	—	—	6·2	N/A	1·5
	1963	5·2	4·5	—	—	—	—	—	—	—	—	7·9	N/A	0·29
	mean													0·7
Hancocks	1960	7·1	6·0	—	—	6·5	3·5	—	—	—	—	0·09	N/A	5·9
	1961	8·3	6·0	—	—	5·5	3·5	—	—	—	—	2·6	N/A	7·3
	1962	9·2	6·0	—	—	4·7	3·5	—	—	—	—	2·7	N/A	8·1
	1963	7·3	6·0	—	—	3·7	3·5	—	—	—	—	3·7	N/A	6·3
	mean													6·9

Notes

1. The bank overdraft of Imperial Tobacco includes other short-term loans.
2. The initials N/A indicate that the interest rate is not available.
3. The proportion of net assets shown is taken from the asset figure shown in column eight of Table N. This is the denominator, the numerator is taken from the group accounts.
4. The loan capital of I.C.I. is divided into many categories. To state each separately would make the table rather cumbersome. Certain of the minor loans have been grouped together with a general heading given.
5. The average for the year has been taken in each instance except where the share or loan capital has been increased or decreased at one date and then at the close of the period.
6. In the instance of Harland & Woolf acceptance credits in 1963 are included with bank overdraft.

already been discussed in other chapters. The question is, does the return compare favourably with the rates of interest paid on raising capital? In considering this it is naturally important to remember the short-term effect, to remember that it may be worth paying more in the short run if this will guarantee success in years hence.

The simplest way to tackle the problem is to examine the figures. It will be best to take the four years (Table R).

The principal objective is as noted previously to pay less for capital than is earned except in rather special circumstances. The object of compiling the table was to note how the various companies stood up to the test.

I.C.I.

The average rate of return seems to be above the rates of interest paid in each year though it is touch and go in 1962. The one problem that will recur in all instances selected will be the unknown and maybe relevant rate of bank overdraft interest. However, in this company the bank overdraft is maintained at a low proportion of capital.

Courtaulds

In 1961 the rate on preference shares of 6% was 0·7% above the rate of return. The preference shares accounted for 2·7% of capital employed. In 1962, 4·4%, i.e. all preference capital, was earning a rate below that paid. In 1963 the position had improved inasmuch as the preference rate was now covered. However, the new debentures at 7·0% were well ahead of the return and amounted to about 9·2% of total capital. For the four-year period the mean return was below the rate paid on 6% preference shares. The bank overdraft seems unimportant.

Imperial Tobacco

There seems no problem here except in the instance of preference shares at 10%. The return on capital never reaches this level yet the amount involved is or seems to be insignificant. On the other hand the bank overdraft is particularly high but no rate of interest is given. It could be higher than the average return of 7·0% in which instance the company is borrowing at more than it can really afford. But unless the actual rate is known the true state of affairs is and must remain hidden. However, the record of this company leads one to believe that the interest paid cannot be particularly high.

Newton Chambers

In 1961 and 1962 the return more than covers the interest paid. In the following two years the story is somewhat different; this company may be going through a difficult period but obviously this cannot be allowed to happen indefinitely. An average of 4·4% does not show well when 3% of capital is paid for at a rate exceeding this amount. Also the bank overdraft is at a figure that gives little encouragement. It is difficult to envisage an overdraft rate at less than 4·4%.

Lancashire Cotton Corpn.

The figures here speak for themselves; two reasonable years precede two years when the return is so much lower than the rates paid on moneys raised that the future must inevitably be looked on with some trepidation if not distrust. The mean is between preference shares and loans, but the variations in return give little promise to this figure and only suggest that averages are not entirely to be relied upon particularly where the deviation is significant, i.e. where it is such as to make the average figure fairly meaningless.

George Wimpey

Here things seem fairly satisfactory but there are unknown factors in the rates applicable to certain loans and to bank overdraft. However, perhaps the amounts involved are not such as to suggest panic.

Harland & Woolf

This company has obviously fallen on hard times and the figures speak for themselves. Post-account information suggests a change of fortune; nevertheless, in looking at the figures as they stand, little hope is promised. In this instance the policy must necessarily be "wait and see".

William Hancock

The average here over the period is sufficiently above amounts paid to breed satisfaction. It is only in 1960, the first of the four years, that disquiet may arise. This is probably a lean year infrequently repeated; nevertheless the figure should not be ignored. Generally speaking although averages please, particular years indicate that policy may be a question of chance rather than informed decision.

CHAPTER 12

A Note on the Incidence of Taxation

To this point no count has been taken of profit after tax. It has been assumed that taxation is an appropriation of profit earned rather than a cost incurred in attaining it. In this, opinion within the profession tends to coincide. Return on capital is considered to be the ratio of net profits before tax to capital employed and the whims and fancies of political economics must not be allowed to confuse the issue. Were tax a defined proportion, easily calculable, of profits all equally computed, then no problem appears, the return is that amount lower in each company. However, in fact, profits are not computed equally for tax purposes, that is to say different allowances may apply to different companies in different years. Consequently to use net profit after tax as a guide to efficiency would be quite confusing and would produce figures that had little if any contribution to make to the state of knowledge.

This is not to say that taxation has no relevance to the discussion but that its incidence is in a direction other than as a factor reducing available profit.

It is necessary to distinguish the larger from the smaller company and direct from indirect taxation.

Direct taxation in the larger concern can have quite a noticeable effect on policy which will show itself in profit variation. It is not proposed to argue this matter at any length, for to do so would involve serious consideration of such nebulous influences as the psychology of State interference in a private economy by the artful use of taxation.

It is, however, instructive to examine briefly the type of pressure that taxation law might exert on profits. In the first place there is the obvious fact that the lower the profits the less the levy, assuming profits to be properly computed. This may appear at first reading a remarkably ridiculous statement. However, remember that profits are strictly the moneys earned by owners of the capital invested. If the capital is in the form of shares then a high net profit would be essential if the members are wanting a steady and adequate return on their investment. However, if the moneys are in the form of loans or securities which are entitled to fixed interest, then these payments will appear in the accounts themselves and the figure representing net profit will be the amount remaining after these are paid.

We may find, therefore, that the return shown on equity capital may tend to be lower as a result of current tax policy or the anticipation of equivalent levies. So does taxation affect certain of the ratios discussed so far. Nevertheless, this is relatively unimportant, inasmuch as the general rate of return cannot be affected owing to the elimination of interest charges in calculating the profit to be related to capital employed (Table N).

There are other factors, however, one or other of which may be rather relevant in weighing up movements in returns.

Firstly, there is the factor of anticipation. The management of the company have certain quite legal methods of spreading profits into other periods. For instance, sales can be pushed into the coming financial year by appropriately dating the contract, or merely holding back delivery and invoicing for a day or so. This could have an appreciable effect on profits of the one period; keeping them low in favour of the following financial year. It may be a sound policy where change of government or tactics has led to the expectation of tax reductions applying to that year.

The reverse can also happen. Sales can be rushed through in the financial year rather than be held over, as natural courses of events may suggest, into the succeeding period. This would occur when political or economic conditions were pointing to a clampdown on profits.

In addition to sales juggling there are other forms of profit spreading by delaying or anticipating expenditure. This applies to both revenue and capital account. Purchase of fixed assets can be quite a complex financial affair. The date of the acquisition may be very relevant. When investment allowances* are high then it is reasonable to push on with reinvestment in fixed assets particularly where there is a suspicion of

*See Appendix B, note 5.

change in the next budget. The same applies to occasions when fixed asset purchase is encouraged by other means such as heavy initial allowances or perhaps development or investment grants. The effect may be in either direction depending on whether the inducements are existing and thought to be temporary or whether they are anticipated in the following period.

Lest it be wondered how this will affect profit, the answer is that the greater the investment in fixed assets either by replacement or new acquisitions for expansion then the greater the depreciation charge in the immediate account and consequently the lower the profit. It may be argued that the new assets will earn additional income and thus compensate for the charge but when purchases are rushed in the manner that has been outlined it is more than likely that the benefit of any additional investment or replacement with more modern plant will be felt at a date later than might be normal due to the delay in putting the plant into most effective use, consequent upon its premature acquisition.

In any event should there be an expansion project it is likely that the depreciation charge will rise very sharply where diminishing balance methods are employed.

The additional depreciation in either instance by lowering profits will be more welcome in a period of high taxation and thus again will taxation demands or expectation thereof have a determining effect on capital expenditure and profits.

It might be noted that whereas the profit will be kept perhaps at a lower figure than would be normal, in more stable economic times, the capital figure in calculating capital employed will tend to be on the high side. Assets which are bought in advance must be included in capital employed, yet profits will not be earned by them till some distant date. It is so that assets not in use are not depreciated and profits are not affected, but nevertheless it is assumed here that the assets will be used as and when purchased but that the period of greater benefit will not have arrived. Again even if profits are not affected as plant is not in use, the denominator will be greater if new capital is raised, for assets idle are employed in the sense that the available moneys were deliberately used to acquire such assets. If new moneys are not raised the profit itself may be influenced in a different and more obscure way by reason that the moneys once freely available for trading purposes are now locked up in fixed assets.

The smaller business brings other problems. Where the concern is controlled by the directors it is likely that more money will be drawn out in the form of salaries than would be so in the non-controlled company. The point is that salaries are an alternative to profits in the sense that where the business is owned and managed by the same persons then they will find it to their advantage to draw the surplus income in the form of salaries rather than profits. This is so because whereas profits are subject to corporation tax, which is usually higher than standard rate income tax, salaries are reduced by the various allowances available before being taxed. Of course, where salaries are high, then the income tax rates applicable may also be high. The maximum rate payable can be as much as 83% (in 1978/9). However, any company director in this pay bracket could be similarly penalised if he chose to leave the profits in the company and pay corporation tax thereon as the Inland Revenue have the power, where they reckon that profits are being retained primarily with the object of avoiding the payment of taxes, to make what is known as a "tax direction" on the company. This has the effect of hypothetically apportioning undistributed profits among those entitled to them and taxing those persons accordingly.

Such directions will not be made unnecessarily, however, particularly when, in times of inflation, it is important to increase effective capital employed in the company by retaining profits for the building up of a better capital base in the shape of reserves. When prices are rising then turnover will rise also and it would be improvident not to maintain the ratio of turnover to capital by increasing the latter. Incidentally, when such benefits as Stock Relief are offered by the Revenue then it is obviously wise to retain profits to the extent that will absorb such relief — these retentions will, by definition, avoid corporation tax also.

In these various ways discussed, the declared profit in the annually published accounts will obviously be influenced by factors which are directly related to the taxation laws in operation. To that extent it must be seen as not solely dictated by market conditions though, admittedly, the dividend policy rather than the pre-tax profit declared is the more sensitive to Exchequer demands and inquisitions.

Another form of direct taxation is capital gains tax. This again can have an indirect effect on the figures sought for comparative purposes. Such a tax is necessarily going to influence capital investment and thereby in its incidence on capital employed and profits have some disturbing effect on what might otherwise have been stable ratios. The incidence here is however somewhat difficult to assess in a short paper and would require a great deal more research than is at present intended.

So much for direct taxation. What of the other and more ubiquitous forms of raising revenue classified rather vaguely as indirect taxation. At present the main components of this are Value Added Tax (VAT) and customs and excise duties.

Again this is a subject which demands a great deal of serious research and careful argument. It is intended here merely to point to the possibilities and indicate the type of influence which these taxes could have on the various ratios being discussed.

Possibly the most important of the various forms of indirect tax is VAT which was introduced in 1973 principally to bring the U.K. in line with the tax systems within the Common Market. Although the method of collection is complex the end-effect is to impose a sales tax on goods and services bought. At present there are two separate rates applicable, being 15% and zero%. The rate charged on any article is obviously going to influence sales, the degree depending on the elasticity of demand among other things. Consequently changes in these levies or anticipations thereof are inevitably going to affect sales or production. Anything which reduces demand reduces sales. Anticipated reductions will have repercussions on production. In both ways profits may be affected and ratios, artificially disturbed.

The word artificially is used because strictly the levy is quite out of control of the producer and the resultant ratios are not then a reasonable gauge of efficiency — except that it may be argued that the producer has chosen to employ his capital in an industry subject to these arbitrary exchequer raids and accordingly they must be taken as a normal risk of the venture.

The latter argument possesses some force. Even more so when considering the manner in which licence or petrol duty might have strong determining effects on the manner in which part of the capital is employed or the method in which goods are distributed. This could be a form of challenge bringing out the more efficient in inter-company comparison, even though it may distort the picture when a time series is being discussed.

It may be suggested that direct taxation could be looked at in similar light. This is so only in a very limited sense.

Taxation expectations do indeed have an influence on profits in ways outlined previously. However this effect is in no way related to the tax charge set against the profit of any specified year. This by income tax or corporation tax is a flat levy on profits which will always tend to be maximised. The tax will vary according to such considerations or impositions as capital gains levies or reductions on account of additional allowances. These are to a certain extent controllable by management but the extent of the power to control and the estimating of its incidence is such a difficult problem that serious discussion seems worthless at this stage in the book, for there is little likelihood of any valuable conclusions being drawn.

Another influence on profit is found in national insurance contributions. They are a form of taxation being an involuntary contribution by the company to the exchequer. The handling of labour can therefore be an important consideration in determining profit. The more the idle time the relatively greater the employers' national insurance contributions and the less the profit. This again can be relevant to inter-company comparisons and should call for more care in the efficient use of labour.

If this chapter has not appeared in any way instructive but rather tended to confuse, the responsibility must be, perhaps from cowardice, put partly at the feet of the subject. It is a delicate matter for discussion for the complexities involved in taxation law make any dogmatic assertions dangerous. The aim has been to show the way and supply the reader a limited amount of food for thought.

If the road seems a little indistinct and the food rather indigestible, it is to be hoped that the blame will be attributed to the intricacies of the subject matter.

CHAPTER 13

A Note on the Doubtful Significance of the Turnover Figure

THE figure of turnover is a figure often asked for by financial analysts but how valuable is this figure? How far can it supply or suggest data not otherwise available? How far is its relation to other totals extracted from the accounts an indication of present or coming difficulties or advantages and of what use are such ratios in endeavouring to compare one company's results with another. The tendency has been to discount comparisons from the point of view of overall efficiency or social value but they are still of interest to the investor who perhaps wishes to invest valuable capital in such a way as to take a minimum risk — though in the hope of increasing income. He is not perhaps looking for instant growth — rather for a steady upward movement in profits, and consequently dividends.

The turnover figure can be set against many other statistics. In Chapter 3 it was shown how it might indicate the average debt collection period. The watching of this figure could be significant — a continual rise disproportionate to an increase in sales would suggest that sales are being made for the immediate purpose of boosting profits, without due consideration of the credit rating of the buyer. It might, alternatively, merely suggest that too much money is being tied up in debtors at the expense of quick payment of creditors, accumulation of extra stocks, or the financing of non-essential repairs or replacements of plant. This often occurs even when the debtor's credit rating is good and the collection period remains more or less steady. It is a matter of what is known as "overtrading" — attempting to do too much on too little capital. It can lead to serious difficulties and at times when money is short even to insolvency. This has already been discussed. The turnover figure is useful then in estimating the collection period of debts and (by watching for any trend) in making assessments of the sales policy of the organisation and the security of profits to come. If it is wished to use it as an indication of possible overtrading, in the sense of over-playing the capital, it would need to be accompanied by such information as materials purchased, etc., in order that an idea may be obtained of the lag in payment of creditors, and the variations in turnover of stocks.

The sales figure is then only valuable for discovering defects in sales policy and is insufficient for commenting on the possibility of overtrading.

It may be hazarded that the relation of sales to working capital is a ratio to watch in this context, i.e. that increases in sales should be accompanied by corresponding increases in working capital for financing this further business. This is a doubtful yardstick because in the first place the working capital may be originally not put to maximum use and, secondly, the increase in sales may be the result of a quicker turnover in stocks and not a greater quantity of sales at the previous rate of stock turnover. An indication might be failure of the stock figure to show noticeable upward movement, but then it is not possible to know whether the company was overstocked in the first place.

All that can really be said is that an increase in the ratio of sales to working capital over a long period *may* be an indication of overtrading particularly if it is accompanied by a steady increase in stocks or work in progress. More than that it would be foolish to assert. As a matter of interest it might be instructive to look at the figures for I.C.I. and Courtaulds and note whether there is any tendency to stability in the ratio, though from what has been said this would be no proof that overtrading is not present — perhaps a sign however that the chances are slightly against its presence.

Taking I.C.I. first. The ratio of sales to net current assets per the "Group financial record" for the years 1954 to 1963 is roughly 3·5, 4·0, 5·0, 4·2, 5·1, 4·3, 4·5, 4·0, 3·8, 3·5. There is little sign of stability here. Although the figures seem not to vary within vast limits in fact the percentage deviation from the arithmetic mean of 4·2 is as much as 10% which would not matter were the trend the same as that of sales, i.e. consistently upward. The only noticeable trend is an upward movement in the first three years and a reversal in the final three. This might suggest an initial failure of working capital to keep pace with sales (a symptom of overtrading) and recently a period of perhaps overstocking. These are, however, mere arrows in the dark and the explanations could be quite different. (Dealing with group accounts the increase in turnover may be accounted for by acquisition of a new company working on a different ratio of sales to working capital. One company is not the same as another in this particular context.) As a matter of interest, reference might be made to the liquidity position disclosed in the third chapter. This shows an increasing liquid ratio for the years 1960–3. This seems to contradict the suggestion of overstocking; it could however indicate an over-enthusiastic sales policy. In fact in both 1962 and 1963 the percentage increase in debtors was considerably greater than that of sales. But all this is mere conjecture.

Courtaulds' ratio for the years 1958–63 is 3·1, 2·9, 3·2, 3·9, 3·8. The ratios in this case tend to follow sales very roughly though, in 1963, although sales rose, the ratio fell slightly which might for reasons already discussed indicate that future trends may be worth watching. The fact that the ratio is lower than in the instance of I.C.I. would suggest that perhaps the latter company is using its working capital more effectively. This again is pure suggestion, it may be that Courtaulds is a company that cannot operate except on a low rate. It may need a great deal of working capital to finance sales but relatively little fixed assets. I.C.I. may work the other way round, which tends to put the question in quite a different light.

However, as has already been established, all these suggestions are extremely nebulous, and founded more on possibility than fact. All in all it cannot be said that the ratio of sales to working capital is a safe basis on which to draw firm conclusions. The only possible exception is in the case of two firms in the same industry — producing identical products. Both quantitative differences and trends may then be relevant in comparisons. So also if it is possible to obtain say a national average for a particular type of business. Here again, however, difficulties can arise for the ratio can be affected by such factors as alternative methods of finance (e.g. loans as against bank overdrafts), or even varying wage policies. It must be concluded then that turnover figures are not of such great value in this particular context.

To what other uses may a turnover figure be put? It can be related to capital employed, fixed assets, total assets or even to profits. Perhaps it would be reasonable to treat with each in turn. Take first the subject of the capital employed. Relating sales to this figure would seem pointless. The resultant ratio would need to be compared with the profit return. It might therefore be sufficient to compare sales with the profit figure — thus obviating the need to introduce capital at all.

What of the relation of sales to fixed assets? This could have some significance, inasmuch as the imagination would suggest that increases in fixed assets should lead to increases in turnover, assuming the increase is real and not a reflection of increases in cost of replacement. This is quite wrong, as the fixed asset increase may have been such as to reduce expenditure rather than increase sales. It is in fact aimed at increasing profits (either through sales or expenditure), and therefore should be related to profit and not sales where there is no information on the nature of the increase in assets. There is another point of view. Increases in fixed assets are usually accompanied by proportionate (in theory) increases in working capital. Having found no satisfactory relation between turnover and working capital it seems unlikely that there would be more chance of success should this sales figure be compared with the total of the fixed assets. Perhaps another attempt might be hazarded to prove our hypothesis by examining actual figures, taking the only two companies for which such figures are available.

The ratio of sales to fixed assets as disclosed by I.C.I.'s accounts for 1963 was for the preceding ten years 1·1, 1·2, 1·2, 1·1, 1·0 (ignoring revaluation), 1·1, 1·2, 1·2, 1·2, 1·2. This ratio seems reasonably stable, but does it mean anything? The company seems to succeed in keeping sales up with increases in fixed assets, but this is of no benefit if it is only done at the cost of increases in trade expenses — which are not disclosed in the accounts. The only position, then, seems to be that if anything is to be related to fixed assets it is profit. Here again there will be certain inconsistencies because the effect of investment in fixed assets may not be felt for some time. There may indeed be some form of correlation between profits and fixed assets (and an increase in the assets must to "prove itself" earn a profit at least equivalent to the arithmetic mean in Table N), but, because of the lag which is an unknown, and may be erratic in its incidence, it is unrealistic to compare these two figures so as to draw any valuable conclusions.

Much the same form of argument applies to the relation between working capital and fixed assets. It is possible that in most cases an increase in fixed assets will demand an increase in working capital — as, for example, an increase in the size of the concern usually demands higher running costs — wage bills, stocks, etc. However, there are certain undeniable facts which make any annual comparison of doubtful relevance.

(a) There is the lag again. It may take time before the new assets are put to full use.

(b) If the assets are a long time in construction, working capital may initially fall, due to the cost of the project — where this is not financed only out of new funds.

(c) This ties up with (a), but is not quite the same thing. When any new project is commenced the first thing that occurs must be an increase in stocks and creditors. This will not affect working capital. It is not until the stock is sold, and the sale is reflected in debtors and cash, that the increase in working capital may be more apparent. True, some increase to cover extra expenses, such as wages, may be naturally necessary, but short term needs may be financed by a bank overdraft. This again would have no effect on the figure of working capital.

(d) The working capital may have been in excess of needs in the first place — no increase being necessary when the new assets are installed. If the investment was to reduce costs, then the eventual effect may be to reduce the working capital that is needed.

(e) Different companies work on different ratios. Dealing with group accounts, increases in fixed assets may represent new members of the group working on different ratios. New fixed assets would be added to the total and also new current assets and current liabilities — but not necessarily in the same proportion as with the other companies.

A brief examination of the significance of the turnover figure apropos capital employed — fixed assets and working capital — has been made, and it has been found that in no case does any useful information appear, nor can any valuable conclusions be drawn. Any put forward are nothing more than possibilities and to rely on them could be dangerous. This is obvious from the points raised. Why, then, is the turnover figure so much in demand — surely it is useless without the cost variations?

The only relationship not examined is that between sales and profit. If there is a definite correlation between sales and profit, then, prior, or interim knowledge of turnover would be a satisfactory guide to the likely profit.

Before studying any figures it may be as well to examine the possible degree of dependence of these two items, and whether there is any theoretical likelihood of a strict correlation in various circumstances.

In the first place, and stating the obvious, profits are not the result of sales, but arise from the difference between sales and costs. Any increase then in sales does not necessarily mean an increase in profits.

In order to assess the significance of an increase in sales in this context it is necessary to know the nature of the sales increase, and any material expense incurred in achieving it. These facts are never or rarely available at the time they are required. Think of the possibilities.

(a)   Sales may rise from purely inflationary price increases — not affecting profits at all. In fact the increase in sales may, on examination, not be keeping pace with the fall in the value of money.

(b)   The increase may be real, but competitive in the sense that it was the result of a large advertising campaign which captured part of the market which may well be lost again the following year. Here again the cost of the advertising may well outweigh the increase in income.

(c)   The increase in sales may in a competitive market be the result of a price cut. This might increase turnover, but the profit margin being now lower, the profit may be less than before.

(d)   The apparent increase may in a group be due only to the acquisition of new subsidiaries, which are actually earning a lower profit rate than the previous average for the group.

(e)   The increase may be ephemeral — it may be the result of a new product or process which has involved much costly research which must be set against the income. The product may have an immediate appeal but due to competition, or the vagaries of public taste, sales of it may fall heavily in the succeeding year or years, perhaps leaving a legacy of investment to be written off against a non-existent income. In a private enterprise type of economy, many projects are speculative in the sense that a "risk" company continually takes chances in putting new products on the counter; these may result in many fat years to come against which initial costs can be set, but the scheme might fail, and the initial additional income may be insufficient to wipe out the various costs of developing the project. In other words turnover may sometimes be a guide to future expectations, but it is a most unreliable guide and unless the investor or analyst has a great deal of "inside" information and knowledge of market conditions, he had best not place too much faith in it or he may be unpleasantly surprised.

(f) Finally to come back to a matter considered in a previous chapter, there is the influence exerted by the stock valuation.

It is not denied that errors in stock taking are self-cancelling on a long-term basis, inasmuch as if they should increase profits in year 1 they will tend to decrease them by an equal amount in year 2 — unless the error is perpetuated by consistent under- or over-valuation. It is, however, impossible to continue each year to reduce profits by 8% by reducing stocks by a fixed amount, for the reduction would be cumulative and would soon become obvious.

However, when considering one year in isolation, it is well to remember that a material increase in turnover does not necessarily foreshadow a proportionate increase in profits, as the eventual profit figure will be considerably influenced by the value put upon the stocks. In fact, a company could make it a policy to manipulate the stock figure in order perhaps to suggest a stable profit.

It will be immediately suggested that the auditor will prevent this. It is a pleasant and reassuring thought but quite untrue. The auditing profession has persuaded itself that it has no responsibility to take stock, and insufficient technical knowledge in many cases to value it. It considers this enough to exonerate itself from responsibility. It will be obliged to examine the stock figure to the "best of its ability", and be expected to discover large and obvious errors if only by comparisons and various reconciliations. However, as was suggested earlier, no auditor is likely to guarantee the accuracy of the stock figure to within 5% or even 10%. In cases such as Wimpey's, it appears from the accounts that they accept a Managing Director's certificate entirely.*

In Chapter 7 the incidence was shown of a 5% error in the valuing of stocks. In the instance of I.C.I. this would affect net profit by 8%. Now if in a particular year turnover was to rise by 10% this might seem an encouraging sign. In 1963 the turnover was in the region of £625 million, a 10% increase would be £62 million. The ratio of profit to sales varies

*See Appendix B, note 7.

considerably. In 1963 it was roughly 14%, this would then give grounds for expecting profits in 1964 to rise by £8·7 million. Is any further comment necessary except to point out that 1963 stocks were £130 million. The profit of £8·7 million could consequently be smartly eliminated by a mere 6·7% error in stock valuation. (In fact, it would be less, as the increase in turnover would probably be accompanied by an increase in stocks.)

The effect of a 10% increase in Courtaulds' turnover would be to increase profits by £2·6 million. Stocks in 1963 were £45 million. The profit increase could therefore be eliminated by a 5·8% error in stock valuation.

If this is true of I.C.I. and Courtaulds where the effect of stock errors is only 8 or 9% then how much more relevant in the case of other companies such as Wimpey's where the effect is as much as 24%?

This problem raised by the effect of stock valuation is of no little importance, and is a matter which the law should take slightly more seriously than it does. It would not be pleasant to have a repetition of the McKesson Robin's affair, or even a minor version of it, as a goad to stir authority into the necessary action. It might be argued that such massive and almost epic frauds are unlikely today where industry is more carefully controlled. Such confidence would be, to say the least, rather prone to be proved false, and is a symptom of the prevalent lack of concern with the ethic of company practice, which leads to the correction of errors long after irreparable damage has been incurred.

This is one reason why such importance is attached to the chapter on asset revaluation, and why in another publication the law relating to capital profits was so sharply attacked.*

There is something dangerously inadequate about a society which encourages participation in ownership by the acquisition of shares by the small man — particularly the employee — and at the same time allows him to be presented with information, and lulled with laws, which give him a sense of security that is entirely without justification. The information is often based on incorrect premises and is stated in terms which are meaningless, and the laws are incapable of righting the situation, or offering any compensation for losses which the system so

*Distribution of Capital Profits, *The Accountant*, March 1962 (the author).

often leads the shareholder to suffer.— sometimes without realisation. If any evidence is needed, it is supplied regularly by the figures offered for shares by take-over bidders, and by the capital profits earned by the financial dairymaid who buys the shares economically, gains control of the organisation, and then proceeds to sell assets which were grossly undervalued in the accounts at a considerable and often tax free capital profit, which he appropriates principally to his own holding in the company. As an alternative he may, rather than withdraw the surplus, rent back the properties and use the new funds to develop the company, thus increasing profits and dividends so as to enable him to sell the shares originally acquired, at a handsome profit. One does not so much complain of the man's initiative, but of the system which allows him to take profits from the original shareholders to whom they properly and in justice belonged.

Private competition is a popular creed, but while it is based on the profit motive, and, unless it is subject to reasonable control, then it is difficult to see how it can be supported by what is thought of as a civilised society, for it is governed primarily by principles which are compatible with no law but that of the jungle. Unfortunately, economic man in his natural self, is even yet "red in tooth and claw". Ethical standards and premises are vital to the wealth of society. Until they prevail, man's reason will be used far more to supplement, than to control, his supposed natural instincts. It is unfortunate but it is true.

CHAPTER 14

The Bullock in the Boardroom

RECENT years have witnessed an increasing demand for direct worker participation in management by appointing representatives of the work-force to sit on the Boards of companies in the private sector as "worker-directors" though the obvious corollary that directors should be invited to sit on works-committees or attend relevant union meetings has not been given much support. This demand for democratic government within companies, although somewhat biased in one direction, has been partly recognised by the publication of the report of the Bullock Committee which was appointed to examine the feasibility of such direct worker-participation. The Bullock Report was given considerable coverage by the press and was accepted by parliament, if not in full then as a base on which reforms might be built.

Worker participation in management may or may not have a dramatic influence on the performance of companies in the battle for profitable business, much depends on the form this participation, if it happens, will take. There is a considerable difference between direct representation on the Board of a company and the restructuring of company law on the basis opted for in Germany where the Board of Directors, or its equivalent, is a body of professional managers responsible to a quite distinct governing body composed of representatives of both capital and labour. The arguments in favour of the latter type of democratisation of companies are the more convincing — perhaps because they are more compatible with the facts of business life.

In order to be in a position to appreciate the force of the various arguments that may soon fly through the headlines it might be helpful to consider the historical background at least in outline.

At one time directors were those persons appointed directly by the owners of a company to manage it on the share holders' behalf. Time passed and companies grew in size and compass. Among other things they tended to become separated into various categories with the major divide being between the private company and the public company.

Private companies were, more often than not, created for convenience, in so far as, firstly, they could continue to exist as legal personae after the demise of the founder and were thus more easily conveyed from one generation to the next and, secondly, they could acquire the benefits accruing from limited liability status plus certain undefined tax advantages. In this era the directors were frequently both the owners and the managers of the share capital.

Public companies were, on the other hand, born of a quite different need, the desire to obtain capital quickly for purposes of expansion without involving the provider of the funds with any risk bar that of losing the agreed sum lent; this being outweighed by the hopeful promise of a return above that commonly available on gilt-edged investments. Certainly, many of these companies began as small family businesses but the greater part were, from the outset, earmarked for trading on the grand scale — the inducement lying in a prospectus inviting the general public to partake in an adventure promising undreamed of rewards.

As these large enterprises grew and lines of communication became tentacles reaching across countries and beyond to the ends of the known world, the whole basic structure, in its organisational mien, tended to change. The old link between the official Board of Directors and the shareholders became more tenuous — particularly as the constituency of the membership was, by grace and virtue of the Stock Exchange, subject to frequent change and was barely recognisable as a constant from one day to the next. The time came when, in the words of the one-time editor of *The Economist*, Mr. Hartley Withers, Boards of Directors became no more than "self-elected oligarchies". The names of the incumbents were rarely known by the shareholders, whose interest was limited to the regular flow of dividends. Only when a company crashed were the members of the Board disclosed; this despite the fact that the information was available to any member who bothered to read the Annual Report, even cursorily.

Needless to say, the birth of the mammoth corporation brought with it a bundle of legislation intended, too often as an afterthought, to protect the interests of the various third parties involved, be they shareholders, creditors, employees or merely the long-suffering general public in its role as consumer. An extensive body of both statute and case law came into being giving lush but lawful pickings to the legal and the accounting professions alike.

There was, however, one rather more pertinent development in company organisation which seems to have either been deliberately discounted or conveniently ignored. This lay, and still does lie, in the almost imperceptible divorce of ownership from management; the repetition in commerce of the distinction that has long existed in government; that between the elected parliament which makes the rules and the permanent civil service that not only keeps the show on the road but desperately tries to maintain a steady course. This separation between the legislative and the executive, more obvious on the other side of the Atlantic, exists to ensure continuity and to avoid the many pitfalls arising from sudden swerves in legislative policy.

This type of separation has already been adopted by some, if not all, public companies and is one which, if universally recognised, would make very good sense of the proposals concerning representation of workers on the Board contained in the Bullock Report. The division accepts the emergence of management as a trade or profession in its own right and as important as any other in the productive process. Like any other occupation it requires special training and the application of certain, even if nebulous, skills. It is management which forms the executive branch of commerce and, as such, it is quite distinct from the occupation, or role of Director. The function of the former is to organise and maintain the everyday running of the business; the function of the latter is to lay down the guide-lines within which management must operate. That is the theory but, alas, it is not always the fact.

In reality, many executives of public companies are also *de jure* members of the Board of Directors — the former position being necessarily allied with the latter as a term in the contract of employment. Alternatively directorships are a perk awarded to long-serving or particularly able executives often with the idea of ensuring that their allegiance does not drift elsewhere. This is obviously a useful ploy where no firm contract of employment exists and loyalties are not otherwise guaranteed.

This "fact of business life" need not necessarily prove a stumbling block in the present context as the status of the company's "executive branch" is in need of a face-lift. There is no reason whatsoever why alongside the "legislature" of the Board made up of delegates from shareholders, unions, consumers, etc., there should not be an Executive Committee which would deal directly with the everyday management decisions and have complete responsibility, with limited but defined powers of discretion, for the implementation of Boardroom decisions. The Board would handle overall strategy but the Executive Committee, whose chairman, possibly a Board member by co-option, would have a free hand in tactical disposition of available economic forces. It would also be answerable to the Board which would have the sole rights of fire and hire over its members.

If this distinction were clarified by law then the present wrangling over recommendations of the Bullock Committee would be seen in its true light as an absurd and pointless preoccupation with non-essentials. What is so desperately needed is the restructuring of the public company in a way that would put the discussions of the directing Board outside the everyday running of the business. There would still be a position of "managing director" but this would arise from his role as senior manager co-opted on to the Board and not elected or appointed from without. His seat would come from secondment, as the link-man, and not for any other reason.

The imagined problems arising from the rivalry between employees as a group and trade unions as an institution in the bid for representation could be resolved overnight and bloodlessly. The present position of trade unions being able to hold a company to ransom by merely calling out members would, so far as the shop stewards are concerned, be unaffected. Rather would a *de facto* position be changed into one of *de jure* with the advantage to the public of putting the union leaders into a position wherein policy decisions would be partly of their own making.

There is, of course, the perennial problem of union vacillation and the fact that elected representatives have no absolute power to commit their members, particularly in the field of demarcation disputes. None the less it is not unreasonable to expect that the National Executive of the T.U.C. would, in exchange for a greater say in company control, put teeth into disciplinary measures and give proper assurances that decisions democratically made at Board meetings would have the backing, not only of the movement, but also of the law. They might agree that defiance of such decisions would be construed as a breach of the law and that the company concerned would be free to take legal action against dissident trouble-makers. On reflection, this could well free the national effort from the threat of unofficial strikes and management might well accept such a blessing eagerly as ample compensation for opening the doors of the Boardroom.

The other problem, more in the mind than in the truth, arises from suggestions that union representatives are not qualified to make Boardroom decisions. It might be pointed out that the House of Commons has long been heavily loaded with men and women whose only true qualification for leadership is located in their trade union origins. If such people are considered able enough to run a country there seems little reason why they should not be trusted to run a company. The Meriden experiment is not irrelevant here; the workforce have shown both that they are willing to direct an industry conscientiously and, more to the point, they have admitted the need to call in outside trained managers to organise production most effectively.

Incidentally there is no earthly reason why employees should not be represented on the Board as a force distinct from the union factor (though, to the unions, the necessity is far from obvious) and there is an exceptionally strong argument in favour of the general public, in its role of ultimate consumer, being allotted the seats that make up the third force — the uncommitted body that must counter the pressures of the unions on the one side and the interest of shareholders on the other. Why if the bullock is to be put into the boardroom should there be any objection to the introduction of the "man in the street" as matador?

In the light of these few suggestions the prospect of worker-participation within companies might be considered with less trepidation than has been witnessed in the past. If the structure of public companies were to be revamped along the lines just discussed and the divorce of management from control effected then the long-term prospects of the investor might even be improved. Surely any changes that give some hope of relief from the industrial anarchy that has prevailed during recent times, and thereby offer the prospect of both higher productivity and greater efficiency in the use of the limited resources, must be greeted if not with open arms then at least with cautious optimism.

CHAPTER 15

Reform of Company Law

THE law relating to companies is a most complex subject. The 1948 Companies Act is no bedtime reading, except perhaps for those who find boredom the best nightcap. To attempt any reform of this Act is inevitably a task to try the patience of the most able legal mind. Who is to feel the confidence necessary to put forward definitions of terms shunned by the original scribe and even now disputed by both the law and the accounting profession?

The Jenkins Committee were given the opportunity to rush in, thankfully they did not do so but produced a report which although smacking of unhappy compromise at least erred on the side of conservatism. If they did no more than offer a crutch where a cure was needed the fault lies not with those who bore the responsibility of the reform but rather more with those who submitted memoranda discovered in archives and who have now for many years made no effort to catalogue and agree upon the meaning of the many and various terms they employ.

It is no surprise to find that legal decisions are couched in such cautious phrases when the law in statute finds it impossible to define adequately the concept of a reserve or to distinguish properly between capital and revenue. Neither is it surprising that the statute hesitates where the profession who employ the concepts are still not agreed on their meaning — this is apparent from many of the accounts they produce. There are occasions when one must be forgiven for accusing them of attempting the wisdom of Humpty Dumpty without possessing the wit of Lewis Carroll.

Nevertheless, in spite of the apparent or implicit obstacles, attempts to tidy up are actually being made. The pity is that the subject is so confused that any effort to establish some order compatible with contemporary needs is likely to end in failure and at best make the issues even more confounded than before. What is necessary is a complete reappraisal of the position and role of the limited company in society having reference to the political structure of the country and the social changes both in standards of behaviour and outlook that have occurred since 1948 or in so far as the 1948 Act was insufficient since 1925. The most recent essay has been the Companies Act of 1967. It does not take more time than is needed to scan the introduction to the Bill that preceded the Act to see that although the need for reform was recognised and steps in the right direction were intended the way was barred and beseiged by political prejudices.

To state that the primary objects were first to abolish the status of exempt private company, secondly to obtain more information as to the income and number of directors, and thirdly to insist on the publication of so-called political contributions, must immediately make both the Bill and the Act suspect.

The point is that the limited company has long been a favourite whipping post for disgruntled politicians. The word limited itself is almost an accusation, the term management or director has become in many circles one of abuse and the company being a legal persona has in spite of Sydney Smith's remark, a body which is most certainly kicked.

Companies in general are in dire need of public relations men. The image needs to be changed. It is true that there is much in the way of malpractice, more so in higher echelons of industry. There is also the question of charging items to the business which should not so be charged. However, it is surely time that it was realised that it is not necessary to form a company to do this except in a minor number of situations and in any event the gap could have been stopped quite simply without the ridiculous step of forcing all companies into the pattern established for public companies.

The administrative cost on both sides is considerable both in preparation of reports and filing thereof at the relevant registry. How many persons realise that the public companies which occupy so many columns in the daily papers represent but 4% of the whole. Of the rest 96% are private companies, and of these over 70% were exempt. That is to say for every company already filing accounts, an additional 2·3 did not do so. These are now obliged to file full accounts and reports, making them available for the inspection of the inquisitive public.

Was this necessary? Why should the accounts and the details of those directors' salaries be the subject of any casual criticism? Is the genuine private company rightfully bound to account to the nation?

It is here that the nature of the limited company needs careful re-examination.

Many persons, not least those involved, have the idea that the company revels in privileges accorded by law, giving it a status far more enviable than any other business is accorded, and that it is consequently reasonable to expect a comprehensive account of stewardship from it at intervals of one year.

If this picture is subjected to careful analysis it is soon obvious that the many privileges exist for the most part in the minds of the public. Much as many would prefer to imagine otherwise it is a sad fact but true, that the South Sea Company is not the archetype of the average private company. No more is Frank Donald Costa the typical entrepreneur, and even were he so it is rather doubtful if the casual layman could detect from a swift or serious perusal of the annual report such deceptions as the trained auditor did not discover.

The limited company is a legal person, i.e. it possesses an identity that is quite separate from those who subscribe to it. It can sue and be sued in its own name. This is a legal convenience rather than a privilege. It is given limited liability provided certain conditions are observed. In other words, the owners are not liable for more than the capital originally subscribed by them. The owner of a share, nominal value £1 sterling, cannot be made to pay any sum above this amount should the company be forced into liquidation, irrespective of the moneys owed. This is ostensibly a considerable advantage. It would seem reasonable that the business should make its accounts available to creditors or prospective creditors for their own benefit. Moneys owed by the company are a relevant factor in deciding whether to lend or give credit. It is also in the interest of the shareholder that access should be had to the annual accounts, for the creditor then acts as a watchdog preventing the shareholder from being effectively and quite silently robbed, being more sensitive to changes in the fortunes of the enterprise and quicker to take action. More important again is the fact that when shares are offered for sale in the open market the buyer should have information at his disposal enabling him to form a sensible decision. He will be assisted by the fact that, in having access to the accounts, experts, self-appointed and otherwise, will be in a position to give private or, through newspapers and other journals, widespread advice and continual commentary on the position and prospects of various companies. Finally there is the more subtle fact that a tidy annual report is a fairly accepted sign of good faith on the part of those presenting it, particularly as it must be signed in part by auditors whose competence has been proved (at least to the satisfaction of the Dept. of Trade). In this way the interest of the casual investor is safeguarded and the creditor can rarely claim to be taking a terrible risk.

Now it is a fact, already stated, that but 4% of registered companies come into the category just discussed, i.e. publish reports and are subjected to the criticism of those whose living depends upon it. The 1967 Act brought the other 96% into the same or an equivalent category. True, of these 96% approximately one-quarter were already, being not entitled to exemption, filing accounts, but they did not normally have a stock exchange quotation and were not generally subject to prying eyes, except when subsidiaries of larger and more well-known businesses.

What of those private companies which claimed exemption, being 70% of all companies registered? Why was it necessary to deprive them of their status? Does the new gain merit the additional work necessarily involved?

A private company, being exempt, did not need a qualified auditor. Yet according to the Jenkins Committee, paragraph 88, at least 90% of these companies employed auditors approved by the Dept. of Trade. This being so, there seemed little reason for complaint. The position could have been resolved by merely making such an audit imperative. This would have safeguarded the interests of the various parties to a substantial degree.

An exempt private company was not allowed to be the subsidiary of any public company nor was any other company allowed to have shares in it. The law was framed to stop a public company obtaining advantages by acting through exempt private companies. These latter were therefore the province of the family business. Shareholders were few (they cannot exceed 50 in any event, except in special circumstances) and they were bound to restrict the right to transfer shares. Generally speaking they tended to be in business in a small way. For this reason among others it was thought to be unnecessary to force them to the expense of preparing and filing proper accounts.

Have conditions changed to warrant a reversal of attitudes? As far as limited liability is concerned, the creditor really gains little from the accounts being available at Bush House, apart from the fact that in most instances he will be unaware as to where Bush House is or even that it is open to the inquirer. He will tend to be wary in giving credit and if in any doubt can always ask to see a copy of audited accounts. Banks tend to do so as a matter of course before granting loans. Any creditor who deals with a "fly by night" customer is unlikely to be affected by the fact that accounts are filed or would have been had the company survived the regulation time. If the creditor is to be protected, the best method is to increase his powers where debts are unpaid after a defined period and to give him a right of access to books or accounts under certain conditions. Otherwise it is best to rely on the acumen of the creditor himself. He takes a risk at any time and if it is or proves to be to his detriment then he is either unfortunate or was guilty of a poor appreciation of the risk involved. In either instance it is the run of the game. There is no evidence that the position has been alleviated by the abolition of the exemption status.

As a result of a simple analysis the Jenkins Committee discovered that of all private companies registered in 1954, by 1961 20% had gone into liquidation, been struck off the register, or were seriously in default in filing returns. This superficially seems to indicate a strong degree of irresponsibility. Many companies are it appears built upon sand or constructed without any proved prospect. Many may be the work of those who walk the shady side of Lombard Street. Must not the public and the unknowing creditor be given greater protection? The answer is yes, but this protection is most unlikely to be afforded by destroying the exemption status. The obstacles thus provided will soon be surmounted by the person who intended to do so, and the result will be to increase the administrative work at the centre, without solving the principal problem. This, as the Jenkins Committee seemed to appreciate, must be tackled in other ways. Differences of opinion will exist, but obvious steps are increases in penalties for default in observing the rules set out in the various acts and greater evidence of integrity of purpose and sufficiency of backing, when the company is initially registered.

On a more ordinary note, it may be observed that the advantages of limited liability to the Artful Dodger are largely illusory. This is no place for detailed discussion but on the two principal topics, tax and liability, it can be safely said that tax advantages so far as income tax are concerned and particularly now that corporation tax has been devised, to all intents and appearances do not exist, except perhaps for those who, by changing from schedule E to schedule D, can obtain greater allowances and can extract all profits in the guise of salaries. Such gaps are easily stopped. As for liability, the man who seeks company status as an insurance policy against the risks of activities which require an acumen not normally to the pleasure of the law, will find that should the venture fail he will be in little better straits than the bankrupt, for he is more than likely to be adjudged to have contributed to the misfortune and may find himself personally liable for the greater part of the liabilities of the business.

Consequently, there seemed little to be gained by forcing the exempt private company to file accounts whilst allowing the non-company to carry on as usual, when the latter is more suitable now for the dealings of the confidence man. To claim that the adoption of the word, or rather the abbreviation "Ltd" after one's name encourages confidence and makes the raising of funds more simple is an admission of innocence. No recognised source of finance is likely to be impressed by such a suffix, for it is no guarantee of respectability and far from giving a sense of security, it means an increase in risk. The lender is likely to be far more interested in seeing a set of accounts properly audited and obtaining some security for his money. Neither of these precautions flows from the registration of accounts, more will flow from compulsory audit.

Generally then it may be fairly suggested that the abolition of exemption status is hardly defended. The main purpose it serves is to open the books of the small retailer to the larger operator and encourage the growth of the greater business unit. This may be a situation to be welcomed by some but the arguments in favour, though economically convincing, are socially irrelevant, for the primary effect of the replacement by the large unit will be the gradual elimination of the family concern, in its narrow sense, the extinction of the shopkeeper and independent craftsman, in favour of the store manager and salaried artisan.

The depersonalisation of the service industries and distributive trades may not seem particularly disastrous, but opinions could well change when the face of the traditional town is lifted. Personal service is to the customer in the greater part as important as independence is to the supplier and by personal service one implies rather more than being served with one's order by the same white-coated assistant each day. The emphasis here is naturally on the market or dormitory town rather than the neon-lit city. The man on his way to work, the ordinary commuter, whether on the Clapham omnibus, or the breakfast special from Brighton, is accustomed to calling for papers or cigarettes at his tobacconist. The word "his" is particularly relevant. There is a form of relationship implied here which cannot be replaced by machine or mammoth organisation. Much the same applies to the purchase of all personal consumer goods whether by the casual visitor or the housewife placing her regular weekly order. This is no middle-class fetish; it applies through all strata of society. The shopkeeper or tradesman dwelling in the area is likely to be more attentive to the needs of his customers, both in goods and gossip, than is the employee who can dissociate himself from the organisation for which he trades.

The psychology of the matter is perhaps beyond the scope of the present work, suffice it to suggest that property ownership is a symbol of security and has always been so and that each man in this country aspires to personal ownership and respects it in others, it is part of the conservancy common to the race.

It is a conservancy shown again in his desire that his name carved on the desk, the oak tree, or the stone, should remain for all time. It is shown in the bookshelf and in the photograph album. It is shown distastefully in the food he eats and delightfully in the ale that he drinks. He may be dragged from these traditions by the allure of the self-service multiple store, by chrome plate and Formica but those who aspire to the reorganisation of society on the basis of cost reduction had best be mindful of the way in which cost is defined. If not, then, when *they* perhaps find themselves at Dunkirk, they may suddenly discover that there are no small boats to bring them back.

This is to stray from the main theme. The issue has been whether the abolishment of the status of exempt private company was necessary or valuable. The answer seems to be in the negative, there seems no adequate reason why the small limited company should be obliged to account to the nation, nor why it should be obliged to disclose the details of its trading to competitor and public alike.

The second main purpose of the 1967 Act was to demand greater disclosure of directors' benefits. The new Act insisted both on names of directors being given and the emoluments of the chairmen and other directors in each bracket of £2,500 beginning at £0–£2,500. Where emoluments are waived this must be stated and the amount involved noted.

These provisions seem reasonable enough were they restricted to the public company where directors' emoluments can be particularly relevant and in some instances indicative of a position not otherwise obvious. It is ridiculous, however, to force the once exempt private company to give similar information. It is of no concern to anyone but the shareholders and they normally have access to it anyway. There is certainly no reason to declare income to the general public, for not only are they by definition not shareholders but to them the business is no different from that of an individual businessman who has not bothered to create a company. The position of creditors has already been discussed.

As has been stated previously the limited company has always been something of a whipping post to the parties of the so-called left, as if it somehow symbolised the capitalist monster. Being so, these provisions cannot be dissociated from the idea of party politics.

If the income of the lesser but ubiquitous shopkeeper and independent artisan is to be spotlighted, then why not also the normally far higher screw of those in the professions which, incidentally, are the breeding ground for members of Parliament. There is something rather absurd in the picture of the Labour Party candidate, a prosperous barrister, reserving the right to conceal his own income whilst persuading his audience drawn from a constituency where the greater part of the shopkeepers are directors, earning rather less than a barrister fallen on hard times, that it is necessary and in the public interest that they should declare their earnings. But perhaps Citizen Schweik does not see it this way.

Number three on the list of principal objectives was the determination to ensure that political contributions are declared. Assuming cards to be put on the table there is little doubt as to the objectivity of this resolution. The idea prevails that the big bad limited company finances the Conservative Party and that by forcing the company to declare the sum of its support, then the contributions may well be decimated. There seems no reason why such contributions should not be made known, but the interesting aspects of this odd and sanctimonious provision lie in the fact that firstly no provision seems to be envisaged to ensure that other sources of finance are made known to the apparently innocent public; secondly nothing is said about trade unions declaring the amounts deducted from subscriptions for political purposes; and thirdly, and this is particularly relevant, the Companies Act 1948 already insists that any item of an unusual nature be shown separately if in the auditor's opinion it is material to an appreciation of the accounts.

This latter provision seems to be quite adequate. However, if it is necessary to disclose each penny placed in the tin on Primrose Day then distinctions are likely to be difficult to explain.

The cheque made out to the particular party headquarters is easy to describe, but what of more subtle contributions? There is an odd tendency for instance for the names of M.P.s to appear on the boards of companies. Now they may have arrived at Westminster through the company; on the other hand, the position may have been donated partly to embroider the annual report and partly to provide additional moneys for party purposes.

Again what of the political portion of the union subscription. The latter is, or must be, indirectly paid by the company being a factor determining the wage paid. Consequently it would seem reasonable to include an estimate of the total amount contributed to party funds through the payroll. This could be a considerable amount. Take for example the number employed in the United Kingdom in 1964 by certain large organisations.

I.C.I.	126,000
Courtaulds	60,000
G.K.N.	75,000

Then there are the marginal items such as providing facilities, particularly in the fleet of company cars for candidates at election time. There is the salary which flows to the account of the employee called forth to Westminster by way of retaining his services though these are probably not justified by the amount paid.

More serious and complex issues are the campaigns waged against government policy.

In certain respects there seems no reason why company funds should not be spent in fighting nationalisation, where directors are of the honest opinion that the profits, allowing for advertising increases, can be maximised by private enterprise and that the latter is to the benefit of the shareholder. The director is the steward appointed by the members and neither he nor they should be *obliged* to consider the benefit of society in such a way as to put it before personal gain. A man must perforce obey the written law but otherwise he is quite entitled to his own opinion and to work in a manner that will obtain for himself the greatest reward.

To disallow political donations for tax purposes is in fact to cut against common practice which dictates that any expenditure directed toward the acquisition of income or rather incurred in the making of profits is justly treated as an expense when sorting out the appropriate tax payable by the organisation.

The whole matter, however, is steeped in party squabbles and chips on shoulders. It is probably best left to be sorted out in the lobby.

Forgetting then the principal purposes of the Act and looking at the other provisions more interest may be aroused. Before discussing these items it would be advisable to set down the aims which the analysis attempted in this work seem to make necessary.

The object should be to provide for the disclosure of sufficient information both in the annual report and otherwise, that the member may not be misled as the the nature or worth of his investment and that both creditor and general public, where their interests are involved, may have access to facts and figures relevant to a proper appreciation of the state of affairs of the company.

Where the general public are concerned they have the right to see that limited national resources are not misused and that innocent parties particularly employees, not being members, are not in any way being victimised. There is a limit, however, to the scope which should be allowed to such assumedly benevolent interference. It is intended principally for the large public company and the claim here made is that the once exempt private company, normally the little family concern, taking company status for administrative reasons alone should not be subject to the same prying eyes, the reasons for this having already been stated.

Dealing first with what may be described as organisational changes, there is a certain section of the Act which deals with the information that should be given regarding groups of companies. Names and location of subsidiary companies must be given, as also must the name and location of any company in which the one has an interest greater than 10% or which represents more than 10% of its total assets.

The above seems a reasonable provision, but why must its effect be muted by a provision that it need not apply where the number of subsidiaries is great. This giving of options to directors seems quite pointless. If such are thought necessary, surely the proper persons to decide on whether information should be given are the auditors. The directors may claim the privilege, but the auditors should be the ones to decide, for they alone profess independence. The same applies to all other clauses in the Act where directors are given this right to decide whether the law applies to them or not.

In certain circumstances Dept. of Trade permission is necessary; this seems a reasonable precaution. It applies to most of the information regarding subsidiaries particularly where a subsidiary does not state the name of its ultimate holding company.

Generally speaking the latter will now be necessary. Is it sufficient that this should be restricted to the annual report which the public rarely sees?

Is it not reasonable to suggest that the subsidiary be made to disclose the identity of its owner on all stationery, advertising material, and in fact whenever its name is given. (Partners not trading in their own names must do this.)

It would be useful to know the real proprietors of the shops in the town. It might save the time wasted and annoyance consequent upon walking into each unique shoe shop in the High Street to be offered the identical and often shoddy pair of shoes. But this is to bay for the moon; it would interfere with the sale of neon signs.

Whilst talking of ownership another provision that might be particularly useful but is not introduced in this Act, would be to force companies to state the names of say the twenty principal shareholders or alternatively the names of all persons or organisations holding over 5% of the shares giving details of each holding. This would be valuable to the member in showing him which way the loyalties of this company might lie. The 1967 Act goes some way toward this in requiring registration of interests in 10% or more in the company's equity.

Another innovation which could have the same type of effect would be the listing of other directorships held by each director. The 1967 Act does not provide for this — more is the pity, as it would give some guide to possible conflicts of loyalties and be more effective than present provisions as to declaration of financial stakes in contracts existing or to be commenced.

Reverting back to the matter just discussed, that is share ownership, the factor of particular importance concerns nominees. Shares are registered in names which do not refer to the beneficial owner. When dealing with the suggestion made of stating principal shareholders, etc., it would be necessary to know the true owners. This is not known at present.

It has always been held that a company need take no notice of a trust, therefore shares are registered in the trustee's name. The position could easily be cleared up to everyone's satisfaction if the beneficial owner's name was stated following that of the nominee or trustee — it would not be necessary to give details of the trust itself.

So far little has been said of the accounts themselves. The Act made certain amendments. It would have companies disclose the principal activities of the group giving details of any changes during the year.

Details of turnover must also be shown with the split between different types of business and amount each contributes to profit before tax, but no comparative figures of turnover, dividends, profit before and after tax, and losses for five years as originally suggested, need be given even though this information is already being given by many of the larger companies and in most instances for ten years.

Other suggested changes, not adopted, concerned share capital and reserves. Totals of these were to have been given for five years. No mention, however, was made of controversial issues such as definition and rights of shares, with the single exception of redeemable preference shares where redemption date and premium must be stated.

It is unfortunate that time was not given to considering the possibilities of reducing possible forms of share capital. In this area it might have been sensible to consider the abolition of non-voting shares and other devices for depriving those who accept the greater risk from a fair share of control.

When it comes to reserves, the sundry provisions follow gamely in the wake of the previous Act. Instead of attempting to define different categories more precisely the question is settled quite simply by dispensing with distinctions. This is naturally absurd for it avoids a real issue.

The point is, that there are differences in kind between reserves. Despite the Dimbula Valley judgement there are still reserves which by law cannot be distributed in cash, i.e. share premium account and redemption reserve funds.

The sensible procedure would be for the profession to agree on three basic categories. Those that cannot be distributed by law, those that the directors have agreed to withhold and thirdly those that are considered available for distribution.

The reserve for replacement of fixed assets presents rather a different and special problem.

The valuation of fixed assets has been discussed at length in a previous chapter. Were assets revalued at current equivalent cost, then the surplus would be shown as a capital reserve falling into category one. If the company has not revalued its assets but provides for replacement by appropriation from profit, it is difficult to see that this reserve could logically be treated in any other way. In fact it is often shown among revenue reserves or at best as if it applied or were better included in category two.

It is suggested here that this reserve must necessarily fall into the first category and that the law should be amended to this effect.

This leads us naturally into a discussion as to the changes necessary to cater for the proper treatment of assets.

The provisions in the 1967 Act are interesting if only because they suggest a situation where a sledgehammer is being used by a man who cannot lift it to crack a nut which he cannot see.

The point is that in the first place the assets are divided into categories as if the category were master and assets must be made to conform — rather like forcing a head to fit one of a limited number of hats.

Secondly the assets are insufficiently distinguished and the traditional labels no longer apply. In addition they tend to confuse by giving the impression that a particular item is or may be something which it is not.

Thirdly there is the whole problem of asset valuation. At what figure should an asset be shown in the balance sheet and if revaluation is commended then what basis is to be used and how frequently should such revaluations be made.

Fourthly, and this is rather more controversial in nature, is depreciation being correctly dealt with in the accounts and is sufficient information being given as to the basis of computation of this charge?

Taking these points in order the first is that of classification. Two basic categories are distinguished at present: fixed assets and current assets. Items which seem to belong to neither category are shown separately beneath arbitrary headings between fixed and current assets. Such items are investments and interests in subsidiaries.

The first question is whether headings are in fact needed. The 1967 Act suggests fixed, current and unclassified. This is akin to the previous attempt to define a reserve. The original or most satisfactory distinction is between assets acquired with the intention of retaining them in their original state or form and using them in the earning of profits until such time as they need to be scrapped and replaced (they are not bought for resale but as aids to production or the increase in some fashion of income), and those assets which are being continually turned over in the course of production or trade.

There is no asset that does not fit naturally into one of these classes. To distinguish investments as a class apart is pointless. There are two types of investment. (The Act effectively denies this.) There are those known as trade investments which come into the first category being acquired for permanent aid or employment in the maintenance of income and those purchased on a temporary basis as a means of employing moneys temporarily idle.

The first type are known as trade investments bought to further the objects of the business or in the instance of shares in subsidiaries to expand the area of operation. These are surely fixed assets.

The second type normally take the form or title of marketable securities being sold, say, when cash is needed for asset replacement or payment of heavy liabilities. These must, by definition, be current assets.

As for unusual assets such as goodwill, patents, etc., these fall fairly into the first category.

Much has already been said concerning valuation of assets. The Act here becomes something akin to a blueprint for the Bellman's chart. It tends to confuse an issue already sufficiently complex. No doubt in an effort to accommodate the many recommendations that have been made, the compiler leant so far over backward that he finished up gazing at the stars.

It is not proposed to repeat the arguments put forward in an earlier chapter. With respect to fixed assets it was stated that these should be shown at present-day equivalent of original cost; that is at original cost, made up to current purchasing price by means of index numbers.

This would apply basically to all fixed assets without exception. In addition it is also time that certain fixed assets were more fully described. The latter is a matter appertaining to the previous question, that of classification, but can be conveniently dealt with here. The Act proposes distinctions between various tenures where land and buildings are concerned. This is good. There is equal reason for separating such items as goodwill, patents, trade marks, etc., where the individual items are material. Any item not material could be described as such. Investments should be more fully detailed where they are trade investments and where the individual amounts are material.

A point that might be made here, is that when the word material is applied to any amount, the decision should not be that of the directors but be an independent evaluation by, say, the auditors.

The method of asset valuation described, must be qualified to a certain extent. In the first place, where market value is known to be above the written-down value of an asset, then this market value should be stated.

Assets particularly relevant to this provision, would be land and buildings and quoted investments. Where unquoted investments are concerned the position is somewhat tricky. How is the market value to be ascertained? The Act overcomes the difficulty in a somewhat clumsy way by stating that where equity shares are held then the accounts should include details of profits and losses for the year, amounts included in the accounts, and amounts held by the other company attributable to the investment. Some such provision does seem inevitable though it might be remembered that other figures could be equally valuable, such as return on capital and break up value assuming these figures were calculated as suggested in previous chapters.

Questions will arise, such as whether in the property category more than one value should be given, e.g. market value in present use and market value in an alternative use, this latter purpose being stated. It is suggested here that both figures are relevant.*

Special factors concern assets which may be termed for convenience rather than clarity "intangible". These include items such as cost of patents or trademarks, copyright, goodwill and payments made for such obscure things as "know-how".

There are two aspects of this type of item which merit consideration. Firstly is the question of whether these have any real value or whether the cost should be written off as soon as possible. Secondly, if they have a value how is it to be calculated particularly when the original cost is not easily identifiable?

The first question is easily answered. Any right possessed by a business which gives them an advantage over a competitor or increases the sales value of the product must be valuable. Whether it is saleable is irrelevant, the point is, has it a value in the business?

A patent or trade mark is naturally valuable and the former would normally be saleable. The same applies also to copyright. The value would be estimated as cost plus an amount to allow for change in money values, i.e. these items are treated as are other fixed assets. Where material, each should be shown separately.

As for the writing off, in course of time this will depend on the life of the asset as is normal practice. There is the additional difficulty in the instance of copyright that this could be lost when conditions are not observed. However, such hazards are not confined to these intangibles: land could be lost by compulsory purchase at less than book figure, plant could be lost through failure to pay instalments. Such possibilities do not merit the writing off in quick time the investments consisting of

*See Appendix B, note 8.

these items, though it may be advisable where the danger is real, to make some provision of a special kind, e.g. provision for contingencies, with perhaps, where the amount is material, a note detailing the contingencies envisaged — except if this would be harmful to the interests of the business.

When determining cost of patents, trade marks and suchlike, it is necessary to distinguish between those where the cost consists of an amount paid to a vendor and others where the asset was developed by the business itself. In the latter circumstance it is wisest to take the sum of all moneys expended in the development as the capital cost and charge renewal fees to revenue.

Goodwill is the one item which presents particular problems. If it is purchased when a business is bought, then it is a real asset having a known value, that being the amount by which the sale price was above the capitalised value of profits normally anticipated from the assets purchased. This may be the result of the business being in a particularly advantageous position, geographically speaking, or having established a name for producing goods of trustworthy quality. There is an argument that the advantage does not necessarily pass to the buyer, particularly in the second illustration. Nevertheless, the asset is initially purchased and other things being equal, would be of fairly constant value.

It may be depreciated where it can be shown that the advantage has declined, or written off when such no longer exists. There is however no reason to write off such an asset, particularly where this is done more quickly than depreciation policy would demand, merely because it is intangible. This is to create a secret reserve which apart from being anathema to the law is a method of withholding valuable information from the shareholder.

True, on break up, the goodwill, however valuable in use, may have no takers, being inseparable from the business. The same applies, however, to many tangible assets and it is a rule that in compiling a balance sheet, break-up value or market value is not relevant except as additional information or as with stock where goods are bought for resale.

The irrelevance of the resale value of goodwill invites another equally thorny question. Should goodwill be revalued along with fixed assets and, if so, then on what basis? Again, what should be done about businesses that show no goodwill not because they do not possess any but because no previous sale of the concern has thrown up a figure? Theoretically one could estimate, from market analysis, the present sale price of any business as a going concern and, after subtracting the current value of the total net tangible assets, arrive at a figure for the goodwill. This could apply whether revaluing existing goodwill or discovering the value of that item in a business that has not previously shown it. Such a process would, however, be as unreliable in finding the true value of goodwill as it would be difficult to execute.

In the first place, the sale price of a going concern is virtually impossible to estimate. It depends upon too many factors; too many variables. It posits both a willing seller and a willing buyer — not to mention an unspecified degree of willingness on the part of both. It also depends totally on prevailing market conditions at the time of sale, the availability of credit and prevailing rates of interest both of which may change from one day to another.

In the second place, the current value of individual assets, in use within a going concern, is as difficult to estimate as is the value of the business itself and for very much the same reasons.

In the third place, the resultant goodwill figure, being the difference between two quite subjective, and possibly unsupportable, valuations will in no way indicate whether it derives from locational advantages or from the more efficient use of resources, or both.

The problem must be tackled from another angle — one which is not dependent upon subjective asset valuation. The obvious starting-point is earnings or rather profits. In this way one can begin from facts rather than from fancies. There are two facts available in the records of any business, the first is the current profit and the second is the figure for capital employed calculated on the basis set out in the preceding chapters, particularly Chapter 7.

The first step in our calculations will be to apply the relevant risk rate of return to the capital employed, excluding any existing figure for goodwill. This will give a figure for anticipated profit which can be deducted from the adjusted profit. Any positive answer will represent super-profit and by discounting this back a provisional goodwill figure may be found. The adjusted profit is the actual profit figure given in the accounts after making revisions necessitated by the inclusion of abnormal items of expense or income, i.e. items that are peculiar to the business in question and which would not appear if that business changed hands.

Consider the following example:

		£	
	Capital employed	100,000	
	Risk rate of interest	6%	
	Actual profit	7,580	
	Adjusted profit	7,800	£
(a)	Anticipated profit on capital employed		6,000
(b)	Difference between present actual and (a)		1,580
(c)	Difference between adjusted profit and (a)		1,800
(d)	Difference between adjusted and present profit		220

Here we have taken figures at random. The risk rate at the level given is probably too low inasmuch as it rather approaches gilt edge rates. This is quite unimportant for illustration purposes; (c) shows the expected super-profit on premises already suggested. This would put the goodwill at £1,800 discounted back at 6%, that is at about £30,000.

Now here the problem, if there is a problem, really begins. We have taken a capital employed figure of £100,000 to which we propose adding £30,000 goodwill to give the value to a purchaser at £130,000 but is this the true value of the business?

Now it could reasonably be suggested that an element of "goodwill" is contained in the valuation applied to the majority of the individual assets making up a balance sheet. This does not mean that goodwill exists irrespective of an intention to sell as the value given to those individual assets is a function both of demand in general and demand in their present context (within the business) in particular. It is self-evident that once the assets cease to be used within that business in a productive capacity due say to the disappearance of the market for the goods produced then both the business and the individual assets it possesses have quite unconnected values — the former is possibly worthless as an entity and the latter will be worth no more than their break-up value which will vary according to circumstances, such as age and condition.

The goodwill of a business then is almost totally dependent on the possibility of selling that business as a going concern. In this sense it is necessarily connected with the economist's concept of extra-marginal utility. In the world of economics, the marginal firm is that firm which, at a given moment in time, and taking into account additional costs of closing down, finds it just worthwhile to stay in business. The marginal firm, be it a company or a sole trader, is that firm which is operating at the minimum profit level acceptable and which would, *ceteris paribus*, be obliged to close down if the balance of trade took the slightest turn for the worse.

Other firms in the same industry may be comparatively better off because they enjoy advantages unavailable to the marginal firm. These advantages may lie in their proximity to the sources of demand for the relevant product or be due to other factors such as availability of suitable manpower or raw materials. Whatever these advantages may be they result in returns which are higher not because of greater efficiency in management but because of geographical location. Businesses which enjoy these extra-marginal advantages are obviously likely to be more saleable than those which do not and the selling price will vary according to the degree of that advantage.

The question that immediately arises is whether what we have previously referred to as goodwill is the measure of that relative advantage. The answer is a qualified yes. It is qualified because we have now found that goodwill, as it is generally described, is not a single entity but a figure compounded of many parts. It could reasonably be argued that the extra-marginal advantage just discussed is the only true goodwill but equally it could be as justifiably argued that such a locational advantage is something quite different from goodwill and that the latter is a quite distinct, albeit intangible, asset which is solely a function both of efficiency and of popularity, i.e. goodwill is a nebulous matter built up in the careful construction, by good management and reliable products, of a saleable reputation.

The only sensible conclusion is that what has long been referred to in commercial jargon as "goodwill" is not one indivisible figure but is an amalgam of separable parts of which the two principal ones are "locational" goodwill, being a function of extra-marginal advantage, and "efficiency" goodwill being a function of good management.

For purposes of illustration and methods of calculating relevant figures consider the following hypothetical company which is being offered for sale to Q.

The Cabbage Company Ltd.

Net capital employed.	£10,000
Prevailing interest rates:	per cent
Actual rate of return earned by company	10⅛
Rate anticipated by Q	15
Consols	5
Risk Capital	9

A risk rate of 9% would seem to demand a profit of £900 on the stated capital of £10,000. If £900 were discounted back at 5%, which being the prevailing gilt-edge rate would be roughly equivalent to the minimum return acceptable and therefore the rate at the margin, we would obtain a figure of £18,000. In perfect market conditions Q would be obliged to pay that sum for the company. He would be paying £10,000 for the business and an additional £8,000 for the extra-marginal advantage. The locational goodwill, in theory, would be £8,000.

However, the business is not earning 9%, the currently accepted risk-rate, but 10⅛%. The current average profit is £1,080. Discounting this back at 9% we have £12,000. Discounting it back at 5% gives £21,600. At present profit levels then the asking price for the business would be between a minimum of £12,000 and a maximum of £21,600. Assuming a perfect market then Q would pay the latter price which would be made up of

	£
Capital acquired	10,000
Locational goodwill	8,000
Efficiency goodwill	3,600
	21,600

But this would also be the price offered by other buyers who foresaw no change in profits; Q, however, reckons that he can lift the rate of return to 15%. This would give him a profit of £1,500. To obtain this he will be prepared to up his offer to £30,000*. He anticipated bettering the

*£1,500 discounted back at 5%.

marginal rate of 5% by another 10% and, should he succeed, then the efficiency goodwill of the business will rise from £3,600 to £12,000. In all probability he will not need to offer this considerably higher price in order to obtain the business but will obtain it at a figure sufficiently over £21,600 to exclude less optimistic competitors.

Suppose he settles the purchase at £24,000. He will have paid £14,000 in excess of the net capital employed. How should this be shown in his opening accounts. Tradition would anticipate that a goodwill figure would appear in his first balance sheet. An opening intangible asset of £14,000. It is suggested that tradition would be badly advised and for the following reason.

Locational goodwill and efficiency goodwill are quite separate matters. In fact, as has been suggested previously, it is doubtful whether what we have referred to as "locational goodwill" should be treated as goodwill at all. It is, after all, merely a quantification of extra-marginal advantage. Efficiency goodwill, on the other hand, is a quantification of good management. The latter is controllable, the former is not. If the "locational goodwill" were not shown as an asset then the higher returns apparently earned by extra-marginal companies would give a quite erroneous impression of higher efficiency. On the other hand, if efficiency goodwill were excluded from the balance sheet then differing returns would be useful indications of varying degrees of good management or efficiency in running different businesses.

So far we have tended to concentrate on the acquisition of businesses. This was mainly for convenience. The same rules would apply to existing businesses which will need to calculate their appropriate goodwill figure and divide it between the two kinds. The locational advantage would then be added to net assets and be complemented by an equivalent Capital Reserve.

The relevant risk-rate would need to be known and will tend to vary between different industries. Approximate figures would be available from the Dept. of Trade. If this is not possible then a fairly reliable guide is the prevailing rate charged for capital within the particular industry where interest is fixed and the capital unsecured.

We must conclude then that what we have established as efficiency goodwill is the only true goodwill and should be excluded from the balance sheet. If it were not so excluded then the rate of return for all business units within an industry would coincide and no conclusions could be drawn as to the efficiency of any one company against others.

To sum up, then, all businesses, whether they be companies, partnerships or sole traders, should take pains to discover the extent of both their "locational goodwill" and where possible their real, or "efficiency goodwill". The former should be shown in the balance sheet. The latter should not. Neither figure is likely to be simple to ascertain as the issues raised are not a little complex. However, provided certain basic rates, i.e. risk rate and basic marginal rate, are established, the exercise is not impossible and clues as to how these rates can be found have been given above.

If rates of return are to be acceptable as a guide to relative efficiency in the use of resources, i.e. good management, then all business entities must start at the same level — without benefiting from accidental advantages. Locational advantages need to be removed by being quantified in ways already discussed and included among assets making up capital employed. Despite the fact that in certain instances management chooses a particular site, the geographical position of the business must, for most purposes, be taken as fortuitous.

Such quantification will obviously present problems (particularly for companies not the subject of acquisition), but the complexity of a task is no excuse for not arriving at some approximate solution where this is shown to be economically desirable. Once this figure has been established and included in capital employed then the rates of return on the capital earned by various companies within any particular sector should be a useful indication of comparative efficiency.

The capital reserve representing the extra-marginal advantage would obviously need to be adjusted periodically as the risk-rate changed, compensating additions being made to various fixed assets or, if such was not feasible, to a form of Sinking Fund. Needless to say such a process is unlikely to be made legally essential and for obvious reasons. Company law is rather sensitive to drastic change.

The question of goodwill has been dealt with at some length. Even now the position cannot be said to be clarified completely. All that has been feasible here is to attempt to sketch a few of the problems involved in ascertaining and valuing this figure.

So much for the manner of valuing fixed assets. It only remains to deal with the vexing subject of depreciation. A vast amount has been said of this already. In Chapter 6 we advocated the separation of the depreciation reserve from the assets and its appearance among reserves. There would need to be an accompanying schedule showing the distribution of the reserve among the various assets and also a breakdown of the provision for the year. It might be remarked here that the figure shown in the profit and loss account is a provision and is credited to a reserve account. No doubt this will be objected to as a confusion of terms. A little thought should show that it is not.

It would be, for reasons that by now should have no call to be repeated, instructive, if not essential, that companies should state the manner in which depreciation is calculated. It would be far better were this method standardised, for there can be no occasions when the straight line method or the diminishing balance method is necessary to proper accounting.

It is unlikely that the law would go so far as this, but it is a possibility to be borne in mind.

Before leaving the subject of fixed assets, it might be noted that the Act states that details should be given of acquisitions during the year. The reasons for this are obscure and no really useful purpose is served barring affording the analyst an opportunity to form a plant register. It would seem that such information has no particular value and may be more useful to competitors than shareholders. It is true that the members might wish to know how their money is being spent and whether any is apparently wasted. Nevertheless, they are unlikely to have the knowledge to make sound judgements and would in any event have the opportunity at a general meeting to ask for information on apparent increases in any asset figure shown. There is the possibility that such would be sometimes hidden by disposals but the latter rarely assume large proportions.

Current assets present their own particular problems. Many of these have been discussed so frequently elsewhere, that to bring out traditional arguments once again would merely be tedious.

The principal item in current assets would normally be stocks and work in progess. These can be a considerable proportion of total assets, for instance George Wimpey's, for 1964, show a stock and work-in-progress figure of nearly half of total assets.

It is obvious that the figure when it reaches this level is very material to a proper appreciation of the accounts. Not only does it indicate the amount invested in stocks but also shows the effect an error could have on profit. The importance of a proper stock valuation is naturally if reluctantly recognised within the accounting profession, but insufficiently by the law. The accountant relies principally on the many recommendations put forward by the Institute of Chartered Accountants, the A.S.S.C., etc.

The effect of errors in stock taking and valuation may be illustrated by showing the effect of an error of 5% in stock and work in progress on the net profit before tax. Taking the companies used previously, the profits would decrease by the percentages stated if the valuation was below actual by this amount. The figures are for 1963.

	%
I.C.I.	8
Courtaulds	9·1
Imperial Tobacco	26
Newton Chambers	60
Lancashire Cotton Corpn.	40
George Wimpey	23
Harland & Woolf	86
William Hancock	5

This shows an average of 32% which is obviously material. True it is considerably influenced by the lean years of Newton Chambers and Harland & Woolf, but there are always likely to be companies with lean years whatever random selection may be taken. Apart from this even 9% as with Courtaulds is a material variance and will have a 9% effect on the return on capital, i.e. it will reduce the rate of return by 9%. This could be important.

There is good reason then why far more attention should be paid to the valuation of stocks and work in progress. The emphasis in the past has been on methods of valuation. This is reasonable except perhaps for the tendency to be rather conservative.

However, far more attention must be paid to the stock-take itself. The law should state categorically that where the auditor has not the technical knowledge to satisfy himself that physical quantities stated are correct then he should call in an expert to assist him. Similarly, with the valuation, the auditor establishing the principles to be followed.

To accept a director's certificate is ridiculous. The directors already have an implicit responsibility. The only method by which the auditor can satisfy his obligation to his employers, the members, is by taking such precautions as will satisfy him that the figure is correctly, or where precision is impossible, reasonably stated in the accounts.

He must be happy that a proper physical count has been made and that the items have been valued according to accepted principles and consistently from one period to another.

How far the law should go in drawing up rules for the auditor's instruction is difficult to say. There seems no need for a complete physical count particularly of minor items where the system of store-keeping is satisfactory and tested sampling techniques are available. On the other hand, when the value of raw materials or finished goods depends on their condition and where this is a matter needing skill, whether it be in technique or knowledge that the accountant does not profess, then it would be sensible to insist on the use of outside assistance.

The important fact is basically that the item stock and work in progress is one that must merit a great deal of attention. Not only does it, in the greater number of companies, tend to be particularly material in the computation of profits and statements of affairs, but this very fact makes it essential that the complicated nature or make up of the figure should in no way influence the attitude of the person acting as auditor. Rather, should it incite his curiosity and put him on guard, for it is often the easiest vehicle for fraud or mistake.

As far as legal changes are concerned, the most important aspect must be the attitude taken by the law to stock valuations. The courts should be particularly strict on this matter and convince the auditor by action that his duties are not light.

Again it might be stated that auditors cannot rely upon directors' certificates to ease their minds. Where they are not satisfied this should be made obvious in the report attached to the balance sheet.

Talking of reports, it seems unfortunate that the auditor's report is so standardised. There is good ground for encouraging fuller reports with comments on certain figures. A qualified report is looked upon as if it were a kind of writ issued by the auditors and aimed at the management. In fact this notion is ridiculous and a little more in the way of qualification might bring about the change necessary to teach the investor the distinction between commentary, and criticism aimed at arousing suspicion. To say that it is impossible to agree the value of the stock figure within say 10% does not necessarily imply a criticism damaging to the management. The condition of the goods or the market may have led to serious disagreement, no reconciliation being possible.

A change which would be valuable concerns the description of the items stock and work in progress in the accounts. It would seem reasonable to distinguish between these two quite distinct things except when the latter was immaterial in amount in which case this would be stated. Better still were three figures given, raw materials, finished goods and work in progress. The method of valuation in all instances should be given and any material amount written off old or obsolete stock should be shown separately by way of note. When the figures differ considerably from those appertaining to the previous period then reasons for these differences could be given — thus giving an opportunity for the investor to watch the tendency to over-stock. Provision might be made for occasions when the providing of the information might be harmful to business. This could occur when stock is being purchased in advance because the price is expected to rise, the relevant indications not being available to competitors.

One particular note with reference to work in progress. This is usually described as work in progress less cash received on account. Three figures should be shown where applicable, work done, work for which architects' certificates have been received, and cash received on account. Each amount should be shown separately, if only by a note. If any profit on work done but not complete has been taken, the amount should be stated together with the method of calculating the profit element included. Similarly with any provision for a loss.

As for other items among current assets, market investments perhaps present one among a number of difficulties. These investments may be quoted or not. Generally speaking, rules for valuation should be reasonably simple. These, as have been explained previously, are purchased for resale. The market price is therefore relevant. Present practice is to show the item at cost with a note of market quotations. The

1967 Act insists on comprehensive information in the instance of investments not quoted.

The type of detail described would be very fitting in the instance of subsidiary companies and companies in which the holding company has an interest over a stated amount, say 10%. Here the undisclosed reserves of the other company could be relevant, though in the instance of the subsidiary the amount of its profit and total capital employed may be sufficient. These investments would, however, be trade investments and be shown with the fixed assets.

The items now being spoken of are current assets purchased as a means of holding liquid resources on short and profitable terms.

The valuation would depend on whether or not the investment was quoted. It is best to distinguish quoted from other, and show both at cost with a note as to present market value.

The valuation of investments whether they be trade or other is a difficult problem and one that has been shirked in this chapter. It is not so much a matter of the difficulties involved in devising a satisfactory system, but that any valuable or comprehensive discussion would demand more space than is available.

One interesting point which might be dwelt on, is that stock exchange prices are determined by many factors, amongst which is a not well-informed public opinion. They are not then always a reliable guide to the value of a particular holding. A second and equally pertinent point is that a holding should be valued with an eye to its size. The larger the size the more influence this factor has on the value, for it could mean that the investor has a degree of control such as would give him a noticeable voice when policy is being considered and dividends declared. Many companies consider that a 10% holding is preferable, taking into account the saving in investment and administrative costs, when sufficient control is needed to sell their goods through outlets possessed by the second company.

Leaving investments behind and looking quickly at other current assets the two most common remaining are debtors and cash. There is little new to be said here. The reason for wanting facts is apparent in Chapter 3. The method of finding the provision for doubtful debts could be stated, i.e. whether a straight percentage or based on an examination of accounts or both.

There should be notes relating to special facts, such as the number or amount of debts guaranteed, if material, and also perhaps reasons for any noticeable change in the level of any figures shown.

Where cash is concerned much has been said already particularly in discussing bank overdrafts. The principal recommendation should be that some proviso be made to minimise possibilities of window dressing.

So much for assets, what of liabilities? In the first place it might be advisable to rethink headings such as *liabilities*. It is difficult for the layman to think of share capital as owed to anyone, though the position was examined in Chapter 2. Something akin to capital available and manner employed might be feasible, though capital itself is a much debased word.

Much has been said regarding share capital and reserves already, the principal recommendations being the abolition of non-voting shares and the creation of new categories of reserves. It was also suggested that companies should be expected to state the names, not nominees, of the twenty, say, largest shareholders with the number of shares held by each.

Another point which might be pondered on is whether the preference shareholders are treated in a logical manner. Could they not be considered as equity providers working to fixed odds, particularly when preference does not apply to return of capital and dividends are not cumulative? Is it reasonable that, in the majority of companies, preference shareholders only enjoy full voting rights if their dividends are in arrears? This obviously has particular reference to preference shareholders who enjoy the right to cumulative dividends. Might it not be reasonable to think in terms of a new class of shares, defined by statute, where the holders have preference to dividends, fixed or not, but only when dividends have been declared on all shares. These preferential dividends would necessarily be cumulative in effect as would other dividends declared and would need to be separately shown, when in arrears, merely to distinguish those unpaid dividends which would themselves be preferential as to payment when funds became available.

If the law allowed such shares then there would be little need to restrict their voting rights except in matters which concerned ordinary shareholders only. As things are at present, holders of fixed dividend preference shares are near enough being in the unenviable position of lacking the rights of the ordinary members to run the company whilst being deprived of the security enjoyed by holders of debentures.

Needless to say, it is not suggested that all companies should emulate Scottish Television Ltd. which, when incorporated by the late Lord Thomson, gave the preference shareholders not only preferential rights to dividends but also, by disenfranchising the holders of ordinary shares, gave them the sole right to vote at meetings of the company. One can only suppose that the average Scot is not so canny as he is frequently made out to be — or that Thomson was cannier by far than the average Scot.

Another important factor brought out in the previous chapter, that on capital gearing, is that the idea behind revaluation of assets should logically support similar revaluation of liabilities. If preference shareholders and debenture providers take no part in reserves, particularly those arising from revaluation of assets they themselves provided, then something needs to be done, if only to compose some sort of protest song.

Suppose a debenture is purchased with a life of twenty years. Let the price be £100 and the interest rate 5%. It would not be unusual for the value of money to be halved during the loan period. Supposing the fall in value to be steady this gives a loss in real terms of capital £100 and interest £50. A total loss of £150 against a total income of £100. Hardly a satisfactory state of affairs. Had the debenture been revalued by transfer from revaluation reserve, then the capital repayment would have been £200 and the interest paid £150.

Unless something of this nature is attempted then it cannot be worth lending on the long term in a period of rising prices unless interest rates are particularly high, and in any event the unwary are in truth being denied social justice.

Were steps taken, how far should the claim be allowed? Preference and debenture holders have been specified but will not the unsecured lender wish to take a slice and will the bank manager sit back with a bemused smile, or the tax inspector wink?

But there is a danger in looking for twice the normal number of reforms even considered. The matter of mentioning employee benefits and suchlike, in a note to the accounts, was but one of a number of rather numerous suggestions previously made, but this is to shout so loud that the only probable result is to find oneself as alone as Ibsen's "Brand" with the feathers of the great white eagle flaking mockingly around.

CHAPTER 16

By Way of an Epilogue

WHEN most of our analysis has led to suggestion, rather than conclusion, and contains so many hypotheses, it takes a certain courage, or perhaps bravado, to attempt a summing up let alone a judgement. The best that can be done is to point out again some of the salient features of the analysis.

Concentration has been continually kept to the return on capital — variously defined. The greater part of the book has dealt with that subject because it was considered that this was, other things being equal, the most promising method of forming satisfactory opinions of the prospects of any chosen company. The reasons for this choice have been (perhaps inadequately) indicated in the text, and the relative unreliability of other recognised ratios has been argued principally in support of this thesis.

The principal distinction that has been made is between the return on total assets and the return on investor's capital. The latter will tell the investor what he may expect from his investment and the prospects of improvement in his income. The former is, however, the more valuable in indicating the real earning potential of a company, and the comparative profitability with which it uses the resources at its disposal — it is this analysis that is of most value both to the investor and to the economist concerned with the way in which the nation's resources are employed.

The principal factors to be borne in mind by the investor, and it was primarily for him that this book was written, are the arithmetic mean return on capital after revaluation of assets, and the percentage deviation from this arithmetic mean; the manner in which increases in profits and dividends compare with variations in the level of retail prices generally; the trends disclosed by the figures for the period of years —

particularly when related to other companies in that sphere (though beware of the limitations that were outlined) and the influence that a relatively marginal change in dividends paid might have on the market price of the shares.

It is very well for the investor to argue that he is principally concerned with market prices and the return on money invested on the "exchange" — *but,* market price depends on dividends and prospects. Both these are either determined ultimately, or immediately, by the return on capital, and the behaviour of that figure over whatever period of years is chosen for the analysis. The most important point on which the investor should concentrate is, therefore, the level and movements in this return. This, assuming that, firstly, the company is not showing dangerous symptoms of insolvency and, secondly, that the profit and market price are both keeping pace with any fall in the value of money over the period.

Until more information is made available by industry, and this does not mean only turnover figures, these principles outlined are the only safe and reliable basis on which to build any satisfactory assessment of the possible future prospects of increasing profits and dividends in any company in which the investor might wish to employ his capital.

The position is far from satisfactory. It may be claimed quite justly that this book has done little more than prove the impossibility of dealing satisfactorily with the subject on the premises chosen. If it is nothing else then, it is a proof on the basic inability of the investor to appreciate the manner in which his money is used, and of the employee to assess the contribution made by his labour. The fault lies with the tradition of industry, so well supported by both the law and the accounting profession, for the inability referred to is not inherent in the individual, it is engendered by a system which considers that the control of industry is the prerogative of the managerial class, and that the details of the daily life of a company, and the manner in which it uses the money put at its disposal, are matters which are again the concern of the director, and, as far as the law will allow, must be kept from the eyes of both the member and the employee, lest in their ignorance, or occasional lapses of apathy, they should suppose that perhaps the money or effort they provide is not being properly employed.

The methods by which these precepts are preserved are various. So far as public accountability is concerned, the problem is amply solved by the manner in which accounts are traditionally prepared. The problem is, with accountants, as Schopenhauer says of the paradox in all men — "they run after that which is new but are prejudiced in favour of that which is old". Today they rush to join the E.D.P. club business and attend an incessant series of conferences in every other seaside town, where, to parody the words of a famous judge, "they are persuaded by people they do not know to study subjects which they do not understand on the supposition that it will enable them to meet problems they will probably never encounter, in circumstances that are unlikely to exist". Seriously, much attention is paid to the mechanics of computers (the intellectual's substitute for the ubiquitous fruit machine) when far more time should be spent in examining the very premises of their subject and looking for new ways of protecting the interests of the small investor and of giving him the information to which he is entitled in a form which he can comprehend.

Let the accountant, whether he be in industry or practice, put his house in order. Let him shed the mystery in which he apparently prefers to cloak his accounts and tell that which is true. There are many men attempting to do this, but it is still as rare as a rich philanthropist, to find a balance sheet which any person not acquainted with the secrets and shibboleths of double entry book-keeping can properly read.

It is the duty of the public company to account to the public and particularly to its members and employees. It is the duty of the accountant and auditor to see that this is done. This duty is, at present, not being performed and will not be so until statements of affairs are presented which give, in a vernacular form, the information which will enable the public, the investor, and the employee to form a proper assessment of the manner in which the resources of the company, and the nation, are being used and the responsibility with which the funds put at its disposal are being administered.

Appendix A

Company	Year	Total capital employed			Ordinary capital employed			Gross profit	Gross profit less pref. div.	Ord. div.
		Opening £000	Closing £000	Average £000	Opening £000	Closing £000	Average £000	£000	£000	£000
I.C.I.	1960	548,271	598,391	573,331	513,534	563,654	538,594	88,044	86,308	35,463
	1961	598,391	640,003	619,197	563,654	605,266	579,460	61,852	60,116	36,658
	1962	640,003	662,061	651,032	605,266	627,324	616,295	70,369	68,633	37,016
	1963	662,061	718,212	690,136	627,324	683,475	655,399	84,909	83,173	41,181
Courtaulds	1960	164,182	185,874	175,018	146,669	168,361	157,515	21,044	20,074	7,364
	1961	185,874	192,238	189,056	168,361	174,726	171,543	18,697	17,727	7,899
	1962	192,238	152,854	172,546	174,726	135,171	154,949	17,707	16,716	9,877
	1963	152,854	156,433	154,644	135,171	138,750	136,961	23,648	22,657	12,268
Imperial Tobacco	1960	154,000*	160,406	157,203	141,142	147,548	144,345	28,032	27,181	13,523
	1961	160,406	169,937	165,171	147,598	156,079	151,888	29,079	28,228	13,523
	1962	169,937	182,391	176,164	156,079	169,533	162,806	30,572	29,721	13,523
	1963	182,391	190,145	186,268	169,533	177,264	173,398	31,664	30,811	14,209
Newton Chambers	1960	11,885	13,312	12,594	11,752	13,179	12,465	950	943	561
	1961	13,312	13,477	13,394	13,179	13,344	13,261	1,146	1,139	528
	1962	13,477	13,393	13,435	13,344	13,260	13,302	630	627	502
	1963	13,393	13,338	13,365	13,260	13,205	13,232	501	494	502
Lancashire Cotton Corpn.	1960	24,283*	24,882	24,582	24,281	24,870	24,575	3,606	3,606	2,026
	1961	24,882	25,197	25,039	24,870	25,185	25,027	3,175	3,175	2,026
	1962	25,197	24,191	24,694	25,185	24,179	24,682	805	805	1,416
	1963	24,191	23,863	24,027	24,179	23,851	24,015	794	794	1,416
George Wimpey	1960	11,343	13,485	12,414	9,798	11,940	10,869	3,151	3,025	400
	1961	13,485	14,971	14,228	11,940	13,426	12,683	3,220	3,108	400
	1962	14,971	16,519	15,745	13,426	14,974	14,200	3,290	3,178	400
	1963	16,519	18,565	17,542	14,974	17,020	15,997	4,128	4,016	600
Harland & Woolf	1960	16,752	16,724	16,738	14,152	14,124	14,138	377	250	256
	1961	16,724	17,065	16,894	14,124	14,465	14,294	312	185	128
	1962	17,065	16,848	16,956	14,465	14,248	14,356	909	1,036	256
	1963	16,848	17,035	16,941	14,248	14,435	14,341	92 loss	35 loss	128
William Hancock	1960	2,260	2,412	2,336	1,810	1,962	1,886	351	324	83
	1961	2,412	3,283	2,847	1,962	2,548	2,255	503	459	140
	1962	3,283	3,522	3,402	2,548	2,787	2,667	622	578	160
	1963	3,522	3,696	3,609	2,787	2,961	2,874	612	568	160

Note. In the case of Wimpey expenses of increasing share capital 1961 and 1963 have been added back.
*Estimated figure.

Appendix B

1. Shortly after this book was written, in fact in the autumn of 1964, the Lancashire Cotton Corporation became a subsidiary of Courtaulds Limited. The reasons may be suggested by the narrative.

2. There have been changes in the tax law since 1963. In the accounts considered in this book the item of "future tax payable" consisted of tax on the profits of the year plus amounts set aside for taxation deferred by capital allowances. It was considered that both these amounts were in the nature of reserves as neither could be said to be liabilities. This was because as tax was on a preceding year basis, the tax calculated on current profit and provided for theoretically need never be paid — it was in the nature of an additional amount set aside. Since April 1965, and the introduction of Corporation Tax, the preceding year basis has been abolished and tax is payable on the profits of the year of assessment. Therefore, in considering accounts now, the only item to be included with capital employed should be tax deferred by capital allowances.

3. Later in 1963, after the accounts had been prepared, William Hancock revalued part of their freehold and leasehold properties. These were the licensed properties. The surplus, in the region of about 125%, was £3,538,114. This was against a balance sheet figure of £2,844,961 in March 1963. No adjustment was made in the accounts. In 1967 the brewery premises were revalued showing a surplus of 95%. The average increase is therefore very much higher than the percentage increase used in the text, this being of the order of 81%. This only goes on to emphasise the conservancy of our estimate.

4. Since the re-allocation of television contracts the holding company has been ordered to decrease its holdings still further.

5. There are now no investment allowances as such.

6. According to the accounts for 1967, J. Lyons and Company are not, so far as is known, a close company as defined by the Finance Act 1965. There are, however, in a Board of Directors consisting of 21 members, 9 Salmons and 4 Glucksteins. Also, the voting equity appears to be a very small percentage of the total share capital, being 3·6%.

7. The reference to the Managing Directors Certificate was discontinued in 1964, but this does not necessarily mean that the auditors have ceased to rely on it.

8. The 1967 Act provides that the Directors Report should state where the market value of interests in land is materially different from the book amount, and the Directors think this significant. It does not distinguish between present and alternative use and hence most published accounts may virtually evade the intent of the Act.

Glossary

Acceptance Credit. Power to borrow up to a stated amount on bills of exchange. The credit is usually with a merchant bank or similar organisation and is normally for a fixed period, often renewable. It is a useful means of obtaining finance to cover a gap between production and income from sales.

Balance Sheet. A statement setting out the assets and liabilities of an organisation at a particular date. It is traditionally shown as a two-sided account, the liabilities appearing on the left-hand side and the assets they finance on the right. More recently the tendency has been to show the balance sheet in vertical form. Here the net current assets are shown and added to fixed assets to give a total of so-called capital employed. Below this the funds borrowed are listed, the total agreeing with the first mentioned. The method was an attempt to escape from a traditional, and what was considered a misleading system. There are excellent grounds for claiming that the escapers were misled by misunderstanding the tradition, and the escape foiled. There seems for instance no purpose in stating capital employed until that term has been defined and agreed.

Blue Chip Investment. This is a stock exchange investment where the risk is very low both where capital and income are concerned. It is the next best to a gilt-edged, and is usually the equity of a substantial and well-known public company.

Bonus Issue. A scrip issue by another name.

Current Liabilities. Those liabilities due for payment in the near future, normally within the following period.

Debenture. A document setting out the terms of a loan. It is usually accompanied by a deed that appoints trustees whose business it is to watch over the interests of debenture holders. Debentures, though normally secured are not necessarily so. However, they have preference over shareholders' moneys in a winding up. Debentures, if secured, may be so on a fixed or floating charge. The former are secured on a specific asset or assets. The latter are charged on all assets together.

Debentures carry a fixed rate of interest and there is normally power to take action when this in in arrear, e.g. appoint a receiver. The interest is a charge against income, rather than an appropriation of profit. In the same way as shares may be converted into stock so also may debentures.

Only investments such as debentures are properly called securities, for a security, as the name suggests, indicates an investment where there is a charge on the assets of the company, where security is offered for the loan in the form of a definite charge on assets. This would not normally apply to shares.

Depreciation. Term applied to the amount written off a fixed asset in any financial period. It is partly a method of spreading the cost of the asset over its effective life and partly a method of providing for its replacement. These are two sides of the same coin. Difficulties arise in estimating the life of an asset when agreeing the amount to be charged against income in early years. Again where replacement is concerned, the idea of providing for replacement is unreal unless the value of money is a constant and the item is replaced with something similar.

The safest view of depreciation is that it is a method of ensuring that when the asset is scrapped the capital position of the business reverts to position one. To make this possible, it is necessary to allow for changes in money values when providing for this item.

There are various basic methods of providing for depreciation. The straight line basis and the diminishing balance basis are the more popular. The former charges an equal amount each year. The latter charges a percentage of the written down value of the asset. This means that higher amounts are charged in earlier years. This is often excused by claiming that no compensation is made for higher maintenance costs. The validity of this argument is doubtful. Companies using this method will tend to show assets in total as a lower figure than those employing the first method.

Other means of charging depreciation include a combination of those stated; also, in the instance of say, land, the leasehold amortisation system or the sinking fund.

Discount: Cash. Cash discount is given in the form of a deduction from invoice price in consideration of early payment.

Discount: Trade. Trade discounts are discounts given by supplier to manufacturer or retailer, either as a mark of favour, or as a method of controlling prices, or fixing maximum profit margins. The invoice would in the instance mentioned, state selling price and deduct a fixed percentage which would mark the purchaser's profit.

Discounting back. To discount a figure back, in the manner discussed in the text, is to find the capital sum that, invested at the rate stated, would produce that figure annually. The position can be complicated by the introduction of the time element. This involves what is known as discounting the cash flow. The point here is that from the viewpoint of the investor in year one, £100 in that year is not equivalent to £100 in twenty years' time. The true answer to the problem posed then is to find the capital sum by taking the income each year separately and find the amount that must be invested to produce that amount in total in each separate year. The twenty separate amounts are then totalled. In practice, the simplest method where income is constant, is to take the period of investment and obtain a quotation for an annuity amounting to the figure given.

Gilt-edged Securities. Those securities where interest rates are fixed and no danger of non-payment appears to be present. These are normally government securities, bonds repayable at a stated date or dates, sometimes at a premium.

Due to the fluctuation of interest rates generally, the price of these bonds varies. It may therefore be that interest earned is outweighed by capital loss on sale. If this is so, it is doubtful if these bonds can command the respect that would be the attribute of a real gilt-edged investment, i.e. one where no risk of loss was likely. In addition to the fall in market price, there is also the almost certain fact of capital loss on repayment owing to the influence of inflation.

Certain industrials are looked upon as gilt-edged but they are subject to much the same hazards as those mentioned above, except that there is a possibility that the market price will rise as the value of money falls and profits increase, enabling dividends to be higher.

Group Accounts. The accounts of a group of companies. Each holding company must prepare such accounts being the figures for the group as a whole. There are certain exceptions, e.g. where subsidiaries need not be included, but this is unimportant in the context and the accounts themselves must state when the law has not been complied with in the manner applicable to the majority of companies.

Historical Cost. The original cost of an asset without any adjustment to allow for changes in money values.

Holding Company. A company owning, or controlling the policy of another company, normally by having a majority of the voting rights.

Insolvency. The inability to pay one's debts as and when they become due. This can occur even though were the business wound up there would be more than enough to pay creditors and must be distinguished from Bankruptcy.

Internal Control. The agglomeration of systems and checking devices aimed at maximising accuracy and minimising fraud.

Mean. May be of various kinds. As used in the text, it is the total of the items in a series, divided by the number of items. This is known as the arithmetic mean.

Mean Deviation. This shows the degree to which the various items in a series differ from the mean. It is found by taking the difference between the mean and each item separately. The answers are summed up and divided by the number of items in the series. The percentage deviation is the deviation expressed as a percentage of the arithmetic mean.

Moving Average. Where a series of figures is given on a time basis, then the moving average is found by taking the mean for the first so many figures, the number depending on circumstances or the size of the series, then the mean of the same number of items where the first in the sequence is dropped and the next added. The process is continued, the final figure being the mean of the ultimate items, e.g. a five-year moving average taken from figures of profit for fifty years would show the mean for the first five years and every other five years, beginning in turn with each year in sequence.

Profit and Loss Account. The account showing the income and expenditure resulting in a profit or a loss for the particular financial year.

The account is strictly divided into three parts, only two (the latter two) being published.

The first part is the trading account recording sales less the cost of putting the goods into condition for sale. The second part shows the gross profit and deducts therefrom all the incidental expenses of selling and administration. This is the profit and loss account proper. The third part will be the appropriation account. This takes the net profit from the previous account and shows how it is dealt with either by distribution or by putting sums to various reserves.

In manufacturing concerns, there is also prior to the trading account what may be referred to as the manufacturing account, showing the cost of putting goods in a position for sale. This account is often combined with the trading account.

Reserves — Capital. Funds appertaining to ordinary shareholders but by law, or in the opinion of the directors, not available for distribution to them.

Reserves — General. Moneys or funds belonging to ordinary shareholders but not subscribed by them — usually arise from appropriation from profit and loss account — moneys kept back for a rainy day.

Rights Issue. An issue of shares by offering to present members the right to take up a fixed number proportionate to their previous holding at a price lower than the market would offer. The shareholder can, if he accepts the option, take the shares to keep, or sell at a profit, or else he may sell the right to purchase the shares from the company.

In taking into account the possible profit, it is well to remember that the number of shares, being increased, will need to be backed by higher distributions of profit. There should be, therefore, an indication of increasing, or prospective, prosperity, or at least a promise that the dividend rate will be maintained.

Scrip Issue. An issue of shares gratis to those holding shares at the date the issue is declared. it is a substitute for a dividend. Reserves, rather than be paid out in cash, are capitalised and the holding of each member is thereby increased.

The form of the declaration is normally say, one for two, i.e. each member receives one additional share for each two shares originally held. Note that the member gains nothing unless profits are expected to be enough to pay the old dividend on the increased number of shares, that is, if the rate of dividend does not fall.

It is a sensible way of disposing of capital reserves which cannot be distributed in cash and has the effect of bringing share capital to a more realistic level.

Shares. Units of capital subscribed to enable a company to be established. Shares may be of various types. These are discussed in the text. The principal types are preference shares and ordinary shares. The former normally have a preferential right to dividend, that is, no dividend is payable to ordinary shareholders until the preferential shareholders have received the agreed percentage. Those shares sometimes have priority in repayment of capital on a winding up. This is not usual. They may also have rights to participate in surplus profits. Generally speaking, their rights are defined in the Articles of Association and they can claim nothing more than is given when this is written.

Ordinary shareholders are the virtual owners of the company taking the ultimate risk and ultimate profit. Normally they control the company by voting at meetings and groups of members may demand meetings be held. These shares are known as equity shares. A class of non-voting ordinary shares has appeared. These, as the title might suggest, are a contradiction and not approved by thinking persons. A non-voting share cannot be considered part of equity.

Shares are transferable in the units, whatever these may be, of issue. That is to say, £X shares are transferable in units of £X. When shares are fully paid they may be converted into stock. The only difference this makes is that transfers can be made of any amount and are not confined to aggregates of the original units. Instead of selling 100 shares at £1 per share, the member now sells £100 of stock.

Share Capital. The total shares issued by a company or authorised to be so issued. Strictly there are two figures. The authorised share capital is the value of shares authorised by the Memorandum as the capital of the company. The issued share capital is the value of shares issued. There is also a third category known as the paid up share capital. This is the amount called up on shares issued.

Share Premium. An amount, in addition to the nominal value of a share, charged on issue. The premium is shown as a separate figure in the balance sheet.

Statement of Affairs. A preferable name for a balance sheet, though a general term including in its ambit many forms of account, e.g. statements of affairs in bankruptcy, etc.

Stock. *See* **Shares.**

Stocks and Work in progress. Stocks are either of raw materials or finished goods in manufacturing concerns. In retail industry, they are goods bought for resale but not yet sold. Work in progress is a term used to describe goods in process of manufacture. It is normally priced by adding to the total expenditure to date on materials and labour, a predetermined percentage, say, for overheads. Occasionally in the instance of a large contract, it includes an element of profit.

Stock Exchange. The largest betting-shop in the country with the added sophistication that bets are placed by an agent who charges a commission and is known as a stock-broker.

To obtain a quotation on the stock exchange, that is, to persuade the proprietors that the shares of the company in question are worth dealing with, one must satisfy stringent conditions as to information to be made available. These conditions are reputed to be supposedly for the benefit of the public or the protection thereof. The information given is less than many would prefer, for the greater the quantity the safer the investment inasmuch as the risk can be judged to a greater degree of accuracy.

The principal complaint against such an organisation as the Stock Exchange must be that because of the grape vine that grows along Lombard Street too much is known by too few, and too little by too many, with the result that too many are too often taken for a ride by too few.

Subsidiary Company. A company controlled by another company, normally by reason of that other company's having acquired a majority of its shares.

Tax: Capital Gains Tax. this is a tax on gains made by the sale of what were previously regarded as capital assets. Certain exceptions include genuine sales of owner occupied houses.

This tax is particularly complex. The intricacies are yet to be examined or even explained, and those responsible for administering the tax admit at the moment that they are not capable of comprehending it in its entirety.

There are two brands of this tax, the short-term gains tax and the long-term gains tax. One relevant criticism particularly applicable to the latter is that persons will pay tax now on the surplus arising on a sale, that surplus, in fact, representing no more than a fall in the value of money. The Government, or, rather, the State, will then be gainers from an inflationary policy.

Tax: Corporation Tax. This is a tax levied on companies, being a fixed percentage of profits.

Tax: Income Tax. A tax levied on all persons in receipt of income. A company is treated as a person.

Tax: Payroll Tax. This is a tax based upon the number of employees in any business. A fixed sum is payable per week for every employee, the amount varying according to sex and age. The idea is to force industry to economise in employment of labour. It will of course also favour the employment of women, the competition for whose services may result in higher or equal pay. This may nullify the advantages and increase the confusion.

Tax: Profits Tax. This is, or was, levied on companies and certain other organisations. It did not apply to individuals or partnerships. It was in addition to income tax.

Trade Investments. Investments made with the purpose of furthering the objects of the investing company, i.e. assisting it to maintain or increase profits.

Working Capital. Current assets minus current liabilities, or in fact, the moneys available to finance expansion of sales or production without increasing fixed assets, or available for purchase of fixed assets once current liabilities are secured.

Name Index

217

Subject Index